FEVER

CABIN

CABIN FEVER

CABIN FEVER

Shelter

Utopia

Porn

Art

The cabin. It is as much a cultural construct as it is an enduring architectural form, as much a symbol of a certain way of life as it is a marker of the human relationship to place. Such complex connotations and meanings have, at times, rendered the cabin indefinable and elusive. But at its essence, the cabin conjures ideas of a simpler, more primal existence.

It stands apart from ordinary life. It provides basic shelter. It allows for communion with nature. Forever associated with Henry David Thoreau and his iconic (and often misunderstood) retreat on Walden Pond, as well as countless other thinkers and writers from Aldo Leopold to Michael Pollan, the cabin has allowed for considerable philosophical inquisition. It is also an object of consumption and a compelling part of our visual culture, popularized by coffee table books and websites such as Cabin Porn. No longer is a cabin simply a cabin. The old associations endure, but we've ascribed it new meaning. Whereas initially it provided a pragmatic solution for shelter, it has come to represent an idealistic vision of an unattainable past. So potent and seductive is this image that increasingly we present it as a panacea to the modern condition. This is both an obvious response to our over-stimulated world and a puzzling outlet for a culture intent on being connected.

Cabin Fever is conceived as part of the Gallery's ongoing commitment to the presentation of visual culture in its myriad forms and it is the first exhibition to address the evolution of this architectural typology in North America, as well as its influence on contemporary culture, in such a comprehensive manner. This edited volume, which includes social, cultural and architectural analysis from a diverse selection of writers, will serve as an important resource on the evolution of cabin culture in North America.

The idea for *Cabin Fever* originated with independent curator and writer Jennifer M. Volland, and we are thrilled to have an opportunity to work with her on another ambitious and innovative project. Bruce Grenville, the Gallery's Senior Curator, and Stephanie Rebick, Associate Curator, were enthusiastic collaborators and worked closely with Jennifer to determine the exhibition's shape and structure. Once again this proved to be a fruitful partnership. I commend Jennifer for her commitment to approaching architectural history from a diverse array of lenses that encourage new ways of understanding familiar subject matter. Her passion for the material, keen eye and creativity are discernible in all aspects of the project. I am grateful to Bruce and Stephanie for their stewardship that brought Jennifer's complex idea to fruition.

An exhibition of this scale would not be possible without the involvement of all aspects of the Gallery and I thank the dynamic and inventive staff of the Vancouver Art Gallery for their significant contributions. The installation of the exhibition was very demanding, and our Preparation, Registration and Audio Visual teams handled each challenge with finesse and aplomb. Michael Lis and his team at Goodweather designed and produced architectural models and large-scale interventions that figure prominently in the exhibition. I thank Michael for his insight, ingenuity and dedication to the subject matter. The publication and exhibition graphics were designed by Information Office, Vancouver; it was a pleasure to work with Derek again and his clear vision and impressive design knowledge helped shape the overall aesthetic.

I extend my deep appreciation to the Board of Trustees of the Vancouver Art Gallery for their continued support of these ambitious, interdisciplinary projects. I would especially like to thank Gallery Trustee Naudia Maché and her husband Mark for their generous donation toward the exhibition, as well as the Richardson Family, the Gallery's Visionary Partner for Scholarship and Publications. *Cabin Fever* benefited greatly from the assistance and encouragement of the many lenders who shared works from their collections—the exhibition would not have been possible without your support. Finally, I would like to extend my deepest gratitude to the architects, artists, designers, photographers, filmmakers and writers who contributed to the book and exhibition; your innovative work deftly approaches the cabin's complicated history and reveals the enduring symbolic and cultural value of this unique architectural form.

Kathleen S. Bartels, Director
Vancouver Art Gallery

Clockwise from top: Scott & Scott Architects, Whistler Cabin, Whistler, BC, 2016. Liddle Cabin, Mount Rainier National Park, WA, 1969. Marcel Breuer, Breuer Cottage, Wellfleet, MA (rear perspective), 1948–49

11

The cabin stands as an iconic building form with a rich and diverse history. A small, single room, gable-roofed structure constructed of wood or stone is invariably identified as a cabin, though no two people will necessarily agree on the details of its making or its genealogy. Like many architectural typologies it is a hybrid form with as many variations as there are locations and building materials. For the vast majority of its existence the form of the cabin has been intimately linked to its location and functional purpose. It is primarily a structure that provides shelter from the vagaries of the natural environment while utilizing materials and methods gathered from that same environment. Writing in the first century BCE Marcus Vitruvius Pollio (aka Vitruvius, *De Architetura*) imagined the origins of architecture in a pre-historic age where early humans sought to sustain fire by erecting a simple post and beam structure over a fire pit in order to maintain that life enhancing element. This rudimentary structure, he proposed, was in turn expanded to provide space for the human builders and their families. The pitched and thatched roof, and the walls of woven branches or mud came later, but were drawn and dependent on the natural materials close at hand.

Indigenous architecture, defined by the materials and the people who made it, is the underlying principle that shaped the evolution of the cabin typology. Geographical terrain, natural materials, climate and culture were the defining criteria for both the form of the building and its use. Large mature trees and effective tools, for example, provided the Indigenous people of the Pacific Northwest Coast with the necessary resources to produce extraordinary log and plank buildings that could house extended families

and provide shelter and context for the production of a rich and multi-faceted social and cultural history. The same is true throughout the world where Indigenous builders utilize stone, snow, sod, rammed earth and adobe, logs and branches, woven grasses and leaves, clay and straw, hides and bones. This impressive integration of materials, method and meaning has produced one of the most remarkable and versatile forms of architecture throughout the world.

This exhibition and publication are focused on cabin typology in North America, with the primary focus on the nineteenth and twentieth centuries when changes in technology and immigration built on, expanded, and more often, destroyed and displaced the Indigenous forms that had emerged in the

millennia prior to first contact with European settlers. There is no doubt that settlers gained significant local knowledge from existing Indigenous building traditions but also brought with them new tools and building practices linked to their own histories and cultural customs. Some of the earliest known examples can be seen in the cabins built by Swedish or Finnish immigrants who settled along Pennsylvania's Darby Creek in the mid-seventeenth century as part of a colonizing strategy formulated by the Swedish South Company, founded in 1626 with a mandate to establish colonies on the east coast of North America. Their round log, one room cabins reflected the building traditions of the Swedes and Finns from central Sweden, and notably that of the Forest Finns, who had been forcibly migrated to Sweden in the late sixteenth century to implement their slash-and-burn technique to transform the northern forests (home to the Indigenous Sami people) into farmland. These same techniques were enacted on the lands of the Indigenous Lenni Lenape (or Delaware) people on the east coast of the North American continent who were pushed out of their homelands to make room for the New Sweden colonies. This devastating intervention set the pattern for much of the immigration and settlement that would follow throughout North America from the seventeenth century to the present.

13

In considering a structure that might describe the fundamental components of the cabin typology within its formal, social and cultural evolution we settled on a tripartite nomenclature—Shelter, Utopia and Porn—that maps the formal evolution of the cabin typology within a changing set of social and cultural desires. The universal need for shelter determined the original parameters of the cabin typology and aptly defines the first section of this exhibition and publication. The second section recognizes a utopian impulse that is most often identified with Henry David Thoreau and his belief that divinity and democracy might be found in a return to an intimacy with nature. His cabin at Walden became an iconic symbol of simplicity and authenticity. The desire for an unencumbered return to nature is manifest in diverse and often conflicted uses of the cabin in the form of early twentieth century "parkitecture"; in the mid-century embrace of the cabin as a second home in the woods or vacation home by the lake, and, only a generation later, in the birth of a counter-culture movement inspired by a "back-to-the-land" sensibility that embraced a rejection of the materialism and emptiness of modern life searching for a more authentic and meaningful relationship to nature. The third section sees this utopian impulse rewritten in a world dominated by commerce and marketing that identified the cabin in the woods as the ideal site for the consumption of nature. The cabin becomes the nexus of a sophisticated cultural movement that strategically links design, pornography and technology to produce a surprising new typology called "cabin porn."

This publication is both a document of the exhibition and an omnibus reader on the subject of the cabin typology in North America over the past three centuries. Co-curator Jennifer Volland's introductory essay, "Cabin Fever," offers a personal account of her lifelong fascination with the cabin through the tripartite narrative of Shelter, Utopia and Porn. Within this narrative she deftly confirms the cabin's deep and fundamental social imperative—an imperative that is often overshadowed by the assumption that a cabin is nothing more than a pragmatic architectural solution to the need for physical shelter.

In both the exhibition and the publication we offer a typological narrative that maps the evolution of the cabin building type from rudimentary shelter to technologically sophisticated retreat. The twenty selected buildings stand for the thousands of closely related typologies and the millions of buildings collectively described as a cabin. In reviewing the chronological timeline of the selected buildings it is possible to trace a dynamically evolving role for building materials as priorities shift from the exclusive use of localized materials, to use of manufactured and standardized building materials, and, more recently, to the widespread adoption of prefabricated and highly technical materials. This shift in materials is intimately intertwined with the changing aesthetic, social, cultural and ideological values that determine the functions of the cabin.

The publication is primarily composed of a selection of notable writings, excerpted texts and iconic images that chronicle the long history of writing and visual documentation of the cabin. From Abbé Marc-Antoine Laugier's eighteenth-century essay that proposed a theory of architecture which identified the structure of the "primitive hut" as a true and fundamental manifestation of the divine in architecture; to the world of mid-century modern mail-order plans for vacation cabins; to a photo essay on the early twenty-first century aesthetics of ruggedness as manifest in the design of contemporary clothing and lifestyle accessories by Roots, Herschel or L.L. Bean—the narrative of the cabin is as diverse as its typology.

The final section of this publication offers an insight into the cabin as an enduring subject of art. Mattie Gunterman's prosaic photographs of settler life on the West Coast in the late nineteenth century reveal the cabin as shelter and an indispensable site of social interaction, while in the early twentieth

15

century Frederick Varley along with other members of the Canadian Group of Seven painted the cabin as a symbol of national identity and the gateway to a focused and intense relationship to nature. For contemporary artists such as James Benning and Liz Magor, the lonely cabin in the woods efficiently holds a double reading as both a site of escape and of containment.

From its earliest rudimentary form to its elaborate present the cabin has, as its first principle, provided shelter within the natural world. For many that achievement was a battle with nature, but there can be little doubt that the most successful cabins have been those that have found their form *within* nature, responding, adapting and integrating with the sites of their building. New technologies and synthetic materials may have expanded the language of this fundamental building typology, but its symbolic narrative has remained focused on the primacy of a fundamental and prioritized relationship to nature that is only possible from within the walls of a cabin.

Bruce Grenville, Senior Curator
Vancouver Art Gallery

<u>Above</u>: Frederick Varley, *Fire Ranger's Look-out*, c. 1932, oil on panel, Collection of the Vancouver Art Gallery, Purchased with funds donated by the Audain Foundation

<u>Opposite</u>: Liz Magor, *Messenger* (detail), 1996–2002, wood, plaster, textile, found objects, Collection of the Vancouver Art Gallery, Gift of the Artist

Jennifer M. Volland

Cabin Fever:
An Introduction

The day I moved to Los Angeles was the day I knew I wanted a cabin. I had just left a simple, rustic house, dubbed "the outpost," on a vineyard property in the Gabilan Mountain Range, ten miles from the sleepy town of Soledad in California's Salinas Valley. From the ramshackle deck, I could see the craggy spires of Pinnacles National Monument and mile after mile of what John Steinbeck describes in *East of Eden* as "light gay mountains full of sun and loveliness."[1] Looking back, I can see that, at times, the transcendent beauty of it all was wasted on my 25-year old self. My roommate and I had parties, played records loudly, ingested illicit drugs and recklessly engaged in target practice with a .300 Winchester Magnum and bowling balls—things that now seem irreverent in this type of setting. But I also had moments of clarity and appreciation. I got to wake up in the morning and see the sunrise through the sliding door of my bedroom, and I got to gaze up at a pollution-free night sky when I returned home from my job in the winery tasting room. Something about the combination of humble shelter and sublime landscape gave me unimaginable pleasure, and while I recognized this would be nearly impossible to re-create in the sprawling metropolis of Southern California, I decided it somehow had to be a part of my life.

There is nothing original about this dream. Many people can relate to the desire to get away, to disconnect, to escape the realities of life—or to really live, if only for a short time. In fact, cabin culture is part of a longstanding North American tradition, inextricably tied to ideas of the frontier and individualism and immortalized in literature by writers such as Henry David Thoreau, Jack Kerouac and Michael Pollan.

The history of the cabin has followed a similar trajectory to that of wilderness in general; as a human creation that has taken on almost mythical proportions. In "The Trouble with Wilderness; or, Getting Back to the Wrong Nature," environmental historian William Cronon exposes how such one-sided, and often paradoxical, experiences of the landscape formed and perpetuated in Western culture. But, more importantly, he challenges readers to rethink this history of wilderness in a way that recognizes the complex intersection between humanity and nature. To understand how wilderness became a cultural construct. To understand why we've come to look at wilderness as a panacea to the ills of civilization and modernity and to acknowledge our role as agents in this idealized vision. "As we gaze into the mirror [wilderness] holds up for us, we too easily imagine that what we behold is Nature when in fact we see the reflection of our own unexamined longings and desires," writes Cronon.[2] In other words, we seek out places and experiences that we believe hold some untapped potential for personal transformation.

After reading Cronon, I wondered if there was a similar exercise to apply to the cabin, the architectural typology that is probably most connected to the natural world, and one that has been, in a way, altered from its original intent as a pragmatic solution to shelter from the elements. Such an inquiry is not intended to elevate the status of a man-made object, but rather to explore how the relationship between human and place might be reframed to accommodate a more comprehensive and nuanced understanding of the cabin. In viewing the evolution of the cabin through a multifaceted lens—one that includes the perspectives of women and children; the tenets of romanticism; the counter-culture movement; consumerism; and the advance of social media—we can see the cabin not simply as a physical form, but also as something that has absorbed, reflected, and even come to symbolize a distinctly North American culture.

Cabin Fever, the title of this exhibition and publication, draws from the idiomatic term for an anxious state of mind resulting from a prolonged stay in a remote or confined place. But it also plays on the more benign definition of "fever:" a contagious, usually transient, enthusiasm. It is this second meaning that drove my recent curiosity about cabins. With a surge of books focusing on cabin architecture and design, an increasing popularity in the neo-homesteading movement, and the advent of *Cabin Porn* and other inspirational hipster websites, mainstream interest in cabins has reached a new level.

Yet a dearth of critical analysis on the subject remains. Academic investigations tend to have specific focus areas (how cabins act as symbols in literature; how the hut causes one to rethink the limits of architecture; how the cabin has influenced or cultivated philosophical inquiry), and scholarly journal articles overwhelmingly lean toward Norwegian cabin culture (appropriately so, given the high ratio of cabins to people in the country).[3] My co-curators and I attempt to fill that void, applying an approach similar to the one we used in *Grand Hotel: Redesigning Modern Life* (Vancouver Art Gallery, 2013); that is, identifying critical forces that give shape and meaning to an architectural typology.

The story of the cabin is global and personal, physical and psychological. Examples exist everywhere—the Russian dacha, the Norwegian hytte and the Swiss chalet, not to mention the many cabin types found in North America. And each cabin enthusiast has their own relationship to the cabin, whether through first-hand experience or through books and magazines or through a virtual reality. My own history touches on all of these. I am someone who was always enamored with cabins and bought one with my family. I am also a researcher who has devoured countless books and articles on the topic, once travelling to Norway for a deep dive into how Scandinavian lifestyles and traditions have both formed *and been formed* by cabin culture. And finally, like a lot of people, I am simply an observer of contemporary culture, one who has seen the idea of the cabin captivate a collective consciousness. In this essay, I construct my own personal narrative of the cabin using the thematic categories of the exhibition and publication—Shelter, Utopia, Porn.

Top to Bottom: Norwegian Hytte, 2012. *Dacha near Kivach Waterfall*, Russia, 1915

Opposite: Cabin remodel, Three Rivers, CA

20

Our cabin is in Three Rivers, California, an unincorporated community in the foothills of the Sierra Nevada, near the entrance to Sequoia and Kings Canyon National Parks. We were first introduced to the area when my brother and sister-in-law got married there in 2007, and despite the triple-digit temperatures during the weekend celebration, it seemed the right place to begin to search for our own cabin. Equidistant from Los Angeles, San Francisco and the Central Coast, we knew our family and friends could get to Three Rivers in about four hours. The community is charming and picturesque with some basic amenities—a small market, a few good restaurants, a mercantile and an old-fashioned candy and ice cream shop—dotting the two-lane 198 Highway. We were drawn to the natural beauty of the area, the way various forks of the Kaweah River converged against a backdrop of snow-capped mountain peaks. Most importantly, though, it was removed from the chaos and traffic of Los Angeles, and easily accessible to miles of hiking trails and backcountry.

We had only a few requirements for a second home, one being that we wanted it to be on or near the water. Real estate in Three Rivers runs the gamut. The town is devoid of tract homes. The lots vary in size and shape; many are rumoured to have been amended over drunken card games. And properties range from working ranches to off-the-grid mountain retreats. We looked at one boulder-studded acreage with a seventy-year-old historic cabin and water tower, a rat-infested former rental with "a lot of potential," and a dilapidated mid-century with a steep, overgrown path to a swimming hole.

Then we saw something online that looked promising. It was an acre of land on the North Fork of the Kaweah River, with a few small structures developed in 2003, none of which were ever inhabited. The main structure was 500 square feet and consisted of a dark and musty L-shaped room; a tiny, narrow bathroom; and a single-car garage. There was also a 200-square-foot studio, a redwood gazebo and

a carport. A middle-aged woman owned the property; her centenarian father, a highly acclaimed Western landscape painter, used the studio. The woman lived in another part of Three Rivers, and she had plans to build a larger rammed-earth house on the land before her premature death. We bought the property from the daughter of her former partner, and set to work making it livable for our family.

It was at the beginning, before we completed any work on the main structure, that our experience felt most true to the idea of cabin as shelter. We stayed in the studio, which was a rough space—four walls, a roof, an unfinished floor and no insulation. We slept in sleeping bags over blow up air mattresses. We had a Coleman stove on the small deck to make tea. There was no bathroom or running water.

This was our modern-day primitive experience. The temporary "hut" defined our relationship to the land. We used the space as a base to assess the possibilities of the property, and it grounded us to our new home

21

away from home. It was a rational solution that served our immediate needs; the motivations behind it not unlike those that early humans must have had toward shelter. In his 1755 "Essai sur L'Architecture" [Essay on Architecture], Marc-Antoine Laugier explored such an origin theory for architecture based on the fundamental relationship between man and nature. He wrote, "man in his earliest origin, without any other help, without other guide than the natural instinct of his needs. He wants a place to settle."[4] And so we settled in the studio and endured the rudimentary conditions, even enjoyed them, because we knew they would soon change.

Provisionality was a key feature of many early residential forms, including the North American log cabin. As French historian Alexis de Tocqueville observed in *Journey to America*, "[The log cabin] is only a temporary shelter for the American, a concession circumstances have forced on him for the moment."[5] Once a family could plant and harvest crops and secure a form of potential income, then they could turn their energies to building a more suitable dwelling.

View of tents at Kaweah Colony, Sierra Nevada, CA, c. 1886

The proximity of a virgin forest determined site, as trees alone were the main—and quite often the only—building material. Construction involved an assessment of natural resources and heavy physical labor. "The settler first selected trees with straight smooth trunks of approximately the same diameters. The trees were then felled, cut into logs of the desired length, then pulled by horse, or dragged by hand, to the site of the cabin where the notching was done," C.A. Weslager wrote in *The Log Cabin in America*.[6] Then the logs were stacked on top of one another, overlapping at the corners. Building techniques were brought over by Europeans, mostly Scandinavians and Eastern Europeans, where similar resources were readily available.

Design did not play a key role, except in terms of practicality; the simplest log cabins consisted of a single room, ten by twelve feet, with no windows and, perhaps, a small sleeping loft. Building one could be an individual effort; at other times, the raising of a cabin involved an entire family or community and could be completed within a couple weeks.

I confess that we were not the ones doing the work on our cabin, and our building materials did not come from the surrounding land. We hired a contractor and got our supplies from the local mercantile or big box home-improvement stores in a town some thirty miles west. Despite all the modern power tools available to our contractor, though, it took him and his crew far longer to renovate the main structure than it did for the pioneers to raise a log cabin: about nine months.

We attempted to keep the cabin as close as possible to the state in which we found it, using the same footprint as the existing structure and veering away from anything visually obscene. Still, we left our mark. We also transformed the surrounding landscape. We cleared ground. We improved access to the river. We planted native trees and plants: Western Sycamore, Fremont Cottonwood, Silver Bush Lupine. And we built a rambling fence around the perimeter of the property.

Undoubtedly, the act of cabin ownership has had a cumulative effect on the community of Three Rivers. The influx of second-home owners, along with investors snapping up properties for vacation rentals, has shifted the socio-economic base of the town, favouring visitors and part-timers over long-term residents. This, coupled with a constant cycle of building and renovating, contributes to an environment in flux. I am acutely aware of what this shift must look like to locals; even more, I wonder what this would look like to the earliest inhabitants of the area. What they call(ed) their home, I call my escape. It is a place of privilege, the relationship to place so far removed from the original.

Once home to the Yokuts Native Americans, the Southern Sierra foothills offered an Edenic landscape with abundant natural resources. On our property, there is still evidence of the tribes' subsistence lifestyle: bedrock

22

mortars for grinding acorns and seeds are carved into the immense slabs of granite. Families lived in simple, framed pole huts, usually cone or oval shaped, covered with grass and branches, and built above a circular hole in the ground. While the huts were typically permanent, their footprint on the earth was delicate and no examples remain. Such was the way of life in this area for thousands of years.

Squatter's Cabin, Sequoia National Park, CA, 2010

Aside from sporadic explorations of mining and ranching by individuals in the 1840s and 1850s, Euro-American settlement in Three Rivers lagged behind the rest of the state. The foothills of the Sierra Nevada range appeared remote and wild, with little opportunity for economic prosperity. However, the enactment of the Homestead Act in 1862 changed that and dozens of families settled here, drawn by the lush grazing land for livestock.[7]

Then there was the short-lived utopian socialist community (1886–92) that sprang up not far from our place. Kaweah Colony was based on the principle of equal work and compensation for men and women. The tent settlement, which varied from 50 to 300 people, included skilled workers but also a cultural contingency of artists, musicians and writers. With an economy based on logging, the colonists built the first road into what would become Sequoia National Park; it took them four grueling years. Ironically, the creation of the National Park—an idealistic and nationalistic endeavor intended to be enjoyed by all people—contributed to their demise, as it included all the lands that had been claimed by the colonists.[8] Today, the government-dubbed Squatters Cabin is the only remnant of Kaweah Colony. Situated amongst a grove of the giant trees that once served as the lifeblood of this experimental co-op, the cabin is now an empty shell, accessed by a marked trail and visited primarily by tourists who, with the help of a sign displaying a few descriptive sentences, are left to imagine who the structure originally served and how it was used. What once was a simple shelter is now part of the park's lore.

UTOPIA

This history underscores the ironies intrinsic in the evolution of the cabin. What started as the seed of Western civilization in North America, the structure that spurred the nation's expansion and exploration, quickly became the vehicle to escape it—and, also, a symbol of how one could experience nature.

So it was that my idealized vision of a cabin was not unlike the Squatters Cabin: a historic relic with a storied past of pioneer life. What we ended up with, of course, was nothing like that. Our cabin is a wood-sided building painted barn red with white trim and a metal roof; the interior has white walls and a scored concrete floor. It is more reminiscent of Scandinavian design (light, simple, uncluttered) than North American. While charming, it possesses none of the characteristics of what I considered a "traditional" cabin: log frame construction, rustic interiors, a quirky floor plan or a stone fireplace.

Despite the absence of these features and the structure's young age, it did have the unique story of the previous owner, as well as the geographic significance associated with the surrounding land's earliest inhabitants. I came to realize that these things alone—what this place meant to people and what it would mean for us—are worth a lot. Worth so much, in fact, that I let go of my preconceived notions of what a cabin is and built my new definition around something much more abstract: the experience.

The notion that a cabin could provide something beyond basic shelter evolved during

Three Rivers Cabin, Three Rivers, CA, 2017

the age of American Romanticism. This movement, which flourished in the years between 1820 and 1860, revolted against the tenets of the Enlightenment period—industrialization, scientific rationalization and social conformity—in favour of the emotional and individualistic experience found in nature. Nowhere was this more apparent than in literature. Henry David Thoreau sought moral high ground by living a life of simplicity in a cabin, which he detailed in *Walden; or, Life in the Woods* (1854). The author's two-year quest to practice the transcendentalist's ideal of introspection was both a social experiment and a critique of the civilized world, and it set the tone for countless others in his wake.

Hippies, poets, writers, philosophers and the generally displaced have all turned to the cabin (and the natural environment) as a place for nourishment and inspiration, if not an outright liberation from the conventions of society.

Novelist and poet Jack Kerouac periodically sojourned to Lawrence Ferlinghetti's cabin in Big Sur, California, to evade the pressure of fame and halt his downward spiral into advanced alcoholism (later recounted in his 1962 semi-autobiographical novel *Big Sur*).

24

Conservationist Aldo Leopold spent weekends in a refurbished chicken coop along the Wisconsin River and wrote about it in *A Sand County Almanac: And Sketches Here and There* (1949). Leopold reminds us "there is value in any experience that reminds us of our distinctive national origins and evolution."[9] Such reenactments—whether living in a cabin or spending time in a national park or, in his example, donning a coonskin cap and going "Daniel-Booneing"—fosters an appreciation of American culture and history.[10]

Top to bottom: Lawrence Ferlinghetti at the "Old West Hotel," Bixby Canyon, CA, 1997. Aldo Leopold and Robert McCabe at the Shack, Sauk County, WI, 1940

Journalist Michael Pollan had his own revelations closer to home. He built a cabin in the woods behind his main house "to remedy the sense that [he] lived too much of [his] life in the realm of There, so steeped in its abstractions and meditations that Here had begun to feel like a foreign country."[11] Pollan created the possibility for a dual existence; in this instance, literally a few steps made a difference in his perception.

I'll be the first to admit that I've been moved and inspired by these accounts, blithely unaware of the gender bias in available literature. Quite simply, I could relate. My primary understanding of the cabin was one of human experience: I have felt Kerouac's desire to disappear; Leopold's sense of nationalism; Pollan's quest to understand architecture's effect on the self.

But upon reading more accounts of women, I am reminded of the unique perspectives they offer. Of course, women have always been a part of cabin history; it's just a matter of visibility and interpretation. The cabin could be read as a place to reinforce a sense of domesticity and also a place to rebel against it. Take early accounts of pioneer life, like Caroline Kirkland's in *A New Home, Who'll Follow?* (1839). On the one hand, the female pioneer appears as though she's along for the ride: a passive participant in the life of her husband, her purpose much the same as it was in "civilization"—that is, to make and keep the home (or in this case, the cabin). But she's also a liminal figure, existing on a geographical and ideological boundary and, just like her husband, getting a taste of the freedom that came with living on the frontier.[12]

Fast forward to ecologist Anne LaBastille's 1976 book *Woodswoman: Living Alone in the Adirondack Wilderness*. Published at the height of Second Wave Feminism, it documents LaBastille's purchase of land, building of a log cabin and other adventures in the Adirondack Mountains in the wake of her divorce. LaBastille's recollections came more than a hundred years after Kirkland's. Considered alongside each other, they reveal an evolution in the perception and practice of women's roles in society. The cabin, in particular, is an important symbol in these narratives. For Bastille, it represents an assertion of independence and self-reliance, for she is not just the cabin's caretaker. She actually built it, and, by doing so, she became an active participant in the wilderness experience.

If anything, women's relationships to nature have only become more complex. Some years ago I read an article in *The New Yorker* about Ree Drummond (a.k.a. Pioneer Woman) who lives on a working ranch in Oklahoma and blogs about her experiences. The story of her ascendancy to stardom is interesting, but what resonated with me more was how writer Amanda Fortini describes Drummond's mass-market appeal: "The amateur country-girl persona works as a literary device because it allows readers to imagine falling in love and ditching their frenzied lives for a calmer, more agrarian existence, without having to abandon the notion that they are sophisticated, independent woman."[13] The story of The Pioneer Woman offers some encouragement that the dream of an alternative lifestyle (vis-à-vis the wilderness experience or the cabin) isn't just *for* men or attainable *by* men. Nor is the expression of that dream.

For me, life at the cabin does offer a break from a conventional domestic existence. I release myself from the drudgeries of day-to-day responsibilities: cooking, cleaning, general house maintenance, childcare. Part of this relates to size. There is simply a lot less to take care of at the cabin, and we live so much of our lives outside. The other part relates to attitude. At the cabin, I tend to do things because I want to, not because I have to. I also feel a sense of liberation from being an adult.

A sense of romanticism about the cabin may start early. It's something that many, including myself, have held since childhood, and I can also see it through the eyes of my own children. They experience a certain kind of freedom when we visit Three Rivers. They have distance from school and lessons and extra-curricular activities. They have no schedule. They write poetry and create artwork. They have the luxury of reading books cover-to-cover, uninterrupted. They swim naked. They roam without care or direction. They are in a constant state of discovery: one day they may find a bird's nest nestled in a tree, another day dozens of tiny frogs by a leaky water pipe.

Although their orientation is to the outdoors, my children also glean physical and emotional comfort from the cabin itself. It is small and cozy: an open kitchen and living area, a bedroom, a bathroom and a bunkroom. Their bunkroom is the size of a pantry and can only accommodate narrow, military-size mattresses. In *The Poetics of Space*, Gaston Bachelard talks about how diminutive, intimate spaces—like nests and shells—"bring out the primitiveness in us."[14] They are places of stability, places to withdraw to, places that allow us to become more in balance with ourselves. The cabin works a sort of magic on my children. Indeed, I've seen an aura of calmness wash over them when they anticipate our arrival to the cabin on the drive north; the vision itself triggers certain emotions.

Our cabin awakens a childlike curiosity in me, too, perhaps in part because it reminds me of the forts and playhouses frequented in the unfettered condition of youth. Bachelard suggests that in such primal images, we imagine that "we could start a new life, a life that would be our own, that would belong to us in our very depth."[15] And it's true. While at the cabin, I'm free of distraction. I have more clarity of thought. I feel empowered to reset my life.

The cabin is also my place of creation. I go there to write. For my last deadline, I transferred two or three plastic bins full of books and research materials from my home office to the cabin, and every morning for a week or two, I would rise at five and work until the heat became unbearable. Then, midday, I'd go to the river with the kids to cool off and rest. It was an idyllic schedule.

Ultimately, the cabin is about what comes together there. For me, it is a place where family, work and life merge. The documentary photographer Dorothea Lange recognized a similar experience when, in the 1950s, she and her second husband, Paul Schuster Taylor, leased a cabin for their extended family at Steep Ravine on the Marin Coast. Although it was just over the hill from their home in Berkeley, it was a world away from their everyday life. Here Lange shot a series of photographs exploring the idea of freedom. While not her most impressive body of work, I appreciate what it signified. For Lange, the cabin was a "device"—a conduit for an elemental kind of satisfaction.[16]

Dorothea Lange, *Steep Ravine*, May 1957, photonegative, © The Dorothea Lange Collection, the Oakland Museum of California, City of Oakland. Gift of Paul S. Taylor

Regrettably, I have found that, on occasion, the euphoria of cabin life has become overshadowed by a desire to make the cabin itself aesthetically pleasing. We've spent countless hours looking for the right furniture and accessories, referencing design websites for inspiration and perusing vintage stores. It's as though we're on a never-ending quest to manufacture the perfect image of the cabin so that ultimately it may guarantee us some sort of utopic experience.

To this day, I read *Dwell* and *Sunset* magazines, like many others, with a mix of daydreaming and annoyance. So much of what they spotlight is outside the financial reach of most people. The featured cabins often look like homes, and cabins often inspire the homes they feature. This is especially true for *Sunset*, where I recently saw a renovation of a lakeside, A-frame cabin with a kitchen island made from three slabs of Calacatta marble and a $6,000-plus freestanding bathtub, among its high-end touches. Such excess seems a deviation from the magazine's original brand, which focused on cabin rentals and vacation homes within reach of the post-war middle class. Not only were these second homes financially accessible, they also called for methods of

building that did not require experts, and builders made a point to utilize only inexpensive and readily available materials.

So I wonder: Is today's fascination with cabins just a logical extension of that movement? Did *Sunset*, along with projects by architects such as Frank Lloyd Wright, John Lautner and Richard Neutra, help redefine the cabin as architecture with a capital A?[17] For today's cabin owners, design seems to carry equal, if not more, importance to setting and experience.

Along with the exterior appearance of our cabin, which we had limited control over, we had specific ideas for what should go inside. The centerpiece

Top to bottom: *Sunset*, November, 2013. Three Rivers Cabin, Three Rivers, CA, 2017

28

(though placed in the corner) of the living area is a Danish-made, cast iron, wood-burning stove—the Morsø 1410 to be exact—with squirrel reliefs on the sides. Even though it is scaled perfectly to the house, it's not the most practical. The chamber only allows for the small pieces of chopped wood, and the bottom draft vent seems to have been locked up since we purchased it. But the stove was non-negotiable; I had to have it.

We purchased an IKEA kitchen during a "30 Percent Off" sale. It consists of white cupboards with black hardware, black appliances and an oak slab countertop. Matte black Heath Ceramics tile "seconds" form the backsplash and are also used in the bathroom shower.

The curation of space trickles down to the smallest details. We have bowls of pocket knives, hand-woven pillows, vintage postcards of Sequoia National

Park, a cuckoo clock and themed kids' toys like a Roy Toy Log Building Set and a miniature cast iron stove I'd saved since childhood. I even have "cabin clothes," pieces that I had set aside for years in hopes that one day I could wear them at my own retreat: cozy sweaters, flannel shirts, Osh Kosh blue jean overalls, Swedish clogs.

In retrospect, the motivations behind all our decisions seem somewhat ridiculous. It's easy to get caught up in trying to create an image of what cabin life should be. And I know we are not alone. We are conditioned consumers, victims of the culture promoted by design magazines, coffee table books and social media platforms such as Instagram and Pinterest.

Whole lines have been built and marketed around the idea of the cabin, from Lincoln Logs and Log Cabin Syrup to Pendleton blankets and home fragrances. These products are not typically consolidated in one place, but they operate like REI merchandise for the outdoor enthusiast: as seductive space fillers. Leopold and others would argue that such products compromise the connection to nature that something like the cabin is intended to provide. "Civilization has so cluttered this elemental man-earth relationship with gadgets and middlemen that awareness of it is growing dim. We fancy that industry supports us, forgetting what supports industry," writes Leopold.[18] Thus cabin Porn has become another form of the commodification of nature, the antithesis of the historical cabin experience: removed from the idea of practice (Shelter), even skewed from the idea of a return to nature (Utopia).

At the cabin, our initial hope was that we could minimize gadgets—whether the accumulation of superfluous stuff or the use of iPhones and computers—and instead focus on more meditative activities of cabin life, like chopping wood, gardening or baking. While we are not big DIYers, we saw value in the ceremonial gesture of process, whereupon these activities are actually pleasurable and not a chore.[19]

Yet sometimes we are distracted. We can't help but bring our other life with us to Three Rivers, and the delineation between home and cabin begins to evaporate.

Traditionally understood as a counterpoint to the "permanent" home, the status of the cabin now seems to be more in alignment. In *Cabins in Modern Norwegian Literature*, author Ellen Rees posits that in literature, as in life, the concept of the cabin has changed. "Whereas the cabins in literature from earlier periods can be identified as heterotopian places, this is less clearly the case with these contemporary uses of the cabin motif. It may in fact be possible to argue that cabins have become so fully integrated and normalized as a part

29

of everyday life, that they less frequently have the separate status upon which the notion of the heterotopia appears to be predicated. This 'domestication' of the 'Other' space of the cabin is why they gain the potential to be uncannily frightening, and why they become the targets of parody."[20]

But today, the cabin is not just a target of parody. It's also a target of lust. What had long been associated with the frontier has now become a frontier of the mind. People can experience the cabin without ever having to leave their computer, thanks to websites like *Cabin Porn* or *Adventure Journal*. Longings are satisfied by beautifully captured images, frozen in a state of perfection. Perhaps there is some value in this type of experience; that is, inducing a cabin frame of mind—a connection to nature, a desire for a simpler existence— within the context of home. But it is also a ruse.

The truth is, just as the stories behind such "pornographic" images are much more complex, our cabin does not exist in a bubble. We have neighbors: at least two houses are visible from ours. Power lines run through our property. The hum of an occasional car can be heard on a nearby road. More unsettling is the routine firing of rounds at a militant Christian fundamentalist compound upriver a mile or two, which immediately stifles any feeling of peacefulness. And perhaps most sobering is the realization that our cabin can't remedy each and every personal crisis. Expectations of catharsis can be undercut by feelings of isolation and dissolution. There are limits to the experience of escape.

To understand the significance of cabins in the twenty-first century, it seems prudent not to just interpret their history, but also to examine what has been produced as a result of this history. The tangible, yes—the structures themselves, the related products, literature, artwork—but even more, the psychological. The meaning of the cabin has evolved over time and is amorphous, blurring the categorizations of Shelter, Utopia and Porn. As a result, it raises further questions about how humans define their place in the modern world.

Just as Cronon felt about attitudes toward nature, specifically the idea of a "mythical wilderness" as an "antidote to our human selves," we turn, too, to the cabin as a remedy for unresolved issues. "My principal objection to wilderness is that it may teach us to be dismissive or even contemptuous of such humble places and experiences. Without our quite realizing it, wilderness tends to privilege some parts of nature at the expense of others," writes Cronon.[21] Similarly, what I find intriguing about the conception of the cabin is not necessarily the cabin itself, but what it exposes about how and where we spend the rest of our time.

From my home office in the city, I can look out the window and see trees, a blue sky and the occasional skunk or possum nibbling on my dog's food. The ability to experience nature, however limited, is something already present. I could also downsize, live in a smaller, simpler house, something more akin to a cabin, in an effort to slow down and appreciate life. But I haven't. My belief has always been that I need a place that exists outside the realm of everyday life and I thought I could only find this in a cabin. In this regard, I have found partial validation. For me, there is something powerful to the idea of an escape, both physically and mentally. I truly feel different at my cabin. At the same time, I'm aware of the fact that it can carry false expectations, never more apparent than when personal crises persist regardless of my location. This complex nature of the cabin is precisely what makes this architectural typology an intriguing topic of study: it throws the dichotomies between home and away, nature and civilization, and freedom and oppression into sharp relief.

Three Rivers Cabin, Three Rivers, CA, 2017

30

I have a morning ritual at the cabin. I wake up with the sunrise and make a pot of tea. Then I step outside and walk about fifty feet to a small, decaying redwood deck that overlooks the river. I settle into a Russell Woodard Sculptura patio chair, a flea market find by my brother, and one of a set of four. I kick up my feet on a wide, weathered board balanced on two concrete blocks. From this vantage, I observe the changes in the water level, the density of the brush, the animals that graze in the small meadows and fly overhead on their migratory routes—seasonal changes made all the more obvious with our weeks-long absences. I find parallels between the examples of impermanence I see around me and my own life. And perhaps it is the fleetingness of it all—the place, the nature, the surroundings and the feelings—that, for me, is the true essence of cabin fever.

—

1.   John Steinbeck, *East of Eden*, 1952 (New York: Penguin Books, 1992), 3.

2.   William Cronon, "The Trouble with Wilderness; or, Getting Back to the Wrong Nature," in *Uncommon Ground*, ed. William Cronon (New York: W. W. Norton & Company, 1996), 69–70.

3.   For more see Ellen Rees, *Cabins in Modern Norwegian Literature: Negotiating Place and Identity* (Madison, NJ: Fairleigh Dickinson University Press, 2014); Ann Cline, *A Hut of One's Own: Life Outside the Circle of Architecture* (Cambridge: Massachusetts Institute of Technology, 1997); Adam Sharr, *Heidegger's Hut* (Cambridge: Massachusetts Institute of Technology, 2006).

4.   Marc-Antoine Laugier, "Essai sur L'Architecture" (Paris, 1753), in Joseph Rykwert, *On Adam's House in Paradise*, (New York: Museum of Modern Art, 1972), 43.

5.   Alexis de Tocqueville, *Journey to America*, trans. George Lawrence, ed. J.P. Mayer (Garden City, NY: Anchor Books, 1971), 357. This book was originally published in French by Editions Gallimard in 1957.

6.   C.A. Weslager, *The Log Cabin in America: From Pioneer Days to the Present* (New Brunswick, NJ: Rutgers University Press, 1969), 13.

7.   United States President Abraham Lincoln signed into law the Homestead Act on May 20, 1862. It helped facilitate westward migration by providing settlers with 160 acres of public land for a minimal filing fee and five years residence and improvement on the land. By 1900, this act had led to the distribution of 80 million acres of public land.

8.   The colonists were convicted of illegal logging. In actuality, they posed a threat to capitalism because their logging operation bypassed Southern Pacific Railroad, which helped facilitate the timber market. They were never compensated for the road that served as the main route into the park for decades.

9.   Aldo Leopold, *A Sand County Almanac, and Sketches Here and There* (London: Oxford University Press, 1949), 177.

10.   Daniel Boone was an American frontiersman who forged a trail through the Cumberland Gap in the Appalachian Mountains. He was an archetypal hero of the West, popularized in nineteenth-century novels and twentieth-century films and television, which often inaccurately portrayed him wearing a coonskin cap.

11.   Michael Pollan, *A Place of My Own: The Architecture of Daydreams* (London: Penguin Books, 2008), 107.

12.   For more on this idea, see Dawn E. Keetley, "Unsettling the Frontier: Gender and Racial Identity in Caroline Kirkland's A New Home, Who'll Follow? and Forest Life," *Legacy*, Vol. 12, No. 1 (1995).

13.   Amanda Fortini, "O Pioneer Woman!", *The New Yorker*, May 9, 2001, https://www.newyorker.com/magazine/2011/05/09/o-pioneer-woman (accessed October 18, 2017).

14.   Gaston Bachelard, *The Poetics of Space* (Boston: Beacon Press, 1994), 91.

15.   Ibid, 33.

16.   For more on Lange's time at Steep Ravine, see Linda Gordon, *Dorothea Lange: A Life Beyond Limits* (New York: W.W. Norton & Company, Inc., 2009), 418–422. Of particular significance is Gordon's mention of an undated note Lange wrote to herself: "Listen, we build up the cabin in our minds, we *create* the myth of THE cabin in order to fill our *human needs*. Way deep back we *know* that these are a sad and sorry string of poor little shacks, with dirty windows, leaky roofs, staring blankly down over the rocks at the cold and restless sea. But our spirits thrive because here we have room to expand and generate and create our world."

17.   This is not to suggest that these architects or others intended to make lofty pronouncements with their cabin projects. One need only consider Le Corbusier's holiday home on France's Côte d'Azur, Cabanon, the architect's most personal project and the only one he ever built for himself. Although he applied his modular principles to the layout, the single room structure was an exercise in restraint, with a log cabin exterior, small windows and no kitchen or indoor washing facilities.

18.   Leopold, 178.

19.   In his 1984 book, *Technology and the Character of Contemporary Life: A Philosophical Inquiry*, philosopher Albert Borgmann introduced the concept of the device paradigm, in which he explains how technological devices have infiltrated contemporary culture to the extent that people can't live a good life. To rectify this, he argues that we must develop focal practices (for example, gardening or long-distance running) that reignite our engagement and intimate connection. To draw a parallel, the cabin serves a function, but if it becomes more about the final product—the "Porn"— than the practice, then one loses the connection to nature, which is critical to a more authentic experience.

20.   Ellen Rees, *Cabins in Modern Norwegian Literature: Negotiating Place and Identity* (Madison, NJ: Fairleigh Dickinson University Press, 2014), 177. French philosopher Michel Foucault used the term heterotopia to describe places and spaces that have layers of meanings and that operate in non-hegemonic conditions; writings on heterotopia were first published in a 1967 article entitled "Des espaces autres" [Of Other Spaces].

21.   Cronon, 86.

Lower Swedish Cabin, Darby, PA, 1937

Lower Swedish Cabin

Reflecting a history of immigration and settlement, the original cabin architecture in North America borrowed established styles and traditions from Europe and the United Kingdom. One of the earliest examples of Scandinavian log construction in the United States, the Lower Swedish Cabin was built by Swedish or Finnish immigrants who settled along Pennsylvania's Darby Creek in the mid-seventeenth century. Constructed from 74 round logs, the U-notched ends of the rough-hewn white oak, corner chimney, and low, wide doorways are typical of Northern European rural architecture of the period. The modest, one-room cabin features a corner fireplace and a loft space that serves as the sleeping quarters. The opaque lime and stone mortar protected the cabin from the elements; with the exception of a small, one-room addition, the Lower Swedish Cabin remains in its original condition more than 300 years after its construction. Its simple and functional design, as well as its efficient construction, made the Scandinavian log cabin a popular vernacular building type in North America from the seventeenth to the late nineteenth century—one intrinsically connected to the settler experience. Despite its European origins, it occupies a central place in American mythology as a romantic symbol of pioneer life.

Location: Darby, Pennsylvania
Year: c. 1640–50

Type: Log, Settler
Dimensions: 4.9 × 4.3 × 9.1 m
Materials: lime and sand mortar, milled barge boards, red cedar shingles, white oak logs

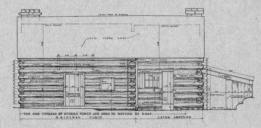

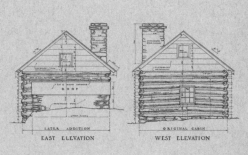

EAST ELEVATION   WEST ELEVATION

<u>Other Examples:</u>
CA Nothnagle Log House, Gibbstown, NJ, c. 1640
Morton Homestead, Prospect Park, PA, 1654
Mortenson-Schorn Log Cabin, Swedesboro, NJ, 1654
Morgan Log House, Kulpsville, PA, c. 1700

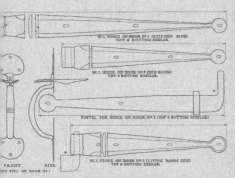

Lower Swedish Cabin, Darby, PA
(measured drawings), 1937
Lower Swedish Cabin, Darby,
PA, 1937

Lone Shieling

Intended to serve as a rudimentary shelter for tourists, the Lone Shieling was one of the first structures built in the Cape Breton Highlands National Park. Modeled on a basic shelter known as a bodhrán—a seasonal dwelling used by shepherds and tenant farmers in Scotland in the eighteenth and nineteenth centuries—the Lone Shieling reveals how vernacular architecture is circulated and adapted through channels of immigration and multicultural expression. Like much of early North American architecture, the history of cabin design manifests varying styles and traditions imported from Europe. With its timber and thatch roof; low, rubble stone walls; stonework detailing; and rectangular form, the Lone Shieling is consistent with this traditional Scottish typology. Selected to honour the heritage of Scottish immigrants in the region and in recognition of the topographical similarities between Cape Breton and the Scottish Highlands, the shelter design deviates from the rustic architecture favoured by Parks Canada and reveals European immigrant influence on the development of Canadian architectural language.

Lone Shieling, Cabot Trail, Cape Breton Highlands National Park, NS, 2009. Couple reading plaque in front of Lone Shieling, Cabot Trail, Cape Breton Highlands National Park, NS, c. 1940s

Location: Cape Breton, Nova Scotia
Year: 1942

Type: Parkitecture
Dimensions: 8.5 × 5.5 m
Materials: fieldstone, flagstone, sod, thatch, wood

Other Examples:
Grey Owl's Cabin, Riding Mountain National Park, MB, 1931
Bunkhouse, Banff National Park of Canada, AB, 1936

Henry Braithwaite Cabins

Henry Braithwaite cabins are examples of simple, one-storey log construction designed to house trappers during hunting expeditions. The fur trade was an important source of revenue for settlers in both Canada and the United States, and the log cabin was adapted to serve as temporary housing during hunting season. Its ease of construction and formal simplicity made its form ideal for provisional shelter erected in backcountry. Henry Braithwaite was an important hunting and fishing guide, among the first to promote New Brunswick as an outdoor sporting destination for international tourists and game hunters. He was known for establishing multiple camps along his extensive network of trap lines. His humble shelters are characteristic of those used by hunters and trappers

across North America from the eighteenth through the early twentieth century. Their modest interiors feature rough plank floors and exposed log walls—sufficient space for sleeping and for storage, and an area to skin and dry hides. They would be outfitted with the necessities for the season—traps, tools, bait, toboggans, food and tobacco—and function as shelter and work spaces, as well as de facto lodges for tourists accompanying him on expeditions. The low-pitched roof with exposed ridgepoles and the use of local peeled spruce logs are typical of the rustic style of architecture that was popular in Canada during the period. While many trappers only inhabited their cabins seasonally, Braithwaite lived well into his eighties alone, full time, in his one-room cabin.

Location: New Brunswick
Year: 1870s–1920s

Type: Trapper, Worker
Dimensions: Variable
Materials: spruce logs

Other Examples:
Trapper Cabin, Commerce City, CO, 1852
Fure's Cabin, Bristol Bay Borough, AK, c. early 1900s
Faille Cabin, Fort Simpson, NWT, 1920

Henry Braithwaite, Frank Risteen and Fred Irland on a hunt, New Brunswick, c. 1893

North Pacific Cannery Workers' Housing

The North Pacific Cannery complex was built in 1889 to house a diverse array of activities related to the fishing industry in British Columbia. Predominantly a salmon cannery, the complex is located at the mouth of the Skeena River and once included a number of wooden structures assembled along a boardwalk, many of which were raised on piles over the river. Relatively isolated in Port Edward, accessible only by boat or rail, the cannery constructed cabin-style accommodation to house labourers during the canning season. The design and layout of these structures reinforced ethnic segregation of its multicultural workforce, and were indicative of prevailing assumptions about the standard of living required for each group. European workers, who primarily held administrative and managerial roles, were provided spacious, two-storey cottage structures to house their families; the cannery manager's residence was the largest on the property. Chinese workers were boarded in two-storey bunkhouses that featured an eating area on the ground floor and sleeping bunks on the upper and lower levels. Intended to accommodate as many workers as possible, the design offered no consideration for comfort or privacy. Japanese fisherman also occupied cavernous bunkhouses divided into small alcoves for each worker, an eating area and a washhouse. The cannery constructed a row of wooden one-room cabins, many without windows, to accommodate Indigenous workers and their families during the fishing and canning season. Indigenous workers were required to outfit their unfurnished accommodations with supplies they brought with them to camp. This collection of modest wood-framed cabins with beveled wood siding and gable roofs reflected the functional design sensibility of the era; canneries along the west coast featured similarly styled administration buildings and residences.

Location: Port Edward, British Columbia
Year: 1889

Type: Worker
Dimensions: Variable
Materials: glass, metal, wood

Other Examples:
Whalers Cabin, Point Lobos State Reserve, CA, c. 1850s
Cannery Row, Steveston, BC, c. late 1800s–early 1900s
Claxton Cannery, Skeena River, BC, x. 1890s–1940s
Inverness Cannery, Skeena River, BC, c. 1890s–1950s
Migrant Worker Houses, Santa Clara, CA, c. 1905–20
Kake Cannery, Kake, AK, c. 1912–40
Cannery Row, Monterey, CA, c. 1920s–40s

North Pacific Cannery, Port
Edward, Skeena River, BC, c. 1910

CABIN FEVER

Shelter

All people at all times have had an inclination toward shelter. The Roman architect Marcus Vitruvius Pollio first commented on the idea of the rudimentary hut between 30 and 15 BC, his commentary later expanded upon and illustrated by Marc-Antoine Laugier in the 1753 treatise *Essai sur l'architecture*. The simple construction method of the first hut, consisting of four poles, four beams and a roof, offered a basis for the origins of architecture, and has since been a recurring subject of investigation in architectural theory. Building a hut, in itself, has served as a rite of urbanization—a way to tame the wild. In North America, driven by European settlement and westward expansion, this practice manifests in the tradition of the log cabin. Its original intent was provisional in nature and, as Alexis de Tocqueville observed, would serve the owner until he "has time to concern himself with the amenities of life, a more spacious dwelling and one better adapted to his needs."[1] Although this building type can be traced to Scandinavia and Eastern Europe, the log cabin helped define a uniquely North American spirit of self-reliance and individualism.

The proliferation of log cabins altered the physical geography of Canada and the United States. This was due in large part to the Dominion Lands Act of 1871 (Canada) and the Homestead Act of 1862 (US), which encouraged western migration by allowing people to claim and develop homesteads; displacing the original inhabitants of the land, homesteaders were part of a larger exercise of colonization by European settlers. The log cabin in North America cannot be divorced from this nefarious history—the architectural typology is central to settler culture and the mythology of the frontier. Literary works by pioneer realist writer Caroline Kirkland and satirist Mark Twain, among others, reveal the cabin's significant role in establishing and shaping larger social consciousness, and contributing to the evolution of a distinctly North American culture.

In addition to offering a simple and expedient housing solution for settlers, the cabin has been adapted over time to service a host of other needs, from temporary workers' housing to alpine hut sanctuaries for mountaineers. Cabins have routinely served as emergency shelters—fire lookout towers, earthquake refugee shacks and other disaster relief structures. Although built as a matter of practicality, the spaces themselves have gathered meaning for their inhabitants. Workers' cabins, ranging from slave cabins and racially segregated labour camps to ice fishing shanties, have protracted and fraught histories. Thus, the cabin has, as a field of study, taken on complex meaning: from its inception, the architectural form has symbolized occupation and dominance; it's been a tool of exploitation and control, and demands to be reconsidered as something beyond mere shelter.

Old cabin, South Dakota, c. 1887–92

—
1. Alexis de Tocqueville, *Journey to America*, trans. George Lawrence, ed. J. P. Mayer (New Haven: Yale University Press, 1960), 334.

43

An Essay on Architecture

Marc-Antoine Laugier

It is the same in architecture as in all other arts: its principles are founded on simple nature, and nature's process clearly indicates its rules. Let us look at man in his primitive state without any aid or guidance other than his natural instincts. He is in need of a place to rest. On the banks of a quietly flowing brook he notices a stretch of grass; its fresh greenness is pleasing to his eyes, its tender down invites him; he is drawn there and, stretched out at leisure on this sparkling carpet, he thinks of nothing else but enjoying the gift of nature; he lacks nothing, he does not wish for anything. But soon the scorching heat of the sun forces him to look for shelter. A nearby forest draws him to its cooling shade; he runs to find a refuge in its depth, and there he is content. But suddenly mists are rising, swirling round and growing denser, until thick clouds cover the skies; soon, torrential rain pours down on this delightful forest. The savage, in his leafy shelter, does not know how to protect himself from the uncomfortable damp that penetrates everywhere; he creeps into a nearby cave and, finding it dry, he praises himself for his discovery. But soon the darkness and foul air surrounding him make his stay unbearable again. He leaves and is resolved to make good by his ingenuity the careless neglect of nature. He wants to make himself a dwelling that protects but does not bury him. Some fallen branches in the forest are the right material for his purpose; he chooses four of the strongest, raises them upright and arranges them in a square; across their top he lays four other branches; on these he hoists from two sides yet another row of branches which, inclining towards each other, meet at their highest point. He then covers this kind of roof with leaves so closely packed that neither sun nor rain can penetrate. Thus, man is housed. Admittedly, the cold and heat will make him feel uncomfortable in this house which is open on all sides but soon he will fill in the space between two posts and feel secure.

Such is the course of simple nature; by imitating the natural process, art was born. All the splendors of architecture ever conceived have been modeled on the little rustic hut I have just described. It is by approaching the simplicity of this first model that fundamental mistakes are avoided and true perfection is achieved. The pieces of wood set upright have given us the idea of the column, the pieces placed horizontally on top of them the idea of the entablature, the inclining pieces forming the roof the idea of the pediment. This is what all masters of art have recognized. But take note of this: never has a principle been more fertile in its effect.

From now on it is easy to distinguish between the parts which are essential to the composition of an architectural Order and those which have been introduced by necessity or have been added by caprice. The parts that are essential are the cause of beauty, the parts introduced by necessity cause every license, the parts added by caprice cause every fault. This calls for an explanation; I shall try to be as clear as possible.

Opposite: Charles Eisen, *Essai sur l'architecture* (frontispiece), 1755

Marc-Antoine Laugier, *An Essay on Architecture* (original French 1753), tr. Wolfgang and Anni Herrmann (Los Angeles: Hennessey & Ingalls, 1977), 11–12.

45

Karl Ove Knausgaard

My Saga — Part 1

The sun was low in the southwestern sky when we arrived at L'Anse aux Meadows. Pierce turned left onto a small driveway. There was a gate; it stood open. That seemed to surprise him as he drove slowly along the access road beyond, which in places was covered with smooth ice. This close to the ocean, the trees grew sparsely and were low and stunted.

On top of a gentle slope, beneath a rock outcrop, there stood a gray, wooden building. Smoke was coming from its chimney. Pierce stopped the car. "We're here," he said.

I got out. The building was obviously some kind of museum or visitor center. Past it was a large plain, and at the end of that was the ocean, which was entirely frozen over. A wooden boardwalk leading down from the building toward the plain where the actual ruins of the settlement lay was in some places covered by snowdrifts, in others bare. I tried the door. Naturally, it was locked.

I walked down the slope, reached the boardwalk and followed it all the way out onto the plain.

In front of me lay a world so beautiful and so cruel that it numbed my senses. The vast expanse of the ice, the dark blue ocean beyond, beneath the pale blue sky, the islands in the distance, sheer cliffs rearing up from the water, and then the strip of land that could be glimpsed to the north, which had to be Labrador.

It was completely silent.

I stood there without moving for a long time, looking out to sea.

The silence did something with the landscape. Usually, something is making a sound. The wind sweeping across the land, whistling past every ridge or rise it encounters. Birds squawking or chirping. And the sea, the constant soughing, night and day, that sometimes in a storm turns into roaring and hissing.

But here everything was still.

All sounds belong to the moment, they are part of the present, the world of change, while the soundless belongs to the unchanging. In silence lies age.

A thousand years is no time at all, I thought.

As I looked out to sea, I had no difficulty imagining a Viking ship approaching land. Green, lush grass, the ocean blue and still, the air filled with the cry of gulls, the smooth rocks crowded with seals.

What were they thinking as they took it all in?

"The Saga of the Greenlanders" describes them as being eager. They had floated into a shallow and been stuck as the tide ran out. "But so much did they desire to land, that they did not give themselves time to wait until the water again rose under their ship, but ran at once on shore, at a place where a river flows out of a lake; but so, soon as the waters rose up under the ship, then took the boats, and rowed to the ship, and floated it up to the river, and thence into the lake, and there cast anchor, and brought up from the ship their skin cots, and made there booths."

Farther out there was a low swaybacked house that had to be a reconstruction of a Viking dwelling. But where were the ruins, the foundations of the actual structures? I looked around. Roughly 50 yards away was a row of humps in the ground. Could that be it?

I had expected fences, signs, like a theme park, something to indicate that this was a tourist attraction. It was, after all, the place where Europeans had set foot on this continent for the very first time.

I walked toward the humps. The scarf I had knotted around my face was already stiff with ice from the moisture in my breath. Just as I thought. These were the remains of their longhouses. Discreet placards offered printed information of a most straightforward kind, such as "A dwelling and small forge."

Left to right: L' Anse aux Meadows, St. Lunaire-Griquet, NL, 2009. L' Anse aux Meadows, St. Lunaire-Griquet, NL (model), c. 1960s

Could that be right? Could this be it?

Yes, it had to be. Here, a small group of Nordic people had lived a thousand years ago. They brought livestock with them, and various tools. They must have lived just as they had back home, hunting, foraging and gathering wood throughout the summer, all in preparation for the hardships of winter.

And yet they were a long way from home, far, far out in the unknown.

The world must have appeared very different to them, I thought. It must have seemed completely open, limitless, uncertain. They sailed west and came to desolate Greenland, with its enormous glaciers, where none of their people had ever been before. They sailed even farther west, without knowing what they would encounter, and landed here.

Were they afraid?

They must have been. Building structures like the ones at home, living in exactly the same manner, must also have been a way to master their fear of the unknown, not to be overwhelmed by it, a way to make the unfamiliar seem familiar.

Ways of Life in Cold Climates: The North American Subarctic

Jean-Luc Pilon

INTRODUCTION

The North American Subarctic is an environmental zone which extends in a broad band from the Atlantic to the Pacific Oceans across the upper portion of the American continent. Its identity combines elements of both physiography and geology. It is essentially a vast tract of land lying between more easily defined regions; it is a land between others.

For the purposes of this general discussion, the Subarctic is considered as those lands lying south of the treeline which defines the southern fringe of the Arctic. Additionally, it is characterized by a tree cover consisting predominantly of evergreen trees, most notably white and black spruce. Most of the North American Subarctic lies between the Arctic to the North and either the Prairies or the Great Lakes/St. Lawrence to the south. Gardner (1981) has presented a survey of the various criteria that have been used to define the Subarctic. Suffice it to say that as a transitional zone different authors will retain certain criteria as more significant than others in setting the limits of the region.

In addition to, and almost certainly as a result of, the physiographic and geologic characteristics of the Subarctic, the region has long been considered a "culture area" in as much as the cultural adaptations documented within the region attest to shared strategies used to cope with common environmental constraints (Wissler 1917; Kroeber 1939). Regardless of how the lines are drawn, the surface area of the Subarctic is second only to that of the Arctic.

The Subarctic is often perceived as being relatively homogenous. However, one should not confuse relative homogeneity with uniformity; the face of the Subarctic is as complex as it is transitory and ever-changing. Its ecological potential, at local levels, is very dynamic and is linked to numerous cycles of birth and death, as much among animal species as plant communities. Thus it follows that the human history of this zone will reflect the efforts of hunter-gatherers, who have lived there over thousands of years, to adapt to the often difficult temperament of this environment.

Map of the North American Subarctic

***

DWELLING STRUCTURES

Archaeologically, remains of distinctive dwelling structures have been documented at several locations within the Subarctic. These are generally of a similar nature regardless of their specific locations and will be described together. It is important to note that what follows is not an extensive list of the types of dwellings known to have been constructed and used in the region (see for example Laliberté 1982). Rather, the few examples presented below provide an archaeological glimpse into the richness and variability of dwelling construction throughout this immense region.

***

2. Western Subarctic

As in the Eastern and Central Subarctic, several different forms of dwelling structures have been documented ethnographically in the Western Subarctic. Some of these have also been documented archaeologically. The overall poor archaeological visibility of many of these different types of houses or shelters can be linked to issues surrounding the perishable nature of the materials employed in their construction as well as the fact that they are surface features which did not leave traces in the underlying soils, and of course, the often cursory nature of the investigations which have taken place to date in many parts of this vast region. In spite of these constraints, it is nonetheless possible to describe some dwellings which attest to strategies aimed at mitigating the harshness of the Subarctic environment.

MOSS HOUSES

Moss houses, or as they are referred to by the Gwich'in of the Mackenzie Valley/Yukon region, ninkun, are a well-known winter dwelling type used throughout the area historically occupied by the Gwich'in and several of their Athapaskan language speaking neighbours (Osgood 1932, 1936). Such houses have been described over a wide area by contemporary chroniclers in the XIXth and XXth centuries in the Mackenzie Valley, Yukon and interior Alaska.

Ninkun were sturdy buildings set into a square depression measuring on the order of 8 metres on each side which was created by the removal of the thick layer of moss, later used to cover the structure's roof. Four center posts supported ridge poles against which roof poles were leaned and covered with an insulating layer of moss. A raised hearth in the center provided the warmth for this dwelling which was occupied for much of the winter season. The interior of such a dwelling was illustrated by Émile Petitot (1889:216) who observed them in November of 1865 among the neighbours of the Gwich'in, the Nné-la-gottiné, or Bâtards Loucheux of the Anderson River drainage in the Northwest Territories. Cornelius Osgood (1936) related similar descriptions that he was given by Gwich'in informants originally from the Fort MacPherson region of the lower Mackenzie Valley and by other Gwich'in informants from the interior of northern Yukon.

Archaeological examples of presumed ninkun-type dwellings are not numerous, but they do exist. For example, Fafard and Le Blanc.(1999:33) reported two shallow depressions at the Dechyoo Nljik site which appear to superficially reflect the ethnographic descriptions. One in particular measured 10m × 6m × 15cm deep before excavation. It had a large hearth in centre, but does not seem to have been excavated.

Well-documented archaeological examples of this type of house construction are reported by A. MacFayden Clark along the Koyukuk River of central Alaska (McFayden Clark 1996). Most of these structures date to the XIXth century. Historic trade goods were among the numerous artifacts recovered from these houses. This leaves the door open to the possibility that EuroAmericans may have influenced the techniques employed in building these dwellings or some of their characteristics. However, a more profoundly confusing situation results from the fact that the study area is at the interface of Koyukuk Athapaskan peoples and Kobuk Inupiat peoples. It is thus not entirely surprising to see that while these houses are quite similar to Gwich'in ninkun, they also have entrance tunnels which are a common feature of Inupiat dwellings.

Drawing of the interior of a Nné-la-gottiné or Bâtard-Loucheux house by Father Emile Petiot

Before excavation the houses looked like shallow but distinct rectangular depressions, with clearly visible tunnels. Surrounding the depressions and further heightening their apparent relief were raised ridges or berms of ground... Protruding from the floor of the pits and from the comers were a few small posts or bases of fallen posts. Along the sides of two houses the tops of some wall sections, which had tilted inward but were not completely caved and buried, were visible (1996:67).

These particular house structures, like the Gwich'in ninkun, were set into depressions excavated into the moss. A raised hearth was located towards the centre of the house. Comer posts supported retainer poles against which steeply inclined poles or planks were placed to form the lateral walls of the structures. Taller paired center posts also supported ridge poles which bore the slightly inclined roof poles or planks. Moss was placed on top of the roof and sheathed with a sewn birchbark covering. The entrance tunnels were excavated below the level of the house floor and covered over with earth and silt atop roof poles.

McFayden Clark (1996:170) makes a worthwhile point in stressing that within the Alaskan Athapaskan house types there were many different construction techniques which could result in superficially similar archaeological remains, especially when excavation is not undertaken.

References

Fafard, M. and R. Le Blanc 1999 "Dechyoo Njik (MIVm-4) and Traditional Land Use Patterns on the Old Crow Flats, Yukon Territory," *Canadian Journal of Archaeology* 23:29-50.

Gardner, J.S. 1981 "General Environment," in Subarctic, Volume 6, *Handbook of North American Indians*, edited by June Helm, Smithsonian Institution, Washington, pp. 5-14.

Kroeber, A.L. 1939 *Cultural and Natural Areas of Native North America*, University of California Publications in American Archaeology and Ethnology, Vol. 38, University of California Press, Berkeley.

Laliberté, M. 1982 La préhistoire du lac Kanaaupscow (*réservoir LG-2- Baie James*), Dossier 53, Ministère des Affaires culturelles, Québec.

McFayden Clark, A. 1996 *Who Lived in This House? A Study of Koyukuk River Semisubterranean Houses*, Archaeological Survey of Canada, Mercury Series Paper No. 153, Canadian Museum of Civilization, Hull.

Osgood, C.B. 1932 'The Ethnography of the Great Bear Lake Indians Annual Report for 1931, National Museum of Canada, Bulletin 70, Ottawa. 1936 *Contributions to the Ethnography of the Kutchin*, Yale University Publications in Anthropology 14, New Haven, Connecticut.

Petitot, É. 1889 *Quinze Ans sous le Cercle Polaire*, Dentu, Paris.

Wissler, C. 1917 *The American Indian*, Douglas C. McMurtrie, New York

Excerpt from Jean-Luc Pilon, "Ways of Life in Cold Climates: The North American Subarctic", in *Revista de Arqueología Americana*, no. 20 (2001), published by the Pan American Institute of Geography and History, pp. 233-288.

51

The Log Cabin in America: From Pioneer Days to the Present

C.A. Weslager

America was settled by restless people...

Whatever their motives, and no matter whence they came, they brought with them their own concepts of the house and the home, of husband and wife relationships, and of child-raising as rooted in Old World sociology. The houses they built when they arrived in America were constructed under the strong cultural influences of their differing European environments, modified by prevailing conditions of the New World climate, the availability of building materials, and social organization.

Englishmen, Dutch, Swedes, Finns, Germans, Swiss, Welsh, and Scotch-Irish carried to the American seaboard individual concepts of their own domestic housing which varied by nationality. As time went on, there was a melding of these nationalities, creating a new social fabric having its own cultural traits in which there persisted strong threads of the past. By the time of the great expansion westward across the continent from the eastern seaboard a century or more later, a recognizable American character was beginning to take shape, and a specialized kind of dwelling ultimately made its appearance—the American log cabin.

In the days of America's expanding frontier, when hundreds of pioneer families left their eastern homes and pushed westward, they faced a hard living without conveniences of any kind.

***

Where woods and trees were plentiful, and this was true in Western Pennsylvania, Maryland, the Virginia and Carolina Piedmont, Ohio, Indiana, Kentucky, Tennessee, Illinois, and elsewhere in the timber-rich areas constituting more than three million square miles of the North American continent, the log cabin became a typical pioneer dwelling. It was young America's answer to the mobile family's gravest problem—a safe and durable haven that an ordinary family man could build with few tools, minimum skills, and little money. It was simple and practical, a direct outgrowth of urgent practical necessity. Log cabins were literally built by the thousands.

***

The availability of trees was the principal factor contributing to the widespread distribution of log housing, but the fact that no nails or spikes were needed to build a log cabin, or to erect a log stockade, was an advantage of the utmost importance. Until the early part of the nineteenth century, nails were hand-wrought by American blacksmiths, and they were relatively high-priced and too heavy to transport in quantity in wagons already overburdened with family necessities. A snug, reasonably tight log cabin could be built without nails, and if necessary, with only one tool—an axe. No pioneer family could long survive without an axe; it was a vital tool used to fell the trees and notch the logs for the cabin. It cleared the land for cornfields and pastures; it was used to sever the spidery roots that held the tree stumps in the earth; to cut wood to size for the fireplace; and to split the rails and posts needed in building fences "horse-high, bull-proof, and pig-tight."

Left to right: Trapper's cabin near Fort Resolution, NWT, 1927. Britton & Rey, *Sunday Morning: Log Cabin*, c. 1908. Log Cabin, Kootenay River, BC, 1887

***

In constructing his cabin, the settler first selected trees with straight smooth trunks of approximately the same diameters. The trees were then felled, cut into logs of the desired length, then pulled by horse, or dragged by hand, to the site of the cabin where the notching was done. The first settler in a new area had to build his cabin alone, or assisted by his wife and children, but as the settlements grew, "raising" a log dwelling was a sort of neighborhood social event. The log cabin became a product of community cooperation with the work carefully divided so that the various materials were ready as needed. A group of choppers felled the trees and cut them to their proper lengths, and a man with a team hauled the logs to the site of the dwelling. There the "corner men" notched and fitted the timbers, and when everything was ready the walls were raised, with all hands assisting in this heavy work. While the roof members were fitted into place, others were wetting down the mud and kneading it with bare hands into the gaps between the logs.

The smaller cabins were usually about twelve to fifteen feet long, sometimes sixteen by eighteen feet, or larger, the axe handle used as a measuring stick. In building a cabin of round logs it was not necessary, or even desirable, to strip off the bark, which, left in place, served to protect the log walls from decay. The logs were laid out and notched at each end to make them fit securely one over the other. Sometimes the top and bottom surfaces of the round logs were axed off to provide a surface for a better fit. The builder had no formal plans or blueprints—he improvised as the cabin took shape. He used whatever trees were nearest to his cabin site—hickory, oak, pine, walnut, chestnut, poplar, and others—but once he had made his choice he preferred to use logs for all four walls of the cabin cut from the same species of tree.

Log cabin construction, Lassen County, CA, 1938

The first four logs were laid in place horizontally flat on the earth, or if the builder intended to install flooring, he placed the four foundation logs on a base of fieldstones or sections of logs set vertically in the earth at each of the four corners. Then he laid other logs across these members to serve as joists, each notched into place. The sidewalls were heightened by laying successive logs one upon the other to a height of seven or eight feet, or sometimes higher. Each log was held in place by its own weight, reinforced by the weight of the log above and supported by the log below. In actuality, the structural technique, although appearing primitive today, was a unique development representing a notable advance in human technology.

If the builder had an auger to make dowel holes, a drawing knife, a frow, a broadaxe, or a crosscut saw he could build a neater cabin than if an axe were his only tool. Most builders allowed the ends of the logs to extend beyond the corners of the dwelling, but a more exacting builder or one adhering to group cultural practice, evened up the ends of the logs and made flush corners if he had the time and tools.

Two limbs at either end of the cabin walls were erected diagonally above the logs to hold the ridgepole, and additional straight limbs were ribbed into place to form the skeleton of the roof, which was covered with tree limbs, or thinner slabs of wood. Shingles or "shakes" held down by "weight timbers" were the preferred roof covering, but their manufacture required skill and riving tools, which many builders did not possess, and so they often covered their roofs with pieces of bark or thatch. The spaces between the logs forming the walls were filled with smaller pieces of wood, or stones wedged tightly, and then caulked with moss, or wet clay, sometimes tempered with animal hair or straw, in the process known as "daubing" or "chinking." Animal skins were sometimes hung on the inside walls to insulate the house in the winter.

After felling the trees, if time permitted—and the builder were sufficiently experienced—he could hew the logs with a short-handled broadaxe or adz

Left to right: Old cabin, location unknown, 1946. Currier & Ives, *The Pioneer Cabin of the Yo-semite Valley*, c. 1800s

before notching and setting them in place. Logs were sometimes hewn only on two surfaces, top and bottom or front and back, but often the complete log was squared by hewing all four sides. Although I have used the term "squared," and will continue to do so, the hewn log seen in cross section was moderately rectangular. Typical of cabins in Pennsylvania are hewn logs measuring six by nine or seven by eleven inches in section. A log can properly be called a "whole timber," and if the log is halved and each half squared, the term "half timber" is applicable. Strictly speaking, therefore, a whole log hewn square, or its halves similarly squared, should be termed a timber, but when used in horizontal, notched construction it was always called a log. In the 1828 edition of his dictionary, Noah Webster said that a piece of timber hewed square was not called a log "unless perhaps in the constructing of log huts," and thus a log could be round or square in its log cabin context. If in the hewing process the logs were reduced in width even smaller than a half timber, the resultant board might properly be termed a plank, and the term "plank house" is sometimes used to describe a structure of logs so hewn. This is a nonspecific term, which I try to avoid, because a house built of unnotched planks conventionally nailed to studding can also be termed a plank house.

The flat surfaces of hewn logs could be made to fit closer together than round logs permitted, and, if carefully notched, there was a minimum of open spaces between the timbers to be chinked. However, no generalizations can be made, because in most American cabins, either of round or hewn logs, interstices were present in the walls; some hewn log dwellings had gaping spaces between the logs equal to, if not wider, than those found in some roundlog cabins. It all depended upon the preference, skill, and cultural background of the builder. Usually a different method of corner notching is found on hewn log houses from that on round logs, and the most common methods of corner notchings characterizing American log construction will be briefly discussed in the concluding chapter of this volume.

55

The front door, which usually opened outward to allow more room inside the cabin, was made of heavy wood slabs fastened with wood pegs before nails were available. The door swung on wood hinges or strips of animal skin, and was usually mounted on the inside with a wood latch and crossbar. Attached to the latch, and threaded through a hole whittled in the door, was a string of buckskin which hung outside the door. When the string was pulled from the outside the latch was lifted from its bracket on the inside and the door could be opened. At night the string was drawn in through the hole, and the door securely barred on the inside. The latchstring hanging outside the door became a symbol of pioneer hospitality and an open invitation for the friendly stranger to enter and share the family table and the warmth of the fireside.

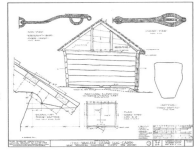

***

To continue with a generalized description of the log cabin, and the reader must realize that there were structural differences varying by area, many of the earliest American cabins were built without windows, and in those having window openings, animal skins or sliding boards were used as coverings. Later, paper greased with animal fat to make it waterproof and translucent was used as a substitute for crown glass, which was not widely manufactured in America until the 1800's. Even when glass was commonly used in city and town dwellings, it was still too expensive for poor cabin builders to buy, and too fragile to transport long distances over rough roads.

***

56

The interior furnishings of the frontier log cabin were simple and practical, and the family's most prized possessions were the articles or utensils brought from the East—dishes, wood or pewter spoons and porringers, a clock, spinning wheel, candlesticks, wooden wash tub, a Bible, and the tinder box with its flint and steel so necessary to start a fire. On the log walls hung firearms, hunting knives, powder horn, gourd dipper, and other domestic utensils. The unpainted benches, stools, tables, and low beds were made of wood, their quality depending on the proficiency of the builder. If there were no candles the cabin was lighted by the knots of the fat pitch pine, sometimes called "candlewood," if it was available, but, if not, the open fireplace provided the only illumination.

Left to right: Woman with spinning wheel outside log cabin, Spokane, WA, c. 1908. Vanleer Cedar Log Cabin, Swedesboro, Gloucester County, NJ (measured drawing), 1938. Cabin interior, Atlin, BC, c. early 1900s

The building of a log cabin required very little time in comparison with modern residential construction, and most cabins were raised in a hurry. There is record of three men felling and trimming the trees, dragging the logs to the nearby house site, notching them, and erecting a one-room cabin complete with chimney and fireplace in two days. Even a solitary builder could construct a cabin alone in a matter of a week or two, although it necessarily had to be small, because one man, unaided, had difficulty lifting heavy logs to a wall position above his head. Six or eight tiers of short logs was about as high as one man could go. Assisted by a second man, or strong boys, he could cut longer logs and raise the walls higher by using skids consisting of two logs placed at an angle against the wall to serve as an inclined plane, and forked sticks or ropes to guide the logs into place.

C.A. Weslager, *The Log Cabin in America: From Pioneer Days to the Present* (New Brunswick, NJ: Rutgers University Press, 1969), 3, 6, 8–9, 13–16, 17–18, 19–20. Reprinted with permission of the author.

Homesteading

Jennifer M. Volland

Above: Covered wagon, Lucille, ID, c. 1800s

Opposite: Poster produced by the Burlington & Missouri River Railroad Co. advertising land in Iowa and Nebraska, 1872

Beginning in the seventeenth century, waves of immigration in North America built on, expanded, and more often, destroyed and displaced the Indigenous forms that had emerged in the millennia prior to first contact with European settlers. When Swedish and Finnish immigrants settled along Pennsylvania's Darby Creek their round log, one room cabins reflected the building traditions of central Sweden and notably that of the Forest Finns, who had been forcibly migrated to Sweden in the late sixteenth century. The Forest Finns implemented a slash-and-burn technique to transform the forests (home to the Indigenous Sami people) into farmland. These same techniques were enacted on the lands of the Indigenous Lenni Lenape (or Delaware) people to make room for the New Sweden colonies. This devastating intervention set the pattern for what would follow throughout North America.

The Homestead Act of 1862 continued to dramatically alter the physical and cultural landscape of the United States, precipitating westward expansion and fostering the pioneer mentality so ingrained in the country's history. This piece of legislation, signed into law by President Abraham Lincoln, offered 270 million acres of the public domain to private citizens. It allowed nearly any person that headed a household or was at least 21 years of age—including newly arrived immigrants, single women and former slaves—to claim a 160-acre parcel of land. Upon paying a filing fee of $18, homesteaders were required to live, build a home or cabin, and farm and improve the land for five years to be eligible for legal possession.

By the time it was repealed in 1976, two million people filed claims under the Homestead Act. While many recall the positive aspects of the legislation—in that it provided a "fair chance" at the American dream of land ownership—the hardships of living life on the land proved too much for many

PRODUCTS WILL PAY FOR LAND AND IMPROVEMENTS!

MILLIONS OF ACRES

View on the Big Blue, between Camden and Crete, representing Valley and Rolling Prairie Land in Nebraska.

IOWA AND NEBRASKA
LANDS

FOR SALE ON 10 YEARS CREDIT

BY THE

Burlington & Missouri River R. R. Co.

AT 6 PER CT. INTEREST AND LOW PRICES.

Only One-Seventh of Principal Due Annually, beginning Four Years after purchase.

.20 PER CENT. DEDUCTED FROM 10 YEARS PRICE, FOR CASH.

LAND EXPLORING TICKETS SOLD

and Cost allowed in First Interest paid, on Land bought in 30 days from date of ticket.

Thus our Land Buyers ☞ GET A FREE PASS in the State where the Land bought is located. These TERMS are BETTER at $5, than to pre-empt United States Land at $2.50 per Acre.

EXTRAORDINARY INDUCEMENTS on FREIGHT and PASSAGE are AFFORDED TO PURCHASERS and THEIR FAMILIES.

Address **GEO. S. HARRIS, LAND COMMISSIONER,**
or **T. H. LEAVITT,** Ass't Land Comm'r, Burlington, Iowa.

Or apply to

FREE ROOMS for buyers to board themselves are provided at Burlington and Lincoln.

COMMERCIAL ADVERTISER PRINTING HOUSE, BUFFALO, N. Y.

CIRCULARS are supplied GRATIS for distribution in ORGANIZING COLONIES and to induce individuals to emigrate WEST.

A SECTIONAL MAP, showing exact location of our IOWA LANDS is sold for 30 Cents, and of NEBRASKA LANDS for 30 Cents.

homesteaders and over half the claims were abandoned. Furthermore, the impact this mass westward migration had on the Indigenous populations was devastating. The government seized and redistributed appropriated land—enticing prospective settlers with posters advertising "free land"—in an effort to control vast amounts of acreage in the United States, and to destabilize and contain the Indigenous populations.

In a similar way, the Canadian government entered into treaties with many of the Indigenous nations of the Prairies region of Western Canada to seize and secure land for settlement. The Dominion Lands Act of 1872 was modelled on the American Homestead Act. Utilizing a similar system, the Canadian government, supported by railways and other commercial enterprises, encouraged mass emigration by European and American immigrants, as well as settlers from the eastern part of the country.

Homesteading cabins were anything but luxurious. They were erected quickly and from readily available materials (mainly sod or logs, depending on location), and they were often thought of as temporary structures until a larger permanent home could be built. The Homestead Act specified a minimum of ten by twelve feet and one glass window; most were a single room that served as the kitchen, dining, living, sleeping and working quarters.

Left to right: Homesteader's cabin, Bitterroot National Forest, Ravalli County, MT, 1906. Poster advertising land in Manitoba to Dutch immigrants, c. 1890. Log cabin, Rideau River, ON, c. 1920s

61

A New Home, Who'll Follow? Or, Glimpses of Western Life

Caroline M. Kirkland

The log-house, was to be our temporary home, was tenanted at this time; and we were obliged to wait while the incumbent could build a framed one; the materials for which had been growing in the woods not long before; I was told it would take but a short time, as it was already framed.

What was my surprise, on walking that way to ascertain the progress of things, to find the materials still scattered on the ground, and the place quite solitary.

'Did not Mr. Ketchum say Green's house was framed?' said I to the *dame du palais,* on my return; 'the timbers are all lying on the ground, and nobody at work.'

'Why, la! so they be all framed, and Green's gone to—for the sash. They'll be ready to raise tomorrow.'

It took me some time to understand that *framing* was nothing more than cutting the tenons and mortices ready for putting the timbers together, and that these must be *raised* before there could be a frame. And that 'sash,' which I in my ignorance supposed could be but for one window, was a *generic* term.

The 'raising' took place the following afternoon, and was quite an amusing scene to us cockneys, until one man's thumb was frightfully mashed, and another had a severe blow upon the head. A jug of whiskey was pointed out by those who understood the matter, as the true cause of these disasters, although the Fates got the blame.

'Jem White always has such bad luck!' said Mr. Ketchum, on his return from the raising, 'and word spake never more,' for that night at least; for he disappeared behind the mysterious curtain, and soon snored most sonorously.

The many raisings which have been accomplished at Montacute, without that ruinous ally, strong drink, since the days of which I speak, have been free from accidents of any sort; Jem White having carried his 'bad luck' to a distant country, and left his wife and children to be taken care of by the public.

Our cottage bore about the same proportion to the articles we had expected to put into it that the 'lytell hole' did to the fiend whom Virgilius cajoled into its narrow compass; and the more we reflected, the more certain we became that without the magic powers of necromancy, one half of our moveables at least must remain in the open air. To avoid such necessity, Mr. Clavers was obliged to return to Detroit and provide storage for sundry unwieldly boxes which could by no art of ours be conjured into our cot.

"Why, law! that's nothing but pride now: folks is often too proud to take comfort. For my part I could'nt do without my pipe to please nobody"   p. 69

While he was absent, Green had enclosed his new house; that is to say, put on the roof and the siding; and laid one floor, and forthwith he removed thither without door, window, or chimney, a course by no means unusual in Michigan.

As I was by this time, truth to speak, very nearly starved, I was anxious to go as soon as possible to a place where I could feel a little more at home; and so completely had my nine days at Ketchum's brought down my ideas, that I anticipated real satisfaction in a removal to this hut in the wilderness. I would not wait for Mr. Clavers' return; but insisted on setting up for myself at once.

But I should in vain attempt to convey to those who know nothing of the woods, any idea of the difficulties in my way. If one's courage did not increase, and one's invention brighten under the stimulus of such occasions, I should have given up at the outset, as I have often done with far less cause.

Excerpt from Caroline M. Kirkland, *A New Home, Who'll Follow? Or, Glimpses of Western Life,* New York: C.S. Francis & Co., 1855

Left to right: Portrait of Caroline M. Kirkland, 1852. Caroline M. Kirkland, *A New Home, Who'll Follow? Or, Glimpses of Western Life* (page 69), 1841

Unsettling the Frontier: Gender and Racial Identity in Caroline Kirkland's <u>A New Home, Who'll Follow?</u> and <u>Forest Life</u>

Dawn E. Keetley

The border separating the gendered ideologies of selfhood that "indoors" and "outdoors" represent is also transgressed, in *A New Home*, when Mary Clavers describes moving from a neighbors' cabin into a log-house of her own. Anxious to move into "a place where I could feel a little more at home," she decides to move when her prospective home unexpectedly becomes vacant, even though her husband is in Detroit. Intent on creating a home from this rude log cabin—moving, cleaning, and preparing supper for her children—the narrator finds that the fire has made the house uninhabitable, so she and her family have to sleep with all the windows and "both doors open, and in this exposed situation," she writes, "passed the first night in my western home": she is kept awake first by the fear of "wild beasts" and then by a "wild storm of wind and rain which drove in upon us and completely wetted every thing within reach"(42–43). This moment of utter absorption in home-building represents the ideological outer limit—or threshold—of domesticity, the point of its possible reversal, at which it potentially becomes something other. The home that Mary Clavers was trying so hard to create and shore up becomes open to the outside. The image of the interior of the home merging with the exterior—the beasts, the rain, the very air—is heightened by the fact that the next day the narrator has to relinquish some of her furniture, leaving it outside (such as the "cup-board," which becomes a corn-crib). The "inside" and "outside" of the home are reversed and in the process of that reversal the home is constituted as a threshold, as neither wholly inside nor outside.

Kirkland's unmaking of the walls of "home" and of the ideology of separate spheres is also figured in a "moving" house, in her tendency to describe homes as in motion, never completely in place. The houses which Mary Clavers and her family inhabit on the frontier are permeated with a certain mobility, thus undercutting the notion of a stable home. At first the Claverses live in a log-cabin, a "temporary" home (Kirkland 1990, 46), but even when they move to their frame-house, the narrator says that this "new house was merely the beginning of a house" (64). "Home" is always

Opposite: Caroline M. Kirkland, *A New Home, Who'll Follow? Or, Glimpses of Western Life* (title page), 1841

64

changing—in the process of becoming a home but never arriving at a fixed end-point. The very title (A New Home, Who'll *Follow*), in its lack of specificity about what exactly is to be followed, suggests that perhaps it is the home itself that is removing and that should be followed. In *Forest Life*, the narrator insists on the impossibility of carrying both the physical and the social structures of ready-made "homes" intact onto the frontier: "To people circumstanced as we are, some modifications of the ordinary relations of society must be absolutely necessary. Colonists must not expect to carry with them the social fabric undisturbed, as houses are transported in the city" (Kirkland 1842, 1: 147). The narrator's use of a domestic trope, the house, suggests that it is particularly the social ideal of womanhood (metonymically connected to the home) that cannot be transferred across space "undisturbed." She goes on to compare the change that a traveller undergoes on the frontier to that "final" change—death: it is "'a separation from all that has hitherto engaged us; a change not only of the *place*, but of the manner of our *being*'" (1: 33; emphasis added). In connecting "place" and "being," and in describing the change, even dissolution, of the familiar self as it moves across the frontier, Kirkland's texts show that women can evade the interiorized, home-bound identities and places of idealized womanhood: both self and space are transformed by travel. And on the frontier, women were transformed, learned to "move" in fact, through traversing the boundaries between the ideologies of domesticity and of free-ranging "masculine" motion.

Republished with permission of University of Nebraska Press Journals, from "Unsettling the Frontier: Gender and Racial Identity in Caroline Kirkland's *A New Home, Who'll Follow?* and *Forest Life*," Dawn E. Keetley, *Legacy* 12, no.1, 1995; permission conveyed through Copyright Clearance Center, Inc.

Democracy in America

Alexis de Tocqueville

Sometimes the progress of man is so rapid that the desert reappears behind him. The woods stoop to give him a passage, and spring up again when he has passed. It is not uncommon in crossing the new States of the West to meet with deserted dwellings in the midst of the wilds; the traveller frequently discovers the vestiges of a log house in the most solitary retreats, which bear witness to the power, and no less to the inconstancy of man. In these abandoned fields, and over these ruins of a day, the primeval forest soon scatters a fresh vegetation, the beasts resume the haunts which were once their own, and Nature covers the traces of man's path with branches and with flowers, which obliterate his evanescent track.

I remember that, in crossing one of the woodland districts which still cover the State of New York, I reached the shores of a lake embosomed in forests coeval with the world. A small island, covered with woods whose thick foliage concealed its banks, rose from the centre of the waters. Upon the shores of the lake no object attested the presence of man except a column of smoke which might be seen on the horizon rising from the tops of the trees to the clouds, and seeming to hang from heaven rather than to be mounting to the sky. An Indian shallop was hauled up on the sand, which tempted me to visit the islet that had first attracted my attention, and in a few minutes I set foot upon its banks. The whole island formed one of those delicious solitudes of the New World which almost lead civilized man to regret the haunts of the savage. A luxuriant vegetation bore witness to the incomparable fruitfulness of the soil. The deep silence which is common to the wilds of North America

was only broken by the hoarse cooing of the wood-pigeon, and the tapping of the woodpecker upon the bark of trees. I was far from supposing that this spot had ever been inhabited, so completely did Nature seem to be left to her own caprices; but when I reached the centre of the isle I thought that I discovered some traces of man. I then proceeded to examine the surrounding objects with care, and I soon perceived that a European had undoubtedly been led to seek a refuge in this retreat. Yet what changes had taken place in the scene of his labors! The logs which he had hastily hewn to build himself a shed had sprouted afresh; the very props were intertwined with living verdure, and his cabin was transformed into a bower. In the midst of these shrubs a few stones were to be seen, blackened with fire and sprinkled with thin ashes; here the hearth had no doubt been, and the chimney in falling had covered it with rubbish. I stood for some time in silent admiration of the exuberance of Nature and the littleness of man: and when I was obliged to leave that enchanting solitude, I exclaimed with melancholy, "Are ruins, then, already here?"

Excerpt from Alexis de Tocqueville, *Democracy in America*, New York: Adlard and Saunders, 1838.

Left to right: Abandoned log cabin, 1910. Log cabin, Adirondack Mountains, NY, 1912. Portrait of Alexis de Tocqueville, 1901

Roughing It

Mark Twain

After leaving the Sink, we traveled along the Humboldt river a little way. People accustomed to the monster mile-wide Mississippi, grow accustomed to associating the term "river" with a high degree of watery grandeur. Consequently, such people feel rather disappointed when they stand on the shores of the Humboldt or the Carson and find that a "river" in Nevada is a sickly rivulet which is just the counterpart of the Erie canal in all respects save that the canal is twice as long and four times as deep. One of the pleasantest and most invigorating exercises one can contrive is to run and jump across the Humboldt river till he is overheated, and then drink it dry.

On the fifteenth day we completed our march of two hundred miles and entered Unionville, Humboldt county, in the midst of a driving snow-storm. Unionville consisted of eleven cabins and a liberty-pole. Six of the cabins were strung along one side of a deep canyon, and the other five faced them. The rest of the landscape was made up of bleak mountain walls that rose so high into the sky from both sides of the canyon that the village was left, as it were, far down in the bottom of a crevice. It was always daylight on the mountain tops a long time before the darkness lifted and revealed Unionville.

We built a small, rude cabin in the side of the crevice and roofed it with canvas, leaving a corner open to serve as a chimney, through which the cattle used to tumble occasionally, at night, and mash our furniture and interrupt our sleep. It was very cold weather and fuel was scarce. Indians brought brush and bushes several miles on their backs; and when we could catch a laden Indian it was well—and when we could not (which was the rule, not the exception), we shivered and bore it.

I confess, without shame, that I expected to find masses of silver lying all about the ground. I expected to see it glittering in the sun on the mountain summits. I said nothing about this, for some instinct told me that I might possibly have an exaggerated idea about it, and so if I betrayed my thought I might bring derision upon myself. Yet I was as perfectly satisfied in my own mind as I could be of anything, that I was going to gather up, in a day or two, or at furthest a week or two, silver enough to make me satisfactorily wealthy— and so my fancy was already busy with plans for spending this money. The first opportunity that offered, I sauntered carelessly away from the cabin, keeping an eye on the other boys, and stopping and contemplating the sky when they seemed to be observing me; but as soon as the coast was manifestly clear,

Mark Twain, *Roughing It* (illustrations), 1872

I fled away as guiltily as a thief might have done and never halted till I was far beyond sight and call. Then I began my search with a feverish excitement that was brimful of expectation—almost of certainty. I crawled about the ground, seizing and examining bits of stone, blowing the dust from them or rubbing them on my clothes, and then peering at them with anxious hope. Presently I found a bright fragment and my heart bounded! I hid behind a boulder and polished it and scrutinized it with a nervous eagerness and a delight that was more pronounced than absolute certainty itself could have afforded. The more I examined the fragment the more I was convinced that I had found the door

to fortune. I marked the spot and carried away my specimen. Up and down the rugged mountain side I searched, with always increasing interest and always augmenting gratitude that I had come to Humboldt and come in time. Of all the experiences of my life, this secret search among the hidden treasures of silver-land was the nearest to unmarred ecstasy. It was a delirious revel.

***

We thought it well to have a strong friend, and therefore we brought the foreman of the Wide West to our cabin that night and revealed the great surprise to him.

69

Higbie said:

"We are going to take possession of this blind lead, record it and establish ownership, and then forbid the Wide West company to take out any more of the rock. You cannot help your company in this matter—nobody can help them. I will go into the shaft with you and prove to your entire satisfaction that it is a blind lead. Now we propose to take you in with us, and claim the blind lead in our three names. What do you say?"

What could a man say who had an opportunity to simply stretch forth his hand and take possession of a fortune without risk of any kind and without wronging any one or attaching the least taint of dishonor to his name? He could only say, "Agreed."

The notice was put up that night, and duly spread upon the recorder's books before ten o'clock. We claimed two hundred feet each—six hundred feet in all—the smallest and compactest organization in the district, and the easiest to manage.

No one can be so thoughtless as to suppose that we slept, that night. Higbie and I went to bed at midnight, but it was only to lie broad awake and think, dream, scheme. The floorless, tumble-down cabin was a palace, the ragged gray blankets silk, the furniture rosewood and mahogany. Each new splendor that burst out of my visions of the future whirled me bodily over in bed or jerked me to a sitting posture just as if an electric battery had been applied to me. We shot fragments of conversation back and forth at each other. Once Higbie said:

"When are you going home—to the States?"

"To-morrow!"—with an evolution or two, ending with a sitting position. "Well—no—but next month, at furthest."

"We'll go in the same steamer."

"Agreed."

A pause.

"Steamer of the 10th?"

"Yes. No, the 1st."

"All right."

Another pause.

"Where are you going to live?" said Higbie.

"San Francisco."

"That's me!"

Pause.

"Too high—too much climbing"—from Higbie.

"What is?"

"I was thinking of Russian Hill—building a house up there."

"Too much climbing? Shan't you keep a carriage?"

"Of course. I forgot that."

Pause.

"Cal., what kind of a house are you going to build?"

"I was thinking about that. Three-story and an attic."

"But what kind?"

"Well, I don't hardly know. Brick, I suppose."

"Brick—bosh."

"Why? What is your idea?"

"Brown stone front—French plate glass—billiard-room off the dining-room—statuary and paintings—shrubbery and two-acre grass plat—greenhouse—iron dog on the front stoop—gray horses—landau, and a coachman with a bug on his hat!"

"By George!"

A long pause.

"Cal., when are you going to Europe?"

"Well—I hadn't thought of that. When are you?"

"In the Spring."

"Going to be gone all summer?"

"All summer! I shall remain there three years."

"No—but are you in earnest?"

"Indeed I am."

"I will go along too."

"Why of course you will."

"What part of Europe shall you go to?"

"All parts. France, England, Germany—Spain, Italy, Switzerland, Syria, Greece, Palestine, Arabia, Persia, Egypt—all over—everywhere."

"I'm agreed."

"All right."

"Won't it be a swell trip!"

"We'll spend forty or fifty thousand dollars trying to make it one, anyway."

Another long pause.

"Higbie, we owe the butcher six dollars, and he has been threatening to stop our—"

"Hang the butcher!"

"Amen."

And so it went on. By three o'clock we found it was no use, and so we got up and played cribbage and smoked pipes till sunrise. It was my week to cook. I always hated cooking—now, I abhorred it.

The news was all over town. The former excitement was great—this one was greater still. I walked the streets serene and happy. Higbie said the foreman had been offered two hundred thousand dollars for his third of the mine. I said I would like to see myself selling for any such price. My ideas were lofty. My figure was a million. Still, I honestly believe that if I had been offered it, it would have had no other effect than to make me hold off for more.

Mark Twain, *Roughing It* (illustration), 1872

I found abundant enjoyment in being rich. A man offered me a three-hundred-dollar horse, and wanted to take my simple, unendorsed note for it. That brought the most realizing sense I had yet had that I was actually rich, beyond shadow of doubt. It was followed by numerous other evidences of a similar nature—among which I may mention the fact of the butcher leaving us a double supply of meat and saying nothing about money.

By the laws of the district, the "locators" or claimants of a ledge were obliged to do a fair and reasonable amount of work on their new property within ten days after the date of the location, or the property was forfeited, and anybody could go and seize it that chose. So we determined to go to work the next day. About the middle of the afternoon, as I was coming out of the post office, I met a Mr. Gardiner, who told me that Capt. John Nye was lying dangerously ill at his place (the "Nine-Mile Ranch"), and that he and his wife were not able to give him nearly as much care and attention as his case demanded. I said if he would wait for me a moment, I would go down and help in the sick room. I ran to the cabin to tell Higbie. He was not there, but I left a note on the table for him, and a few minutes later I left town in Gardiner's wagon.

Mark Twain, *Roughing It*, Hartford: American Pub. Co., 1891, 202-205; 281-284

The Problem of Housing the Negro: The Home of the Slave

W.E.B. Du Bois

Above: Uncle Ben's Cabin, c. 1868–1900

Opposite: Walker Evans, *Negro Cabin, Hale County, Alabama*, 1936

It is always difficult to discuss questions connected with American slavery in a scientific spirit because that institution varied so in different places and periods and because the term connotes such different facts in different minds. In speaking therefore of the houses in which the slaves lived we must discriminate between conditions and phases of development. The first American slavery was in the West Indies. Stolen and sold from their African huts the Negroes went through all the horrors of the "middle passage" i. e., the sea voyage to the New World. Sea voyages under modern conditions are very pleasant things; but in small sailing vessels, sweeping through the heat of the torrid zone, with human beings crowded and jammed together amid filth, dirt and disease, helpless before the lust and brutality of their captors—it was a foretaste of hell, and half and more of the slaves welcomed death long before they sighted the palms and flowers of the West Indies.

Once landed and "seasoned" to the new climate and surroundings, the houses they built were not unlike those they had left at home. Nothing was provided for them save some rough building material. From this the slaves constructed their homes, driving four posts into the ground and weaving the walls of wattles so as to make a room 10 × 15 feet and 5 or 6 feet high, or possibly two rooms. There was no floor, window, or fire-place, and the roof was thatched with palms. Furniture was scanty; a rough platform raised the sleepers from the often wet earth, and this sometimes had a mat or blanket; then there was perhaps a table, some low stools, an earthern jar for water, an iron pot for cooking and calabashes for eating. The cooking was done out of doors usually and if the fire was made indoors there was no place for smoke to escape, save through the doorway.

72

When slaves were few and land plentiful these rude homes were not unpleasant. They often had two rooms, could be kept clean and shady; and something like the old African life, with quasi-chief, medicine man and polygamy appeared. Such tendencies, however, quickly passed, and the cold brutality of slavery soon appeared, where life was nothing and sugar was all. The homes of the slaves became dirty one-room lodges where, crowded like cattle, men slept in dreamless stupor after endless hours of forced and driven toil. All pretense at marriage and the protection of black women was virtually swept away, and herded and whipped like cattle, the black men existed until like beasts they fell in their tracks and died, and fresh loads of half-putrid new-comers were emptied on the shores by the thrift of British noblemen and New England deacons.

Early slavery in Virginia and Carolina was scarcely a system. The pioneers needed, above all, "help," and they secured it in the best and cheapest manner. They bought English bond servants, they impressed Indians, they clamored for Negro slaves. In two of these cases, however, a strong social organization protected and mitigated the severity of the bondage. Community of blood secured in the end only temporary slavery for the white, and the fear of the strong tribal organization of the Indians made Indian slaves dangerous. With the Negroes it was different: they were far from home, of various nations and languages, and in long centuries the better element of them was eliminated. Negro slavery therefore soon became a system with laws and organization. At first the slaves were housed in rough log cabins near the master, and the accommodations of the two were not widely different. Thus arose the first type of slave home in America—the "Patriarchal Group." The central idea of this arrangement was distinctly mediæval and feudal, and consequently familiar to its founders. First, then, was the house of the master—a large log house of two or four rooms; near it were grouped the one-room log cabins. With the light building material of the Indies it cost little more trouble to build two rooms than to build one. But with the heavy logs of Carolina pine, one room was as much as could be afforded. The room was larger and higher than formerly, perhaps 15 × 20 feet, and 6 or more feet high; it had still the dirt floor. A cooler climate, however, made some other provisions necessary: a rough fire-place of stones, clay and wood was constructed and a hole in the wall, closed by a wooden shutter, served with the door for light and ventilation. The slave cabin was thus a smaller and meaner edition of the Big House; there the chimney was stone or brick, the house of logs, with board floor, and partitioned into two or four rooms and a hall. Here the group lived as master and men. At first the bond between them was almost purely legal and economic. The slaves were white and black, and the social station of the master not usually high. The condition of the bondsmen therefore depended largely on accident and whim. Here they were squalid, dirty and driven with the lash; there, a lazy dawdling crowd, or again, simply thrifty farm-hands. Out of this chaos evolved the Virginia ideal. The white bond servants became gradually free and migrated southward; a rigid slave-code carefully fixed the status of the black slave; he was no longer allowed to intermarry with white servants or to become a full-fledged freeman; on the other hand excessive and wanton cruelty toward him was in some degree restrained. The slave had learned the English language and had assumed Christianity. Bonds of friendship and intimacy grew up between black and white; the physical group of Big House and cabins came nearer together and the group formed a great feudal family of lord and retainers.

The Hermitage, Savannah, GA, c. 1907

But the curse of such families, with slaves at the bottom and a privileged aristocracy at the top—ever was and ever will be, sexual debauchery. The morals of black women and white men are found to be ruined under such an arrangement unless long-revered custom and self-respect enter to check license. But the African home with its customs had long ago been swept away and slavery is simply a system for crushing self-respect. Nevertheless time was slowly beginning to provide remedies. White fathers could not see their black daughters utterly neglected, and white mothers saw the danger of surrounding their sons with vice and ignorance. Thus, gradually, the better class of slaves were brought closer into the bosom of the family as house-servants. Religion and marriage rites received more attention and the Negro monogamic family rose as a dependent off-shoot of the feudal slave regime. The first sign of this was the improvement in the Negro home: the house of the house-servants became larger, sometimes with two rooms; a more careful regard for outward decency was manifest and the direct intercourse between the cabin and Big House brought better manners and ways of living.

One can easily imagine in this development how slavery might have worked itself out for the good of black and white. And usually those persons North and South who dwell on the advantages and training of slavery have this phase of development in mind. The truth is, however, that this was but a phase and a rapidly disappearing phase of American slavery in 1861.

74

Slave quarters, The Hermitage, Savannah, GA, c. 1907

The cotton-gin doomed the patriarchal slave group. Commercial slavery, which looked upon the slave primarily as an investment, meant death to the Negro home. One of the first signs of the changed condition of things was perhaps the "Detached Group" as I shall designate the second type of slave homes. The "Detached Group" was the group of slave cabins without a Big House—i. e. removed from the direct eye of the master, either to a far part of the same plantation or to a different plantation. The Big House has turned to brick, with imposing proportions, surrounding trees and gardens and a certain state and elegance with which the old South was flavored.

The house servants are now either lodged in the Big House or in trim cabins near. The mass of the slaves are down at the "quarters" by themselves, under the direct eye of the overseer. This change was slight in appearance but of great importance; it widened the distance between the top and bottom of the social ladder, it placed a third party between master and slave and it removed the worst side of the slave hierarchy far from the eyes of its better self.

At first thought it might seem an advantage to remove thus the extremes of society from each other. Nineteenth century experience has, however, taught us better. It not only deprives the helpless of their sole source of help, but among the lowest orders themselves it strengthens the hands of the worst element. Thieving, sexual looseness and debauchery could now be spread among the slave cabins by the act of the Negroes themselves far faster than occasional visits of the mistress could counteract the evil. The Negro home, deprived of nearly every method of self-protection, received here its deadliest hurt, from which it has not yet recovered.

75

From the "Detached Group" to "Absentee Landlordism" was but a step. The rich lands to the southwest, the high price of cotton, and the rapidly increasing internal slave trade, was the beginning of a system of commercial slavery in the gulf states which will ever remain a disgraceful chapter in American history. In its worst phase there was no Big House and cultivated master, only an unscrupulous, paid overseer, lawless and almost irresponsible if he only made crops large enough. The homes of the field-hands were filthy hovels where they slept. There was no family life, no meals, no marriages, no decency, only an endless round of toil and a wild debauch at Christmas time. In the forests of Louisiana, the bottoms of Mississippi, and the Sea Islands of Georgia, where the Negro slave sank lowest in oppression and helplessness, the Negro home practically disappeared, and the house was simply rude, inadequate shelter.

Belle Kearney, *A Slaveholder's Daughter* (plate), 1900

But whither went the Big House, when so entirely separated from the slave quarters? It moved to town and with it moved the house-servants. These privileged slaves were trained and refined from contact with the masters; they were often allowed to accumulate a *peculium*; they were in some cases freed and gained considerable property, holding it in some friendly white man's name. Their home life improved and although it was far from ideal, yet it was probably as good as that of the Northern workingman, with some manifest differences; sexual looseness was the weakest point, arising from subordination to the whites and the lessons learned therefrom by the servants themselves. They lived often in small one- or two-room homes behind the masters' mansions, reached by alleys—a method which has since left the peculiar alley problem in Southern cities. Some of the slaves and the freedmen lived in a Negro quarter by themselves, although the distinctive Negro quarter of towns is largely post-bellum.

76

Thus we have in slavery times, among other tendencies and many exceptions, three fairly distinct types of Negro homes: the patriarchal type, found at its best in Virginia, where the housing of the field hands might be compared with that of the poorer of the Northern workingmen; the separate group and absentee type where the slaves had practically no homes and no family life; and the town group where the few house-servants were fairly well housed. In discussing slavery and incidents connected with it these varying circumstances are continually lost sight of. Nowhere are they portrayed with more truth and sanity than in "Uncle Tom's Cabin," and yet to this day there are unbalanced minds that, having known personally only the Shelbys or the St. Clairs, refuse absolutely to believe in the reality of Legree.

The house of the slave, which I have sought to show in its various relationships and degrees of squalor, had certain general characteristics which we must notice carefully. First, there was the lack of comfort; the African knew nothing of the little niceties and comforts of the civilized home—everything of beauty and daintiness had disappeared with the rude uprooting of the African home, and little had been learned to replace them. Thus, even to this day, there is a curious bareness and roughness in the ordinary Negro home, the remains of an uncouthness which in slavery times made the home anything but a pleasant lovable place. There were, for instance, few chairs with backs, no sheets on the beds, no books, no newspapers, no closets or out-houses, no bed-rooms, no table-cloths and very few dishes, no carpets and usually no floors, no windows, no pictures, no clocks, no lights at night save that of the fire-place, little or nothing save bare rough shelter.

Secondly, and closely connected with the first, was the lack of hygienic customs: every nation has its habits and customs, handed down from elders, which have enabled the race to survive. But the continuity of Negro family tradition had been broken and the traditions of the white environment never learned; then too the rules and exactions of the plantation favored unhealthy habits; there ensued a disgusting lack of personal cleanliness, bad habits of eating and sleeping, habits of breathing bad air, of wearing inadequate clothing—all such changes and abuses in everyday life for which the world's grandchildren must eventually pay.

Thirdly, there was in the slave home necessarily almost an entire lack of thrift, or the ordinary incentives to thrift. The food and fuel were certain and extra faithfulness or saving could make little or no difference. On the other hand, cunning and thieving could secure many a forbidden knick-knack, far more than honest cultivation of the little garden spot which each family often had. The thriftiest slave could only look forward to slavery for himself and children.

Fourthly, there was the absence of the father—that is, the lack of authority in the slave father to govern or protect his family. His wife could be made his master's concubine, his daughter could be outraged, his son whipped, or he himself sold away without his being able to protest or lift a preventing finger. Naturally, his authority in his own house was simply such as could rest upon brute force alone, and he easily sank to a position of male guest in the house, without respect or responsibility.

Fifthly, and correlated to the last, was the absence of the mother. The slave mother could spend little or no time at home. She was either a field-hand or a house-servant, and her children had little care or attention. There was consequently in the family no feeling of unity or permanence; it was a temporary, almost fortuitous agglomeration of atoms—it was not an organism, and it had neither force nor pride.

Such was the home and the family which slavery bequeathed to freedom.

W.E.B. Du Bois, "The Problem of Housing the Negro: The Home of the Slave," *Southern Workman* 30 (1901): 486–95.

Railway Cabins

During construction of the trans-Canada railway, the Canadian Pacific Railway (CPR) built cabins—both temporary and more permanent structures—close to the tracks, to accommodate its workforce and house regional offices. To subsidize the enormous cost of railway construction, the Canadian government granted the CPR a significant parcel of land (equivalent to the size of England) in 1881; the CPR sold it for profit and constructed on it, laying tracks and building stations, offices and housing. The log cabin—its simple form and efficient construction—proved to be the ideal structure to serve the CPR's diverse needs. Dispersed throughout vast territory, the CPR cabins were built from the abundant first growth pine being cleared to make way for the tracks. Their simple log construction mirrored that used by trappers, prospectors and early European settlers. Assembled from locally cut and peeled logs, the cabins varied in size, proportion and corner notch style. Their design influenced the rustic style that dominated park and wilderness architecture in Canada in the early twentieth century.

The styles of cabin selected to be built in a given area reflected regional materials and intended use. The CPR relied on Canadian and immigrant labour to supplement its workforce, and housing was often segregated based on national origin. Cabins that served as offices and homes for regional managers were the most spacious and well-constructed; Chinese labourers were often relegated to rudimentary shelters, such as tents and boxcars, in camps that housed hundreds of workers. [SR]

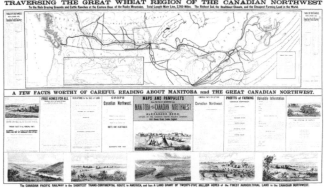

Dianne Newell

The Industrial Archaeology of the Organization of Work: A Half Century of Women and Racial Minorities in British Columbia Fish Plants

Virtually nothing that we know about the history of manufacturing industries, industrial or fishing communities, workers' housing, or gender-segregated and ethnic work forces holds true for the west coast salmon cannery operations and their camp-like villages. With salmon canning we have an industry that until the last few decades did not fall into the category of large, centralized factories that operated year round, were located in urban settings, and drew upon local labour supplies.[1]

A scattering of historic accounts and secondary sources, written mostly by white males, gives us information about various aspects of the industry's development, including valuable glimpses of life and work at the canneries, but not a coherent picture.

***

We know that cannery work was segregated by gender, age, and race-ethnicity, and the particular tasks assigned to the males and females of various ages, races, and ethnic groups varied over time and from region to region, even plant to plant.[2] Until World War II, most work was piecework under contract.

***

The various housing quarters, which were always segregated according to race and, where applicable, to occupational status, flanked the main canning complex. Since the Chinese were strictly shoreworkers, the China House was usually, but not always, close to the canning plant. The native, and to a lesser extent, Japanese, housing was more plentiful and varied, and therefore was scattered around the site.

Here, we are primarily interested in the domestic sphere. The plans indicate that despite the spatial limitations of the site, ethnic boundaries were maintained in housing. There was spatial segregation of racial groups and a variety of housing accommodation for each of them. Thus, the work force was ethnically mixed, but not intermixed, on the site.

***

80

Often there was quite extensive and varied housing, especially at the isolated sites away from the Fraser River district, where seldom was off-site housing available. Cannery camp-village dwellings were of many types, ranging from separate or attached houses for the manager and senior staff, to individual cabins for Japanese fishermen and their wives, to multi-storied crowded bunkhouses for the Chinese male contract workers and rows or clusters of "shacks" or "huts" for the native families, most of whose members shed and worked in the canneries.[3]

The China House (alternatively, "Chinese," "Chinese Bunkhouse") sheltered the Chinese contract labour. While at the canneries, the main canning plant and the bunkhouse were their entire world. Because visitors to the China House were numerous, we have some idea about life inside. Tiers of short, narrow shelves, each serving as a bunk for one man, narrow aisles between the tiers, and a mess room made up the cramped interior. At Bones Bay in the 1930s, about 85 Chinese lived in the bunkhouse.[4] In the kitchen portion, the Chinese cook fed the crew from enormous woks built into brick fireplaces. At the LeRoy Bay cannery, recalls Lloyd Stump, the Chinese contractor, or "China boss," and his young son lived in a separate compartment in the China House.[5] As a small child, Lloyd spent summers at the Stump cannery and often ate in the China House.

Unlike the case of the China House, rarely did anyone other than Japanese visit the Japanese dwellings. After the Japanese were removed from the coast and interned in the winter of 1941–42, the Japanese housing was renamed on the insurance plans to describe the replacement work force—usually "girls," or "Indians." One old cannery worker remembers that the one Japanese dwelling at Bones Bay cannery became a house for Finnish girls (likely from the Finnish settlement at Sointula).[6]

Balmoral Cannery, Skeena River, BC, c. 1890s

Agnes Alfred ("Axu"), who is another of the old cannery workers, recalls the great variation in native accommodation from one cannery to another.[7] At Brunswick cannery, native girls lived in large houses with temporary, semi-partitions separating them. At a neighbouring cannery, Kildala, the native dwellings were divided into four rooms, each of which housed one family, with one common stove in the centre of the building. At Bones Bay cannery, the native housing comprised both individual dwellings and a series of long building complexes, with solid partitions creating individual rooms.

At the Knight's Inlet cannery, native families lived in one-room dwellings that were arranged in rows. The same held true at the Wallace cannery camp, Smith's Inlet. Katie Adams recollects that at this cannery, large families got larger shacks; James Henderson remembers that in the early years many of the shacks had neither a floor nor stove.[8] Typically, however, canning companies provided every native family with a stove and supply of wood. Seldom was there electricity or indoor plumbing, only coal oil lamps, outdoor privies, and cold water taps. All in all, cannery owners provided natives with crowded, primitive accommodation, but as far as many natives were concerned, their cannery housing was only meant to serve as temporary summer accommodation.[9]

The cannery manager and his staff typically lived further from the main plant than those who worked in it. Gordon Stead, who as a 16-year-old white engineering student at the University of British Columbia worked at Claxton during the summer of 1928, recalls that the prestige living sites at Claxton were on the mountainside, located a distance away from the main canning plant. These were reserved for the manager, the senior staff and, interestingly, Haidas from the Queen Charlotte Islands.[10] According to Stead, the Haidas were the best fishermen at the cannery. Next in line were the Norwegians, Japanese and then the "Indians" (by which he simply meant the local natives). At the Bones Bay cannery, the "white girls" lived "up the hill."[11]

Where no ethnic or racial identification for dwellings are given on the fire insurance plans, it is to be assumed that the occupants were "white." The plans indicate that in addition to actual dwellings, portions of industrial and administrative structures, such as the boat building works, mess house, and store/office, also housed a staff member.

1.   For a more hill description of the industry, see Dianne Newell, "Dispersal and Concentration: The Slowly Changing Spatial Pattern of the British Columbia Salmon Canning Industry," *Journal of Historical Geography* 14, no. 1 (January 1988): 22–36.

2.   See Dianne Newell, *The Development of the Pacific Salmon-Canning Industry: A Grown Man's Game* (Montreal and Kingston: McGill-Queen's University Press, 1989).

3.   There is no mention in the record of Chinese women at the canneries—except for one interviewee who reported that Chinese girls, along with white female students from the University of British Columbia, were recruited from Vancouver to help replace the Japanese girls. Tapod interview with Ann Brochie and Lucy Smith, Campbell River, by Colleen Hemphill, 8 September 1984 (in possession of author).

4.   James Henderson, Campbell River, taped interview by Colleen Hemphill, 16 June 1984 (in possession of author).

5.   Lloyd Stump, Vancouver, taped interview by Logan Hovisand Gaylo Horsfall, 15 August 1984 (in possession of author).

6.   James Henderson, Campbell River, taped interview by Colleen Hemphill, 16 June 1984 (in possession of author).

7.   Agnes Alfrod, Campbell River, tapod interview by Colleen Hemphill, 31 May 1984 (in possession of author).

8.   Katie Adams (19 June 1984) and James Henderson (14 June 1984), Campbell River, taped interview by Colleen Hemphill (in possession of author).

9.   James Henderson, Campbell River, taped interview by Colleen Hemphill, 16 June 1984 (in possession of author).

10.   Based on the author's conversation with Gordon Stead, Vancouver, 27 June 1984.

11.   Ann Brochie and Lucy Smith, Campbell River, taped interview by Colleen Hemphill, 8 September 1984 (in possession of author).

Excerpt from Dianne Newell, "The Industrial Archaeology of the Organization of Work: A Half Century of Women and Racial Minorities in British Columbia Fish Plants," *Material Culture Review* 33 (1991): 25–36.

Left to right: Workers' housing, Claxton Cannery, Skeena, BC, c. 1890s

Housing reconstruction after the catastrophe: the failed promise of San Francisco's 1906 "earthquake cottages"

Marie Bolton and
Nancy C. Unger

Measures to remake the city began even as the fires still burned. The U.S. Army organized San Franciscans into refugee camps and imposed martial law. Mayor Eugene Schmitz appointed a flurry of committees drawn largely from the city's business elite. James Phelan incorporated his powerful finance committee as the San Francisco Relief and Red Cross Funds, known as the Relief Committee, in July of 1906 (Kahn, 1979, 137–139); resident Theodore Roosevelt sent the influential Dr. Edward Devine to oversee the initial operations of the Red Cross, which coordinated the work of local charities, including the most prominent, the Associated Charities of San Francisco (ACSF), headed by Katherine Felton.[1] Pursuing their objective of fundamentally reforming San Francisco's housing for the benefit of the working poor, the Relief Committee constructed 5,610 two and three-room wood frame cottages. Although Kevin Rozario suggests that the quality of the cottages was deliberately kept minimal by business leaders unwilling to "interfere with the private property market", they were enthusiastically described by Devine as "attractive, sanitary, safe, and yet comparatively inexpensive dwellings which will have a beneficial effect not only in the immediate future but for the coming generation."[2]

The small green transportable "earthquake cottages", as they came to be known, were placed in parks and on other public lands. The U.S. Army, under the leadership of General Adolphus Greely, presided over these refugee camps

84

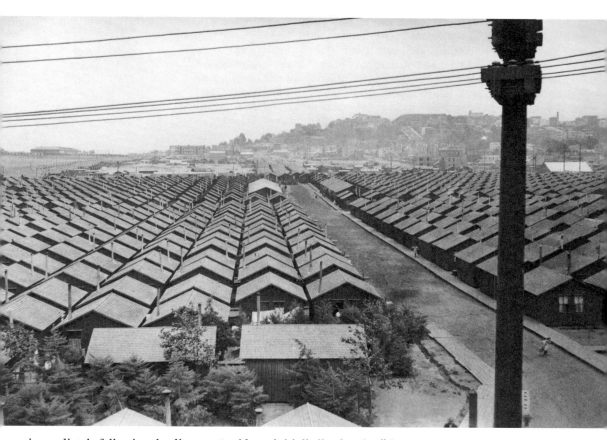

immediately following the disaster. Residents initially lived under "the most rigid [military] supervision".[3] After the withdrawal of the military on 30 June 1906, Felton and F. W. Dohrmann, vice-chairman of the Relief Committee, managed the camps, helped relocate the cottages onto lots throughout the city, and eased the refugees' transition into non-supervised city life.[4]

The ultimate goal of the cottage-lease system was single-family home ownership. The cottages were leased for one year at $2.00 a month. The monies collected were later refunded to the lessee. At the end of the year the cottager became a homeowner, although he or she still had to secure a private lot on which to move the cottage. After losing their homes and often their jobs in the 1906 disaster, many families found respite and recovery in their new houses as they worked successfully to reconstruct their lives. ACSF caseworkers identified especially worthy families that owned or were buying the lot on which their earthquake cottage was placed. For instance, the Hamlins' small two-room cottage provided inadequate space for the family of eight, but it was on a lot that they owned. Impressed by their self-sufficiency, the caseworker recommended that the ACSF give the family a rare building grant of $300.00, "as this family has not applied to us for assistance".[5]

Earthquake cottages relocated to residential districts of the city came to social workers' attention nation-wide as bright spots in the years of the stubborn recession that began in 1907, aggravated in San Francisco by the lingering effects of the earthquake and fire as well as a prolonged streetcar strike. In 1909, some observers recognized the beneficial influence of these single family homes: out of the "unlikely heritage of the calamity [...] a miracle was wrought". Hundreds of families "are to be found in many of the residence districts of the city [...] learning the art of home making".[6] That same year, an observer commissioned by the Red Cross noted the durability of the earthquake cottages and reported approvingly on improvements made to the

85

original structures: "It was very nice indeed how the little cottages seem to endure the rigors of the rain and hot sun of the Pacific Coast [...]. As a rule they have been somewhat rebuilt; have been raised off the ground; front porches and rear kitchens have been added; they have been shingled and painted and set in the midst of gardens of blooming plants and shrubs and form beautiful little suburban homes, in which anyone would be content and happy. The wood work as far as I observed was in good state of preservation. There did not seem to be any rotting of the sills; the roofs seemed tight and altogether the wisdom of issuing these houses has been more than proved."[7]

Opposite: Desolation Peak Lookout, North Cascades National Park, WA, 2009

As the most ardent supporter of cottage living, the ACSF regularly sent social workers to foster its experiment. They encouraged vegetable gardens and proudly reported families weathering hard times by living off their own produce. The modest size of the cottages was praised for encouraging healthy outdoor living. The Associated Charities concluded that even the most humble cottage was "infinitely better than the best tenement", providing the beneficial "influence of a comfortable home upon men and women".[8] Those fortunate enough to live in the earthquake cottages enjoyed all the benefits of single-family home life so celebrated by the experts as being conducive to establishing proper values and good citizenship.

—

1.   Judd Kahn, *Imperial San Francisco: Politics and Planning in an American City, 1897-1906* (Lincoln, University of Nebraska Press, 1979), 137-138; Paul Boyer, *Urban Masses and Moral Order in America, 1820-1920* (Cambridge, Harvard University Press, 1978) 224; see Katherine Felton, "Work of the Associated Charities in Connection with the Clearing of Camps and the Permanent Housing of Refugees", *Annual Reports of the Associated Charities*, 1907.

2.   Kevin Rozario, *The Culture of Calamity: Disaster and the Making of Modern America* (Chicago, University of Chicago Press, 2007) 97; Edward Devine to James D. Phelan, "Recommendations submitted to the Finance Committee, July 10, 1906", in Russell Sage Foundation, *San Francisco Relief Survey* (NY: Survey Associates, Inc., 1913) 394-95.

3.   A. W. Greely, *Report of Major General A. W. Greely on San Francisco Relief* (Washington, D.C.: Government Printing Office, 1906), 129.

See Philip Fradkin, *The Great Earthquake and Firestorms of 1906: How San Francisco Nearly Destroyed Itself* (Berkeley: University of California Press, 2005) 224.

4.   ACSF Case Studies 1912, carton 2, SFLCP, Bancroft Library, UC Berkeley. In accordance with Bancroft Library guidelines, names have been changed to protect the privacy of families.

5.   Anna Simpson, *The Story of the Associated Charities since the Fire of 1906* (San Francisco, 1909), 9-10.

6.   Joseph A. Steinmetz, Pennsylvania Branch Red Cross, to Mabel T. Boardman, National Red Cross, August 11, 1909; August 20, 1909, Red Cross Papers (RCP), National Archives, Washington, D.C.

7.   Simpson, *Story of the Associated Charities*, 14-17, 19.

Marie Bolton and Nancy C. Unger, "Housing Reconstruction After the Catastrophe: The Failed Promise of San Francisco's 1906 'Earthquake Cottages'", ed. C. Rollet and V. Gordon, *Annales de Demographie Historique* 120, no. 2 (2010): 217-40.

Fire lookout towers predate the United States Forest Service, which was founded in 1905; they were built sporadically by local municipalities, lumber companies and state forestry organizations. A massive fire that burned three million acres in parts of Washington, Idaho and Montana in 1910 shaped the future of the Forest Service, shifting its priority to fire detection and suppression. Fire lookouts were constructed in fervent step with government regulation of natural resources. In 1933, President Franklin Delano Roosevelt created the Civilian Conservation Corps; its workforce participated in a large-scale campaign of construction projects, which included many fire lookouts and continued in earnest through 1950. At one time, there were more than eight thousand fire lookouts in the United States; today fewer than two thousand remain, and only a quarter of those are staffed. New technologies—satellites, aircraft and phone service—supplanted the towers as the primary forms of fire detection.

Typically small and remote, fire lookout towers were built on mountain summits or in other advantageous viewing positions. They usually consisted of a single room, known as a cab, perched upon a steel or wood tower, natural rock or, in certain terrain, directly on the ground. The resident fire lookout cooked, ate, slept and washed in the cab. This ensured the lookout was always in a favourable location to survey the landscape.

Over the years, the isolated setting of a fire lookout post has enticed writers seeking escape from the pressures of society, and served to inspire their creative endeavors. Norman MacLean, Edward Abbey, Jack Kerouac, Gary Snyder and Philip Connors all spent seasons serving as fire lookouts, in many cases producing some of their best-known work at the post. Such romanticized notions of living in nature have elevated the status of this otherwise practical architectural form. [JMV]

Fire Lookouts

Mid-August at Sourdough Mountain Lookout

Gary Snyder

Down valley a smoke haze
Three days heat, after five days rain
Pitch glows on the fir-cones
Across rocks and meadows
Swarms of new flies.

I cannot remember things I once read
A few friends, but they are in cities.
Drinking cold snow-water from a tin cup
Looking down for miles
Through high still air.

Gary Snyder at Crater Mountain
Lookout, Mount Baker National
Forest, WA, 1952

Alone on a Mountain Top

Jack Kerouac

After all this kind of fanfare, and even more, I came to a point where I needed solitude and just stop the machine of "thinking" and "enjoying" what they call "living," I just wanted to lie in the grass and look at the clouds —

***

I was a fire lookout and after two nights of trying to sleep in the boom and slap of the Forest Service floats, they came for me one rainy morning—a powerful tugboat lashed to a large corral float bearing four mules and three horses, my own groceries, feed, batteries and equipment.— The muleskinner's name was Andy and he wore the same old floppy cowboy hat he'd worn in Wyoming twenty years ago. "Well, boy, now we're gonna put you away where we cant reach ya—you better get ready."

"It's just what I want, Andy, be alone for three solid months nobody to bother me."

"It's what you're sayin' now but you'll change your tune after a week."

I didnt believe him.— I was looking forward to an experience men seldom earn in this modern world: complete and comfortable solitude in the wilderness, day and night, sixty-three days and nights to be exact. We had no idea how much snow had fallen on my mountain during the winter and Andy said: "If there didnt it means you gotta hike two miles down that hard trail every day or every other day with two buckets, boy. I aint envyin' you—I been back there. And one day it's gonna be hot and you're about ready to broil, and bugs you cant even count 'em, and next day a li'l ole summer blizzard come hit you around the corner of Hozomeen which sits right there near Canada in your back yard and you wont be able to stick logs fast enough in that potbelly stove of yours."— But I had a full rucksack loaded with turtleneck sweaters and warm shirts and pants and long wool socks bought on the Seattle water front, and gloves and an earmuff cap, and lots of instant soup and coffee in my grub list.

"Shoulda brought yourself a quart of brandy, boy," says Andy shaking his head as the tug pushed our corral float up Ross Lake through the log gate and around to the left dead north underneath the immense rain shroud of Sourdough Mountain and Ruby Mountain.

"Where's Desolation Peak?" I asked, meaning my own mountain (*A mountain to be kept forever,* I'd dreamed all that spring) (O lonesome traveler!)

"You aint gonna see it today till we're practically on top it and by that time you'll be so soakin' wet you wont care."

Assistant Ranger Marty Gohlke of Marblemount Ranger Station was with us too, also giving me tips and instructions. Nobody seemed to envy Desolation Peak except me.

***

What strange sweet thoughts come to you in the mountain solitudes!— One night I realized that when you give people understanding and encouragement a funny little meek childish look abashes their eyes, no matter what they've been doing they weren't sure it was right—lambies all over the world.

For when you realize that God is Everything you know that you've got to love everything no matter how bad it is, in the ultimate sense it was neither good nor bad (consider the dust), it was just *what was,* that is, what was made to appear.— Some kind of drama to teach something to something, some "despised substance of divinest show."

And I realized I didnt have to hide myself in desolation but could accept society for better or for worse, like a wife—I saw that if it wasnt for the six senses, of seeing, hearing, smelling, touching, tasting and thinking, the self of that, which is non-existent, there would be no phenomena to perceive at all, in fact no six senses or self.— The fear of extinction is much worse than extinction (death) itself.— To chase after extinction in the old Nirvanic sense of Buddhism is ultimately silly, as the dead indicate in the silence of their blissful sleep in Mother Earth which is an Angel hanging in orbit in Heaven anyway.—

I just lay on the mountain meadowside in the moonlight, head to grass, and heard the silent recognition of my temporary woes.— Yes, so to try to *attain* to Nirvana when you're already there, to attain to the top of a mountain when you're already there and only have to stay—thus, to *stay* in the Nirvana Bliss, is all I have to do, you have to do, no effort, no path really, no discipline but just to know that all is empty and awake, a Vision and a Movie in God's Universal Mind (*Alaya- Vijnana*) and to stay more or less wisely in that.— Because silence itself is the sound of diamonds which can cut through anything, the sound of Holy Emptiness, the sound of extinction and bliss, that graveyard silence which is like the silence of an infant's smile, the sound of eternity, of the blessedness surely to be believed, the sound of nothing-ever-happened-except-God (which I'd soon hear in a noisy Atlantic tempest).— What exists is God in His Emanation, what does not exist is God in His peaceful Neutrality, what neither exists nor does not exist is God's immortal primordial dawn of Father Sky (this world this very minute).— So I said:— "Stay in that, no dimensions here to any of the mountains or mosquitos and whole milky ways of worlds —" Because sensation is emptiness, old age is emptiness.— 'T's only the Golden Eternity of God's Mind so practise kindness and sympathy, remember that men are *not responsible in themselves as men* for their ignorance and unkindness, they should be pitied, God does pity it, because who says anything about anything since everything is just what it is, free of interpretations.— God is not the "attainer," he is the "farer" in that which everything is, the "abider"—one caterpillar, a thousand hairs of God.—So know constantly that this is only you, God, empty and awake and eternally free as the unnumerable atoms of emptiness everywhere.—

I decided that when I would go back to the world down there I'd try to keep my mind clear in the midst of murky human ideas smoking like factories on the horizon through which I would walk, forward...

When I came down in September a cool old golden look had come into the forest, auguring cold snaps and frost and the eventual howling blizzard that would cover my shack completely, unless those winds at the top of the world would keep her bald. As I reached the bend in the trail where the shack would disappear and I would plunge down to the lake to meet the boat that would take me out and home, I turned and blessed Desolation Peak and the little pagoda on top and thanked them for the shelter and the lesson I'd been taught.

The Journey Home:
Fire Lookout: Numa Ridge

Edward Abbey

We've been here ten days before I overcome initial inertia sufficient to begin this record. And keeping a record is one of the things the Park Service is paying us to do up here. The other, of course, is to keep our eyeballs peeled, alert for smoke. We are being paid a generous wage (about $3.25 an hour) to stay awake for at least eight hours a day. Some people might think that sounds like a pretty easy job. And they're right, it is an easy job, for some people. But not for all. When I mentioned to one young fellow down at park headquarters, a couple of weeks ago, that I was spending the summer on this fire lookout he shuddered with horror. "I'd go nuts in a place like that," he said, thinking of solitary confinement. I didn't tell him I was cheating, taking my wife along. But that can be risky too; many a good marriage has been shattered on the rock of isolation.

Renée and I walked up here on July 2, packs on our backs, two hours ahead of the packer with his string of mules. The mules carried the heavier gear, such as our bedrolls, enough food and water for the first two weeks, seven volumes of Marcel Proust, and Robert Burton's *Anatomy of Melancholy*. Light summer reading. Renée had never worked a fire lookout before, but I had, and I knew that if I was ever going to get through the classics of world lit it could only be on a mountain top, far above the trashy plains of *Rolling Stone*, *Playboy*, the *New York Times*, and *Mizz* magazine.

Edward Abbey at Aztec Peak Fire Tower, Tonto National Forest, AZ, 1977

The trail is about six miles long from Bowman Lake and climbs 3,000 feet. We made good time, much better time than we wished because we were hustled along, all the way, by hordes of bloodthirsty mosquitoes. We had prepared ourselves, of course, with a heavy treatment of government-issue insect repellent on our faces, necks, arms, but that did not prevent the mosquitoes from whining in our ears and hovering close to eye, nostril, and mouth.

***

We reach the lookout without fulfilling any fantasies. The lookout is a two-room, two-story wood frame cabin at timberline, 7,000 feet above sea level. On the north, east, and southeast stand great peaks—Reauter, Kintla, Numa, Chapman, Rainbow, Vulture. Northwest we can see a bit of the Canadian Rockies. West and southwest lie the North Fork of the Flathead River, a vast expanse of Flathead National Forest, and on the horizon the Whitefish Range. Nice view 360 degrees of snow-capped scenic splendor, lakes, forest, river, fearsome peaks, and sheltering sky.

We remove the wooden shutters from the lookout windows, shovel snow from the stairway, unlock the doors. The pack string arrives. The packer and I unload the mules, the packer departs, Renée and I unpack our goods and move in. Except for a golden-mantled ground squirrel watching us from the rocks, a few Clark's nutcrackers in the subalpine firs, we seem to be absolutely alone.

Edward Abbey at Aztec Peak Fire Tower, Tonto National Forest, AZ, 1977

***

What *do* people do on a lookout tower when, as now, the season is wet and there are no fires? Aside from the obvious, and reading Proust and *The Anatomy of Melancholy*, we spend hours just gazing at the world through binoculars. For example, I enjoy climbing the local mountains, scaling the most hideous bare rock pitches step by step, hand by hand, without aids, without rope or partners, clinging to fragments of loose shale, a clump of bear grass, the edge of an overhanging snow cornice, above a nightmarish abyss, picking a route toward even higher and more precarious perches—through these U.S. Navy 7 × 50 lenses. The effortless, angelic, and supine approach to danger.

It's not all dreaming. There are some daily chores. Ever since arrival I've been packing snow to the lookout from a big drift a hundred yards below, carrying it up in buckets, dumping it into steel garbage cans, letting it melt in the sun. Now we've got 120 gallons of snow water in addition to the drinking water brought up by muleback. Then there's firewood. Although we have a propane stove for cooking, the only heat in the lookout comes from an old cast-iron cook-stove. And with the kind of rainy, windy weather we've been having, heat is a necessity. Even in July. So a couple of times a week I go down the trail with ax and saw, fell one of the many dead trees in the area—fir, whitebark pine—buck the log into eighteen-inch lengths, tote it up the hill armload by armload.

Three times a day we take weather observations—wind speed and direction, temperature, relative humidity—or my wife does, since she is the scientist in this family. We wash windows, occasionally. We patch and repair things. We listen to the Park Service radio and the Forest Service radio, ready to relay messages if necessary. I entertain the deer and the squirrels with my flute. Renée bakes things, studies the maps, memorizes the terrain. But mostly we sit quietly out on the catwalk, reading about aristocratic life in *fin-de-siècle* Paris and looking at northwestern Montana in the summer of '75.

This is a remote place indeed, far from the center of the world, far away from all that's going on. Or is it? Who says so? Wherever two human beings are alive, together, and happy, there is the center of the world. You out there, brother, sister, you live in the center of the world, no matter where or what you think you are.

Alpine (or backcountry) huts provide basic, temporary shelter in wilderness or national park areas. Common in Europe as early as the mid-nineteenth century, they often form part of a system, connected by trails or other forms of navigation. Their main purpose is protecting visitors from the elements, which facilitates remote access to a range of outdoor recreational activities like mountaineering, hiking, ski touring and climbing. Distinguished from commercial lodges, these huts have common sleeping areas and offer simple amenities, like propane for heating, cooking and lighting; they do not typically have staff. In the early twentieth century, the Alpine Club of Canada began constructing a network of huts in backcountry and mountainous areas to provide permanent shelter for its members during expeditions. The club now operates the largest network of backcountry huts in North America. The *Canadian Alpine Journal*, published continuously since 1907, communicates detailed accounts of hut design and construction—for example, Helen A. Burns' report, from 1940, on the Disaster Point Hut. [JMV]

Alpine Huts

Alpine Hut, Rogers Pass, BC,
c. 1921–37

94

Disaster Point Hut

Helen A. Burns

Have you ever climbed an easy peak on a cloudless summer day? Have you slogged up the last scree slope to the summit and turned to survey a widespread panorama of snow-capped peaks and boundless prairie? Have you tramped down the trail after the descent, and five minutes later found yourself soaking out the tiredness in a hot pool whose sapphire blue was visible all day, like a little jewel in the valley? And then, after a satisfying supper, have you luxuriated in front of a blazing fire in the great stone fireplace, or relaxed on the wide verandah and watched the sun set over river and lake and mountain?

No, this is not a description of Banff and Sulphur mountain, of the upper hot springs and the Club House. It is a brief glimpse of Mount Utopia and Miette springs, of the Athabaska valley and "the little club house in the north"—Disaster Point hut.

It all began during a Labor Day week-end four years ago. The active members of the Edmonton section had made a plot to take a group of our section associates up to Pocahontas and show them some real climbing. The Skipper had told us about Roche Miette, the great rock tower which marks the northern gateway to Jasper Park. He told us how he failed to reach the summit in 1919, and made some excuse involving a train he had to catch, but knowing the Skipper we accepted that story with our tongue in our cheeks!

So nineteen of us started for Pocahontas that Saturday afternoon. In those high and far off times the Jasper highway was still "under construction" and what with long delays while our cars were hauled through gumbo by tractors, and what with Rex Gibson dropping the battery out of his car and sailing on blissfully without it; and what with Lil Chapman picking up the truant battery and bringing it back to its master; yes, in spite and because of these sundry other adventures it was the wee small hours of Sunday morning before we reached our camp site at the spot where the mining town of Pocahontas once stood.

This is no place to tell of how we slogged through the bush to the cliffs of Roche Miette, or of how we too beat an ignominious retreat with the gathering darkness as an excuse. We returned to Edmonton on Monday with two things we had not taken with us: a group of budding "actives" and a firm resolve that we would have a section hut somewhere near the foot of Roche Miette. Most of those budding actives have long since burst into full bloom, and the section hut which was nothing but a dream has awakened into reality as a Club hut far more pretentious than anything we had pictured—a centre of activity which fully justifies the affectionate title, "The Little Club House in the North."

The first question was money, and a modest building fund was not long in materializing. The second was a site. Fortune was with us and the ideal site was found, but thereby hangs a tale. Back in the big, bad boom days before the first Great War, when the tracks of the Grand Trunk Pacific occupied the roadbed which is now the Jasper highway, two young men started a limekiln just north of Disaster Point, which is the end of the great buttress running down to Athabaska river from Roche Miette. The brothers erected a substantial stone dwelling house near their kiln, put in a spur line to the railway and settled down to make their fortunes. Then came the war. The brothers dumped the lime from the flat cars, where it still lies in a huge heap to attract the mountain sheep from many miles around. The railway tracks were torn up and sent to France, where the two brothers followed them. The stone house was deserted and the peace of the primitive wilderness settled back once more upon Disaster Point.

The years passed. Pack rats made their home in the silent rafters. An occasional hobo tore up planks from the floor to build his fire. But the two brothers had built well, and the four stone walls stood four-square to the winds until, two decades later, we found the old house and recognized it as the much-desired nucleus of our Disaster Point hut.

Then followed prolonged negotiations with the Dominion Government. At last, through the generous cooperation of the Hon. J. A. McKinnon, the site was ours, together with the building "as is." Our ambitions were modest: a new floor, new doors and windows, needed repairs to the walls where frost had loosened the limestone blocks. The Skipper made plans, Dr. Bulyea produced an oil painting of the finished hut, we were confident that with plenty of volunteer labor our section home would be ready for occupation by the end of next summer. But now we struck a snag. This was the year of the Columbia icefield camp, and every member of the section was going to camp or bust!

A.O. Wheeler Hut, Glacier National Park, BC, c. 1950

However, we did succeed in getting together a little work party, and then followed ten days of strenuous labor compared with which the ascent of Mt. Columbia was a mere summer picnic. The Skipper, who was engineer in charge, had insisted on one thing, "strict union hours," and we obeyed his ruling; we worked eight hours in the morning and eight in the afternoon and evening! Our only relaxation was the occasional dip in the newly opened Hot Springs.

At the end of ten days we left for Edmonton with a long-drawn sigh of relief. The hut was not finished, but at least it was habitable. The party who visited it on the following Labor Day admitted as much with a certain restrained enthusiasm, but—. Sadly we came to the conclusion that the section had bitten off more than it could chew. Funds were exhausted, and the hut was far from finished. What should we do? The Skipper came to our rescue with a suggestion.

At the same time that the two brothers abandoned their lime kiln, Charles Robert Cross of Boston, U.S.A., bequeathed to the Club the sum of one thousand dollars in memory of his son, C. R. Cross Jr. who lost his life in the early days of the war. There was a proviso in Mr. Cross' will to the effect that the money was to be used for the benefit of the Club "and especially of the Edmonton section." The money was lying untouched. Here, perhaps, was the solution of our difficulty.

After long discussion, we decided to approach the executive of the Club with a suggestion. We proposed that the Cross Fund should be divided between the Disaster Point hut and the Stanley Mitchell hut, which also needed money; in return the section would turn the finished hut over to the Club to be used as a sort of Jasper Park Annex to the Club House. To our delight, the grant was approved, and a building committee was set up with the writer as chairman. Realizing that the Club would require something much more commodious than the simple one-room structure which now existed, we drew up new plans and went to work. We felt that we owed it to the Club to provide the best possible in the way of building and equipment, so for two years volunteer work parties spent every holiday week-end at Disaster Point. A group of five young men who were "handy with tools" were enlisted to do much of the carpentering work. The climax came in the summer of 1940 when Dr. Bulyea built with his own hands a stone fireplace which is a memorial to his son John, who was one of the original party during that exciting Labor Day trip which saw the beginning of the project.

Today, the Disaster Point hut is a worthy addition to the growing list of Club property. It stands on the Jasper highway, twenty-four miles north of Jasper, and fourteen miles from Miette Hot Springs. The original stone building forms the assembly room, where the activities of the day culminate around the great fireplace. In front is a wide verandah, forty feet in length, affording a wide view across the rushing Athabaska to a background of peaks, from Pyramid mountain to Roche Ronde. On the north side is a spacious ladies' sleeping porch, with screens and shutters, and on the south side a similar sleeping porch for men.

At the back of the building are two rooms, a kitchen and a ladies' room, the latter opening into the sleeping porch. The hut is equipped with sixteen cots, but no bedding has been provided, as cars can be driven right to the door and members are expected to bring their own blankets. Provision has been made for the installation of four bunks in the attic, when more sleeping accommodation is needed. There are books and pictures and even a boat for use on nearby Talbot lake, where fishing is reported to be good, but a boathouse is still a project for the future.

The attractions of Disaster Point are manifold. For the climber there is Roche Miette, whose cliffs rise a sheer four thousand feet above the hut, and many other lesser peaks. For the hiker there are numerous trails leading to canyons, lakes and streams. The nature lover will rejoice in the abundance of wild life, for it is a common experience to wake and find deer or mountain sheep browsing on the front "lawn." Best of all, the hut is ideally situated as a stopping place for the motorist on his way over the famous Jasper-Banff highway.

The key of the hut may be obtained from the Park Warden, whose cabin is two miles north of Disaster Point, or from the warden at Park Gate, seven miles north of the hut.

The name Disaster Point, which appears on government maps of Jasper Park, had its origin in an incident which happened to Sir Sandford Fleming seventy years ago. Fleming was exploring a possible route for the Canadian Pacific Railway in 1872 when he traversed the slopes of Roche Miette on his way to the present site of Jasper. Principal Grant, who was acting as secretary to the expedition, describes the following event: "The Chief's bag got a crush against a rock, and his flask that held a drop of brandy carefully preserved for the next plum pudding, was broken. It was hard, but on an expedition like this the most serious losses are taken calmly and soon forgotten."

There has been some criticism of the use of the name in connection with a Club hut, but we are sure that when our members become familiar with the historic incident described above, this prejudice will disappear. At the time when the hut was still a section project, a vote was taken with the result that the members were almost unanimously in favor of retaining the name. We hope that the Club will agree with our viewpoint and that no disaster more serious than Fleming's may ever take place at "The Little Club House in the North."

Helen A. Burns, "The Disaster Point Hut," *Canadian Alpine Journal* 27, no. 2 (1940): 188–193. Reprinted by permission of The Alpine Club of Canada.

While ice fishing huts are utilitarian by nature—their purpose to provide respite from treacherous conditions during winter fishing expeditions—they vary widely in formal quality, material and stylistic flair. Builders, revelling in DIY spirit, create unique, idiosyncratic structures that reflect their distinct personalities and interests—all in thirty square feet or less. For more than a decade, Toronto-based photographer Richard Johnson has documented this vernacular architectural tradition in Canada, in a typological study comprising more than one thousand photographs. In tightly cropped compositions devoid of human presence, Johnson fixes his lens on formal and material qualities of the architecture, and examines its relationship to site, revealing the creativity and humour with which builders approach hut design. [SR]

Ice Huts

Photographs by Richard Johnson

Ice Hut #885, La Baie Des Ha! Ha!,
Saguenay River, Quebec, Canada,
2016

The refugee camp after the fire of
April 18, 1906. From Geary Lake
& From Funston to 14th Avenue,
San Francisco, CA, 1906

Ice Shacks

Ice fishing has a lengthy history in the Canadian North, from Indigenous communities who sustain on the bounty to sport practitioners who revel in the comradery of the hunt. Rudimentary, often ephemeral structures were erected in the wilderness to provide respite from the elements during a hunting or fishing expedition, and an inventive, vernacular architecture developed to serve this need. Usually smaller than 30 square feet and built on sled runners for easy transport, ice huts can accommodate the bare necessities: a kerosene stove, sleeping bunks and shelves for supplies. The huts vary widely in size and formal quality, but each features the essential requirements for spending the day fishing in frigid temperatures: four walls, a roof, a floor with a hole to access the ice through. While the pragmatic structures must be weather resistant, be transportable and expose the ice, the huts vary greatly in sophistication; the form and design are often indicative of owner preference. Their bright colours dot the otherwise barren landscape—marks of a local architectural tradition rooted in site, climate and culture.

Location: Various
Year: Ongoing

Type: Worker, DIY
Dimensions: Variable; typically smaller than 2.8 m²
Materials: Variable

Top to bottom: Ice fishing hut, Lake Simcoe, ON, 1975. A horse pulls an ice fishing hut, Sainte-Anne-de-la-Pérade, QC. Ice fishing huts, Lake Simcoe, ON, 1988

Top to bottom: Ice fishing huts, Sainte.-Anne-de-la-Perade, QC, 1956. Ice fishing, Lake Simcoe, ON, 1956. Ice fishing village, La Baie des Ha! Ha!, Saguenay River, QC, 2009. Illustration from Lester Walker, *The Tiny Book of Tiny Houses*, 1993

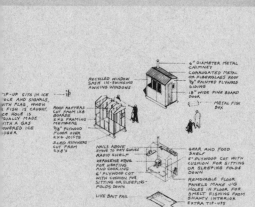

"TIP-UP SITS IN ICE
HOLE AND SIGNALS,
WITH FLAG, WHEN
A FISH IS CAUGHT.
ICE HOLE IS
USUALLY MADE
WITH A GAS
POWERED ICE
AUGER.

RECYCLED WINDOW
SASH IN-SWINGING
AWNING WINDOWS

6" DIAMETER METAL
CHIMNEY
CORRUGATED METAL
OR FIBERGLASS ROOF
3/8" PAINTED PLYWOOD
SIDING
18" WIDE PINE BOARD
DOOR

ROOF RAFTERS
CUT FROM 1X6
BOARDS
2X2 FRAMING
MEMBERS
3/8" PLYWOOD
FLOOR OVER
2X6 JOISTS
SLED RUNNERS
CUT FROM
2X8'S

METAL FISH
BOX

NAILS ABOVE
STOVE TO DRY GLOVES
RADIO SHELF
KEROSENE STOVE
FOR HEATING
AND COOKING
6' PLYWOOD COT
WITH CUSHION FOR
SITTING OR SLEEPING-
FOLDS DOWN

LIVE BAIT PAIL

GEAR AND FOOD
SHELF
6' PLYWOOD COT WITH
CUSHION FOR SITTING
OR SLEEPING FOLDS
DOWN

REMOVABLE FLOOR
PANELS MAKE JIG
HOLES IN FLOOR FOR
SMELT FISHING FROM
SHANTY INTERIOR
EXTRA TIP-UPS

107

Earthquake Relief Cottages

A devastating fire ravaged San Francisco after the city was hit by a 7.8 magnitude earthquake in 1906, destroying 500 city blocks and over 80 percent of the city's infrastructure. More than 250,000 residents were left without shelter and required immediate rehousing. In response, the Army hastily erected refugee camps in city parks, providing tents for the homeless; unable to withstand exposure to cooler temperatures, these temporary accommodations proved inadequate upon the arrival of winter. In response to this escalating housing crisis, San Francisco Relief & Red Cross Funds, with support from the San Francisco Parks Commission and the Army, constructed more than 5,600 rent-to-own wooden cottages that housed more than 16,000 people. Tenants were required to pay $2 a month until they paid off the $50 purchase fee, at which time they became the owner provided they transported their dwelling to a permanent location before the camps closed the following year.

The modest cottages, which came in three sizes, were constructed out of redwood with fir floors and cedar shingled roofs. They were painted "park bench green," a hue selected specifically for its likeness to their city park surroundings. The uniform design of the cottages favoured utility and simplicity with gabled roofs, metal chimneys, one door and three windows—an adaptation of the traditional front-gabled cottage style that originated in Medieval England. While the cottages were not prefabricated, all materials, except the floorboards, were precut at the mill to reduce the work required on-site and to maximize construction efficiency. Despite the haste of their design and construction, the cottages proved quite durable, and a number remain scattered throughout San Francisco today. An early example of disaster relief architecture, with their simple design and speedy construction the cabins would be replicated in subsequent emergency response projects.

Location: San Francisco, California
Year: 1906

Type: Worker, DIY
Dimensions: Type A: 3.0 × 4.3 m; Type B: 4.3 × 5.5 m;
Type C: 4.6 × 7.6 m and 4.9 × 24.7 m
Materials: redwood walls, fir floors, cedar shingled roofs, glass

Other Examples:
Chicago Fire Relief Cottage, 1871, Chicago, IL
Buckminster Fuller, Dymaxion Deployment Unit, 1940
Jean Prouvé, Demountable House, 1944
Shigeru Ban, Paper Log Houses, 1995
Bellomo Architects, House Arc, 2011
IKEA/UNHCR, Better Shelter, 2013
New Panel Homes, Katrina Cottage, 2016

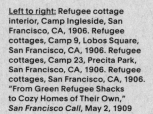

Left to right: Refugee cottage interior, Camp Ingleside, San Francisco, CA, 1906. Refugee cottages, Camp 9, Lobos Square, San Francisco, CA, 1906. Refugee cottages, Camp 23, Precita Park, San Francisco, CA, 1906. Refugee cottages, San Francisco, CA, 1906. "From Green Refugee Shacks to Cozy Homes of Their Own," *San Francisco Call*, May 2, 1909

Signal Peak Lookout

The Signal Peak Lookout was originally constructed as a 12' × 16' ground house in the Sierra National Forest, at an elevation of nearly 7,000 feet, to house US Forest Service rangers stationed in backcountry on forest fire prevention duty. Part of a larger network of lookouts and towers built by the National Park Service on high peaks with unimpeded views, the Signal Peak Lookout featured a large observation platform and small log cabin to shelter rangers. It has the distinction of being among the first lookouts to incorporate a traditional log cabin form into the tower design, and it would serve as a prototype for subsequent towers constructed mid-century. Earlier versions featured observation decks with no capacity for live-in accommodation—until a report in 1914 encouraged combining tower with cabin to improve the rangers' ability to detect and prevent fires. The bottom floor was designed for sleeping and eating. The second floor was outfitted with windows on every side to ensure the ranger had an unobstructed view of the forest from any position in the cabin. Like most rural architecture of the period, the design of the Signal Peak Lookout was determined by the materials available locally and the vernacular style preferred in the region. A product of the burgeoning conservation movement, during the "golden age" of fire lookouts in the 1930s there were more than 8,000 installed on mountain peaks across the United States.

Location: Sierra National Forest, California
Year: 1911

Type: Fire Lookout
Dimensions: 3.7 × 4.9 m
Materials: wood, glass

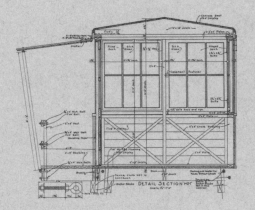

United States Department of Agriculture, Forest Service, 7 × 7' Lookout House (plans), 1936. Signal Peak Lookout, Sierra National Forest, CA, c. 1916

Other Examples:
Devil's Head Lookout, Douglas County, CO, 1919
Blue Point Lookout, Boise National Forest, ID, 1920
Summit Fire Lookout, Mount Revelstoke National Park, BC, 1927
Blue Mountain Lookout, Modoc National Forest, CA, 1930
Watchman Lookout Station, Crater Lake National Park, OR, 1932
Hayes Lookout, Nantahala National Forest, NC, 1939

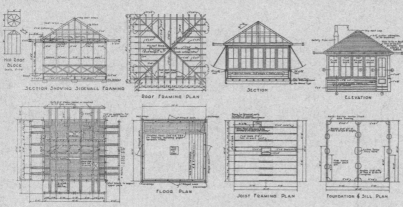

HIP ROOF
BLOCK

SECTION SHOWING SIDEWALL FRAMING   ROOF FRAMING PLAN   SECTION   ELEVATION

FLOOR PLAN   JOIST FRAMING PLAN   FOUNDATION & SILL PLAN

111

Abbot Pass Hut

Originally financed and operated by the Canadian Pacific Railway (CPR) to encourage alpine recreation in western Canada, the Abbot Pass Hut was built in 1922 as a refuge for hikers, mountaineers and backcountry skiers. Swiss mountain guides, hired by the CPR to lead climbing expeditions in the region, provided the design for the one-and-a-half storey, rectangular cabin—almost an exact replica of the hut design found in Switzerland's alpine regions. Building materials were carried to the remote location by horse and on the guides' backs; locally quarried stone was used for the facade. Drawing on both the lengthy history of Swiss high-mountain shelter design and the rustic design tradition popular in the early twentieth century, the Abbot Pass Hut was designed to harmonize with its natural surroundings—leaving the barren and remote mountainous landscape largely undisturbed—and uses stone in its construction, which is rare in Canada's national park buildings. Sitting at 2,926 m elevation, it is the second-highest permanent structure in Canada.

Location: Rocky Mountains, Alberta
Year: 1922

Type: Alpine Hut; Mountaineering
Dimensions: 11.0 × 5.8 m
Materials: cement, glass, lime, metal, stone, timber

Left to right: Climbers at the Abbot Pass Hut on the continental divide between Alberta and British Columbia, c. 1921–37. Abbot Pass Hut, Rocky Mountains, AB, 2017. Abbot Pass Hut, Rocky Mountains, AB, c. 1900–20s. Abbot Pass Hut, Rocky Mountains, AB (building sections), 2000. Abbot Pass Hut, Rocky Mountains, AB, c. 1940s

Other Examples:
Wiwaxy Lodge, Yoho National Park, BC, 1919
The Glacier Circle Alpine Hut, Glacier Circle, BC, 1922
Stanley Mitchell Hut, Yoho National Park, BC, 1940
Ostrander Ski Hut, Yosemite National Park, CA, 1941
Pear Lake Winter Hut, Sequoia National Park, CA, 1941
Arthur O. Wheeler Hut, Glacier National Park, BC, 1947
Ludlow Hut, Lake Tahoe, CA, 1955
Mint Hut, Talkeetna Mountains, AK, 1971

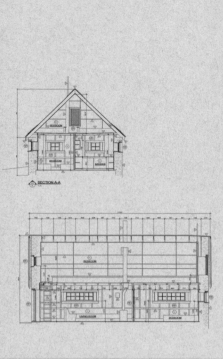

SECTION A-A

Walden Cabin

Henry David Thoreau's celebrated one-room cabin emerged from a desire to reject social dictates and pursue a more authentic life in seclusion, surrounded by nature. In an attempt to find the solace he required to focus on writing, in 1845 and at age 28, Thoreau retreated to Walden Pond in Concord, Massachusetts and built a 10' × 15' single-room cabin with two windows on land owned by his friend and mentor, the Transcendentalist philosopher Ralph Waldo Emerson. By immersing himself in the landscape, Thoreau hoped to align with the wisdom of nature. Built by hand from recycled and locally-sourced materials for less than $29, Thoreau modelled his design on what he viewed as the economy and authenticity offered by early hut architecture as well as the lengthy history of the pastoral English cottage.

By publishing his cabin design in *Walden; or, Life in the Woods*, Thoreau presented his rustic structure as both a philosophical vision and proto-DIY construction plan; the building sparked a utopian dream that still burns persistently in the minds of cabin builders and inhabitants. His straightforward construction method and experiment in the minimum requirements for living continues to inform architectural practice today.

Architect: Henry David Thoreau
Location: Concord, Massachusetts
Year: 1845

Type: Requirements for Living; DIY
Dimensions: 3.0 × 4.6 m
Materials: brick, chalk, hair, latch, laths, lime, mantle-tree iron, sand, second-hand windows with glass, shingles, stones, timber, wood

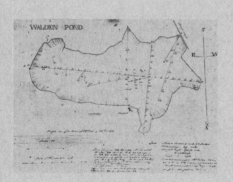

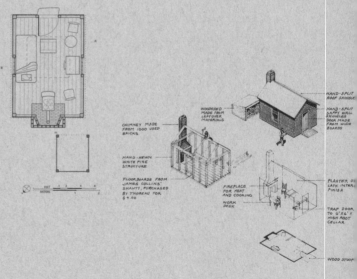

Left to right: Walden Pond (manuscript survey), 1846. Floorplan of Thoreau's House published in Urs Peter Flueckiger, *How Much House? Thoreau, Le Corbusier and the Sustainable Cabin*, 2016. Illustration of Walden Cabin, Concord, MA, 1850. Illustration from Lester Walker, *The Tiny Book of Tiny Houses*, 1993

Other Examples:
Le Corbusier, Cabanon de vacances, Roquebrune-Cap-Martin, France, 1951
Mats Theselius, The Hermit's Cabin, 2000
Texas Tech University, Lubbock, Sustainable Cabin, Crowell, TX, 2008–10
Renzo Piano, Diogene, 2013

Western Duplex Cabin

The Western Duplex Cabin is an excellent example of rustic design style, which came to define US National Park Service architecture in the first half of the twentieth century. Designed by Gilbert Stanley Underwood, who was well known for his sensitivity to site and respect for the natural environment, the cabins at the Grand Canyon Lodge combine log cabin tradition with a California craftsman style. The Western Duplex Cabin, along with the Grand Canyon Lodge, was built during a period when railroad companies were actively promoting adventure tourism. The railroad companies encouraged construction of destination resorts to accommodate their passengers. The idea of integrating nature into architecture flourished in the National Park Service during the early decades of the twentieth century. Architects, landscape architects and engineers combined locally sourced wood and stone to create visually appealing structures that integrated seamlessly within the parks' majestic landscapes.

Architect: Gilbert Stanley Underwood
Location: Grand Canyon National Park, Arizona
Year: 1928

Type: Parkitecture
Dimensions: 5.5 × 12.8 m
Materials: glass, limestone, metal, stone, wood

Left to right: Western Duplex Cabin, Grand Canyon Lodge, Grand Canyon, AZ, 1982. Western Duplex Cabin, Grand Canyon Lodge, Grand Canyon, AZ (measured drawings), 1982

Other Examples:
Jasper Park Lodge, Jasper, AB, 1922
Bryce Canyon Lodge and Deluxe Cabins, Bryce Canyon National Park, UT, 1929
Arthur O. Wheeler Hut, Glacier National Park, BC, 1947
Cal Poly Pomona Architecture, The Wedge, Julia Pfeiffer Burns State Park, CA, 2014
Le Chalet EXP, Mont-Tremblant, QC, 2014

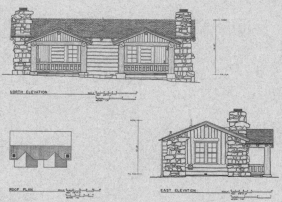

NORTH ELEVATION

ROOF PLAN

EAST ELEVATION

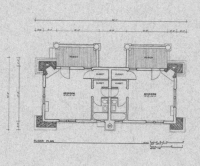

FLOOR PLAN

117

Gisela Bennati Cabin

The Gisela Bennati Cabin, designed by renowned Modern architect Rudolph Schindler, is one of the earliest known A-frame vacation houses constructed in North America. The all-roof structure was an ancient utilitarian building form revived in Switzerland and Germany after the First World War—a response to both the need for cheap, sturdy housing and burgeoning popular nostalgia for a simpler way of life. The catalyst for Schindler's embrace of this traditional form was the restrictive building conditions enforced in the Lake Arrowhead resort community. In response to the requirement that all new construction reflect Norman house style, Schindler proposed this dramatic, triangular structure that merged roof and wall, convincing the board it represented a variation of the Alpine style. While the cabin departs stylistically from much of Schindler's work, it reflects his ongoing interest in geometrical proportions—specifically disrupting rectangularity—functional design of interior spaces, and experimentation with materials and form. The triangular form also references the pine trees that populate Lake Arrowhead, yet more than a design conceit, Schindler placed the sleeping quarters in the loft space formed by the sloping roof. With its open plan, significant use of plywood and all-roof design, Schindler's design anticipated what became the dominant style of cabin architecture in the mid-century.

Architect: Rudolph Schindler
Location: Lake Arrowhead, California
Year: 1937

Type: A-frame; Modern
Dimensions: 7.3 × 17.7 m
Materials: fir plywood, glass, metal, stone, wood

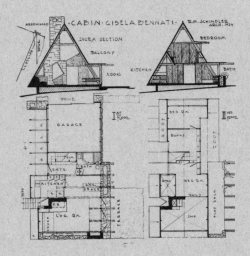

Other Examples:
Rudolph Schindler, Lovell Mountain House, Wrightwood, CA, 1924
Rudolph Schindler, Popenoe Desert Cabin, Coachella, CA, 1924

Left to right: Rudolph Schindler,
Bennati Cabin, Lake Arrowhead,
CA (floorplan), 1934–37. Rudolph
Schindler, Bennati Cabin, Lake
Arrowhead, CA, 1934–37

CABIN FEVER

Utopia

The cabin occupied a unique role in negotiating North American terrain: it served as both the seed of European expansion, and the almost immediate retreat from it. By the mid-1800s, the American Romantics were revolting against the tenets of the Enlightenment period—industrialization, scientific rationalization and social conformity—in favour of an emotional, individualistic experience, as found in nature. Henry David Thoreau's *Walden; or, Life in the Woods* details the author's two-year quest to practice the Transcendentalist's ideal of introspection. Countless people since have turned to the cabin (and the natural environment) as a place for nourishment and inspiration, if not outright liberation from the conventions and demands of society.

The cabin has often been experienced through the lens of romanticism, beginning with the individual and cultural movements of the mid-nineteenth century, but it has also taken on a more expansive and critical role, shaping the national identities of Canada and the United States. Often depicted in paintings by the Group of Seven—who produced images heralded for their distinctly Canadian perspective—the subject of the cabin, set against a majestic landscape, helped locate the country's nascent identity among its abundant natural resources and established a correlation, however problematic, that still resonates. Starting in the early twentieth century, the US National Park Service appropriated the rustic design of the cabin for numerous national park buildings and structures in an effort to attain harmony with the natural environment. In effect, it institutionalized "parkitecture." Similarly, Parks Canada applied the vernacular log construction favoured by trappers and railway workers to recreation buildings housed in the nation's parks, drawing on and perpetuating the historical connotations intrinsic to this style of architecture.

The post-war era brought opportunities for leisure and second-home ownership to the middle class. Cabin design and construction became a burgeoning industry, with popular magazines like *Sunset* serving as launch pads for new ideas. The A-frame cabin, one of the forms most touted, was seen as an entry-level vacation home because it tapped into DIY spirit and called for inexpensive, readily available materials—not unlike its centuries-old predecessor, the log cabin.

As second-home ownership boomed, renowned modern architects such as John Lautner, Marcel Breuer and Rudolf Schindler, best known for residential commissions on a grander scale, experimented with the humbler cabin typology. By applying the utopian language of Modernist architecture to this traditional building type, these architects contributed to a fundamental shift in popular conceptions of the cabin: what was once considered a pragmatic response to the need for shelter became a manifestation of romantic desire for life in nature.

Counterculture movements of the 1960s and 70s also redefined the cabin typology in service of an alternative way of life; geodesic domes, experimental living structures and inflatable architecture introduced new, radical approaches to shelter, yet remained firmly entrenched in the longstanding tradition of the cabin as a site of escape. Stewart Brand's *Whole Earth Catalog* (regularly published between 1968 and 1972, and periodically thereafter), which offered a compendium of products to foster self-sustainable lifestyle, proved to be an effective channel to promote new modes of living.

The utopian impulse that inspired Thoreau to withdraw to the woods in the nineteenth century is at times indistinguishable from the rage that drove former UC Berkeley professor Ted Kaczynski to disavow a world he felt had been destroyed by commercialization and over-reliance on technology. Kaczynski, who moved to a remote Montana cabin to sow his seeds of discontent and mount a twenty-year, nationwide bombing campaign, used his isolated cabin to shelter subversive behavior. The cabin—once a symbol of purity and simplicity—devolved into what architectural theorist Mark Wigley calls "an unsettling agent of horror." Such dystopian interpretations of the cabin, which present it as the locus of transgression and evil, have spawned an entire genre of filmmaking—the emergence of which underscores the increasingly complex representation and understanding of this architectural typology in material and visual culture.

Left to right: The Owen's cabin, Banff National Park, AB, 1935. Sunset, *Cabins and Vacation Houses* (cover), 1974. Marcel Breuer, Caesar Cottage, Lakeville, CT, 1952. Anshen & Allen, Diamond Mountain Cabin, Squaw Valley, CA, 1967–60. Andrew Geller, Reese House, Bridgehampton, NY, 1956

123

Walden; or, Life in the Woods

Henry David Thoreau

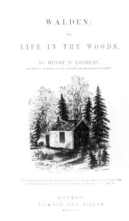

Henry David Thoreau, *Walden; Or, Life in the Woods* (title page), 1854

When first I took up my abode in the woods, that is, began to spend my nights as well as days there, which, by accident, was on Independence Day, or the Fourth of July, 1845, my house was not finished for winter, but was merely a defence against the rain, without plastering or chimney, the walls being of rough, weather-stained boards, with wide chinks, which made it cool at night. The upright white hewn studs and freshly planed door and window casings gave it a clean and airy look, especially in the morning, when its timbers were saturated with dew, so that I fancied that by noon some sweet gum would exude from them. To my imagination it retained throughout the day more or less of this auroral character, reminding me of a certain house on a mountain which I had visited a year before. This was an airy and unplastered cabin, fit to entertain a travelling god, and where a goddess might trail her garments. The winds which passed over my dwelling were such as sweep over the ridges of mountains, bearing the broken strains, or celestial parts only, of terrestrial music. The morning wind forever blows, the poem of creation is uninterrupted; but few are the ears that hear it. Olympus is but the outside of the earth everywhere.

The only house I had been the owner of before, if I except a boat, was a tent, which I used occasionally when making excursions in the summer, and this is still rolled up in my garret; but the boat, after passing from hand to hand, has gone down the stream of time. With this more substantial shelter about me, I had made some progress toward settling in the world. This frame, so slightly clad, was a sort of crystallization around me, and reacted on the builder. It was suggestive somewhat as a picture in outlines. I did not need to go outdoors to take the air, for the atmosphere within had lost none of its freshness. It was not so much within doors as behind a door where I sat, even in the rainiest weather. The Harivansa says, "An abode without birds is like a meat without seasoning." Such was not my abode, for I found myself suddenly neighbor to the birds; not by having imprisoned one, but having caged myself near them. I was not only nearer to some of those which commonly frequent the garden and the orchard, but to those smaller and more thrilling songsters of the forest which never, or rarely, serenade a villager—the wood thrush, the veery, the scarlet tanager, the field sparrow, the whip-poor-will, and many others.

I was seated by the shore of a small pond, about a mile and a half south of the village of Concord and somewhat higher than it, in the midst of an extensive wood between that town and Lincoln, and about two miles south of that our only field known to fame, Concord Battle Ground; but I was so low in the woods that the opposite shore, half a mile off, like the rest, covered with wood, was my most distant horizon. For the first week, whenever I looked out on the pond it impressed me like a tarn high up on the side of a mountain, its bottom far above the surface of other lakes, and, as the sun arose, I saw it throwing off its nightly clothing of mist, and here and there, by degrees, its soft ripples or its smooth reflecting surface was revealed, while the mists, like ghosts, were stealthily withdrawing in every direction into the woods, as at the breaking up of some nocturnal conventicle. The very dew seemed to hang upon the trees later into the day than usual, as on the sides of mountains.

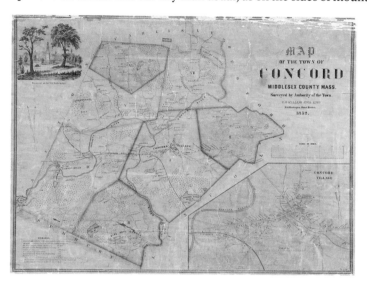

Henry David Thoreau, Walden Pond (manuscript survey), 1846

This small lake was of most value as a neighbor in the intervals of a gentle rain-storm in August, when, both air and water being perfectly still, but the sky overcast, mid-afternoon had all the serenity of evening, and the wood thrush sang around, and was heard from shore to shore. A lake like this is never smoother than at such a time; and the clear portion of the air above it being, shallow and darkened by clouds, the water, full of light and reflections, becomes a lower heaven itself so much the more important. From a hill-top near by, where the wood had been recently cut off, there was a pleasing vista southward across the pond, through a wide indentation in the hills which form the shore there, where their opposite sides sloping toward each other suggested a stream flowing out in that direction through a wooded valley, but stream there was none. That way I looked between and over the near green hills to some distant and higher ones in the horizon, tinged with blue. Indeed, by standing on tiptoe I could catch a glimpse of some of the peaks of the still bluer and more distant mountain ranges in the northwest, those true-blue coins from heaven's own mint, and also of some portion of the village. But in other directions, even from this point, I could not see over or beyond the woods which surrounded me. It is well to have some water in your neighborhood, to give buoyancy to and float the earth. One value even of the smallest well is, that when you look into it you see that earth is not continent but insular. This is as important as that it keeps butter cool. When I looked across the pond from this peak toward the Sudbury meadows, which in time of flood I distinguished elevated perhaps by a mirage in their seething valley, like a coin in a basin, all the earth beyond the pond appeared like a thin crust insulated and floated even by this small sheet of interverting water, and I was reminded that this on which I dwelt was but *dry land*.

Though the view from my door was still more contracted, I did not feel crowded or confined in the least. There was pasture enough for my imagination. The low shrub oak plateau to which the opposite shore arose stretched away toward the prairies of the West and the steppes of Tartary, affording ample room for all the roving families of men. "There are none happy in the world but beings who enjoy freely a vast horizon"—said Damodara, when his herds required new and larger pastures.

Both place and time were changed, and I dwelt nearer to those parts of the universe and to those eras in history which had most attracted me. Where I lived was as far off as many a region viewed nightly by astronomers. We are wont to imagine rare and delectable places in some remote and more celestial corner of the system, behind the constellation of Cassiopeia's Chair, far from noise and disturbance. I discovered that my house actually had its site in such a withdrawn, but forever new and unprofaned, part of the universe. If it were worth the while to settle in those parts near to the Pleiades or the Hyades, to Aldebaran or Altair, then I was really there, or at an equal remoteness from the life which I had left behind, dwindled and twinkling with as fine a ray to my nearest neighbor, and to be seen only in moonless nights by him. Such was that part of creation where I had squatted;

"There was a shepherd that did live,
   And held his thoughts as high
As were the mounts whereon his flocks
   Did hourly feed him by."

What should we think of the shepherd's life if his flocks always wandered to higher pastures than his thoughts?

Every morning was a cheerful invitation to make my life of equal simplicity, and I may say innocence, with Nature herself. I have been as sincere a worshipper of Aurora as the Greeks. I got up early and bathed in the pond; that was a religious exercise, and one of the best things which I did. They say that characters were engraven on the bathing tub of King Tchingthang to this effect: "Renew thyself completely each day; do it again, and again, and forever again." I can understand that. Morning brings back the heroic ages. I was as much affected by the faint hum of a mosquito making its invisible and unimaginable tour through my apartment at earliest dawn, when I was sitting with door and windows open, as I could be by any trumpet that ever sang of fame. It was Homer's requiem; itself an Iliad and Odyssey in the air, singing its own wrath and wanderings. There was something cosmical about it; a standing advertisement, till forbidden, of the everlasting vigor and fertility of the world. The morning, which is the most memorable season of the day, is the awakening hour. Then there is least somnolence in us; and for an hour, at least, some part of us awakes which slumbers all the rest of the day and night. Little is to be expected of that day, if it can be called a day, to which we are not

Henry David Thoreau, *Walden; Or, Life in the Woods* (plates), 1910

126

awakened by our Genius, but by the mechanical nudgings of some servitor, are not awakened by our own newly acquired force and aspirations from within, accompanied by the undulations of celestial music, instead of factory bells, and a fragrance filling the air—to a higher life than we fell asleep from; and thus the darkness bear its fruit, and prove itself to be good, no less than the light. That man who does not believe that each day contains an earlier, more sacred, and auroral hour than he has yet profaned, has despaired of life, and is pursuing a descending and darkening way. After a partial cessation of his sensuous life, the soul of man, or its organs rather, are reinvigorated each day, and his Genius tries again what noble life it can make. All memorable events, I should say, transpire in morning time and in a morning atmosphere. The Vedas say, "All intelligences awake with the morning." Poetry and art, and the fairest and most memorable of the actions of men, date from such an hour. All poets and heroes, like Memnon, are the children of Aurora, and emit their music at sunrise. To him whose elastic and vigorous thought keeps pace with the sun, the day is a perpetual morning. It matters not what the clocks say or the attitudes and labors of men. Morning is when I am awake and there is a dawn in me. Moral reform is the effort to throw off sleep. Why is it that men give so poor an account of their day if they have not been slumbering? They are not such poor calculators. If they had not been overcome with drowsiness, they would have performed something. The millions are awake enough for physical labor; but only one in a million is awake enough for effective intellectual exertion, only one in a hundred millions to a poetic or divine life. To be awake is to be alive. I have never yet met a man who was quite awake. How could I have looked him in the face?

We must learn to reawaken and keep ourselves awake, not by mechanical aids, but by an infinite expectation of the dawn, which does not forsake us in our soundest sleep. I know of no more encouraging fact than the unquestionable ability of man to elevate his life by a conscious endeavor. It is something to be able to paint a particular picture, or to carve a statue, and so to make a few objects beautiful; but it is far more glorious to carve and paint the very atmosphere and medium through which we look, which morally we can do. To affect the quality of the day, that is the highest of arts. Every man is tasked to make his life, even in its details, worthy of the contemplation of his most elevated and critical hour. If we refused, or rather used up, such paltry information as we get, the oracles would distinctly inform us how this might be done.

I went to the woods because I wished to live deliberately, to front only the essential facts of life, and see if I could not learn what it had to teach, and not, when I came to die, discover that I had not lived. I did not wish to live what was not life, living is so dear; nor did I wish to practise resignation, unless it was quite necessary. I wanted to live deep and suck out all the marrow of life, to live so sturdily and Spartan-like as to put to rout all that was not life, to cut a broad swath and shave close, to drive life into a corner, and reduce it to its lowest terms, and, if it proved to be mean, why then to get the whole and genuine meanness of it, and publish its meanness to the world; or if it were sublime, to know it by experience, and be able to give a true account of it in my next excursion.

Henry David Thoreau, *Walden; or, Life in the Woods*, New York: The Macmillan Company, 1910, 83-90.

Pond Scum: Henry David Thoreau's Moral Myopia

Kathryn Schulz

Like many canonized works, [Walden] is more revered than read, so it exists for most people only as a dim impression retained from adolescence or as the source of a few famous lines: "I went to the woods because I wished to live deliberately." "If you have built castles in the air, your work need not be lost; that is where they should be. Now put the foundations under them." "Simplicity, simplicity, simplicity!"

Extracted from their contexts, such declarations read like the text on inspirational posters or quote-a-day calendars—purposes to which they are routinely put. Together with the bare facts of the retreat at Walden, those lines have become the ones by which we adumbrate Thoreau, so that our image of the man has also become simplified and inspirational. In that image, Thoreau is our national conscience: the voice in the American wilderness, urging us to be true to ourselves and to live in harmony with nature.

This vision cannot survive any serious reading of "Walden." The real Thoreau was, in the fullest sense of the word, self-obsessed: narcissistic, fanatical about self-control, adamant that he required nothing beyond himself to understand and thrive in the world. From that inward fixation flowed a social and political vision that is deeply unsettling. It is true that Thoreau was an excellent naturalist and an eloquent and prescient voice for the preservation of wild places. But "Walden" is less a cornerstone work of environmental literature than the original cabin porn: a fantasy about rustic life divorced from the reality of living in the woods, and, especially, a fantasy about escaping the entanglements and responsibilities of living among other people.

***

Only by elastic measures can "Walden" be regarded as nonfiction. Read charitably, it is a kind of semi-fictional extended meditation featuring a character named Henry David Thoreau. Read less charitably, it is akin to those recent best-selling memoirs whose authors turn out to have fabricated large portions of their stories. It is widely acknowledged that, to craft a tidier narrative, Thoreau condensed his twenty-six months at the cabin into a single calendar year. But that is the least of the liberties he takes with the facts, and the most forgivable of his manipulations of our experience as readers. The book is subtitled "Life in the Woods," and, from those words onward, Thoreau insists that we read it as the story of a voluntary exile from society, an extended confrontation with wilderness and solitude.

128

In reality, Walden Pond in 1845 was scarcely more off the grid, relative to contemporaneous society, than Prospect Park is today. The commuter train to Boston ran along its southwest side; in summer the place swarmed with picnickers and swimmers, while in winter it was frequented by ice cutters and skaters. Thoreau could stroll from his cabin to his family home, in Concord, in twenty minutes, about as long as it takes to walk the fifteen blocks from Carnegie Hall to Grand Central Terminal. He made that walk several times a week, lured by his mother's cookies or the chance to dine with friends. These facts he glosses over in "Walden," despite detailing with otherwise skinflint precision his eating habits and expenditures. He also fails to mention weekly visits from his mother and sisters (who brought along more undocumented food) and downplays the fact that he routinely hosted other guests as well—sometimes as many as thirty at a time. This is the situation Thoreau summed up by saying, "For the most part it is as solitary where I live as on the prairies. It is as much Asia or Africa as New England.... At night there was never a traveller passed my house, or knocked at my door, more than if I were the first or last man."

Does this disingenuousness matter? Countless Thoreau fans have argued that it does not, quoting by way of defense his own claim that "solitude is not measured by the miles of space that intervene between a man and his fellows." But, as the science writer David Quammen pointed out in a 1988 essay on Thoreau (before going on to pardon him), many kinds of solitude *are* measured in miles. Only someone who had never experienced true remoteness could mistake Walden for the wilderness or compare life on the bustling pond to that on the mid-nineteenth-century prairies. Indeed, an excellent corrective to "Walden" is the work of Laura Ingalls Wilder, who grew up on those prairies, and in a genuine little house in the big woods. Wilder lived what Thoreau merely played at, and her books are not only more joyful and interesting than "Walden" but also, when reread, a thousand times more harrowing. Real isolation presents real risks, both emotional and mortal, and, had Thoreau truly lived at a remove from other people, he might have valued them more. Instead, his case against community rested on an ersatz experience of doing without it.

Begin with false premises and you risk reaching false conclusions. Begin with falsified premises and you forfeit your authority. Apologists for Thoreau often claim that he merely distorted some trivial facts in the service of a deeper truth. But how deep can a truth be—indeed, how true can it be—if it is not built from facts? Thoreau contends that he went to Walden to construct a life on the basis of ethical and existential first principles, and that what he achieved as a result was simple and worth emulating. (His claim that he doesn't want others to imitate him can't be taken seriously. For one thing, "Walden" is a guide to doing just that, down to the number of chairs a man should own. For another, having dismissed all other life styles as morally and spiritually desperate, he doesn't leave his readers much choice.)

But Thoreau did not live as he described, and no ethical principle is emptier than one that does not apply to its author. The hypocrisy is not that Thoreau aspired to solitude and self-sufficiency but kept going home for cookies and company. That's just the gap between aspiration and execution, plus the variability in our needs and moods from one moment to the next—eminently human experiences, which, had Thoreau engaged with them, would have made for a far more interesting and useful book. The hypocrisy is that Thoreau lived a complicated life but pretended to live a simple one. Worse, he preached at others to live as he did not, while berating them for their own compromises and complexities.

Kathryn Schulz, "Pond Scum," *The New Yorker*, October 19, 2015.

Structures in State Parks —An Apologia

Herbert Maier and A.H. Good

Lamentable is the fact that during the six days given over to Creation, picnic tables and outdoor fireplaces, footbridges and many another of man's requirements, even in natural surroundings, were negligently and entirely overlooked. This grave omission persistent efforts have long endeavored to supply, with varying degrees of success, or lack of it, as one may choose to view it.

Man, confronted with this no less than awesome task of assuming to supply these odds and ends undone when the whistle blew on Creation, may well conclude, pending achievement of greater skill and finesse, that only the most persistent demands for a facility shall trap him into playing the jester in Nature's unspoiled places. He may well realize that structures, however well designed, almost never really add to the beauty, but only to the use, of a park of true natural distinction. Since the primary purpose of setting aside these areas is to conserve them as nearly as possible in their natural state, every structure, no matter how necessary, can only be regarded as an intruder.

Man has come slowly to realize that, if trespass is unavoidable, it can be done with a certain grace. The need proved, his undertaking is somehow legitimatized or not, by harmony or lack of it. As he comes vaguely to sense that he cannot improve on Nature, but rather can only improve and facilitate the way to his understanding and enjoyment of her manifestations, he tends to a kindred humility toward the historic past.

In usual practice it is considered that the plan of a building is more important than its elevations, since, after all, a particular function is the primary reason for the erection of a building. In the case of park structures, however, it may be said that the design and treatment of exteriors are equally important with the plan, and at times more so. Next to the natural features of a park, buildings are the most conspicuous units on the landscape.

In determining the proper design for our park structures we must first consider that we are dealing generally with wilderness and semi-wilderness areas. To most people, therefore, what is commonly known as "rustic" architecture comes first to mind when considering the treatment of park buildings. But we find ourselves installing park structures in all sections of the continental United States. There is the heavy conifer forest region of the

Mount McKinley Headquarters, Comfort Station, Denali National Park, AK, 1985

130

Rockies, contrasting with the drifting sands of the dunes at Goose Island State Park on the Gulf, and parks in the semi-arid mesa country of New Mexico require appropriate structures just as do State park areas in the Maine woods. It is obvious, therefore, that the usual type of rustic architecture will find itself inappropriate in many of our State parks.

Since the primary purpose in setting aside semi-wilderness areas is to conserve them in as nearly a primitive state as possible, it follows that every structure, no matter how necessary, must be regarded as an intruder and should be designed with an eye to lessening its importance. These primitive areas are most beautiful in the native condition in which the Lord made them, and the introduction of man-made structures cannot improve the beauty of the whole but tends rather to rob the picture which Nature has painted of much of its wholesome effect upon the visitor.

The term "improvement" is certainly an anomoly in dealing with parks. Right at the start, in undertaking the development of a new area, is the proper time for the park officials to begin to wage a fight to keep down the number of structures in an area. Where functions are closely related at a given location, two functions or even three or four should be combined under one roof. By that we do not mean that we should go in for excessively large buildings, but many small areas are ruined by the large number of small structures, and it is sometimes not possible to enjoy a single vista or long view without being conscious of the presence of a man-made structure somewhere in the picture.

The number of buildings which are desired by park officials under the State Park ECW program, and which they consider necessary for the needs of the visitors, is frequently found upon study to be erroneous. Only at picnic areas or at particular vantage-points at the termination of long walks are shelters really justifiable. It is not necessary, except for fire-protection, to top off every peak with a lookout. It is much better for the hiker to absorb an expansive panorama from an open promontory rather than to be invited into a lookout or shelter from which he must peek through bull's-eye openings or, in any case, have the picture broken up into segments.

131

There are several ways of lessening the importance of a structure. One of these is screening the building by locating it behind existing plant material or in a secluded nook in the terrain partly screened by some natural feature. Where sufficient plant material does not exist at the site otherwise best suited for the building's function, an adequate screen should be planted, preferably by repeating the same plant material which exists nearby. It is sound theory, however, that structures should be so located and adapted to the natural features of the landscape that it will not be necessary to plant them out. The tendency on the part of some park officials "to make a feature" of their buildings indicates a lack of the proper sense of values.

In a treatment of exteriors the proper use of indigenous or native materials is perhaps the happiest means of blending the structure with its surroundings. The colors used on the exterior of wooden buildings or wooden portions of buildings are another most important factor in bringing about good blending. Naturally, such colors as occur in and are commonest to the immediate surroundings are best. In general, warm browns will go farther toward retiring a wooden building in a wooded or partly wooded setting. A light driftwood gray is another safe color to use. Where contrast is desired to give architectural value to minor items, such as window muntins, a light buff may be sparingly used. Green is perhaps the hardest of all colors to handle correctly, because it is so difficult to get just the correct shade in a given setting and because it usually takes on either a caustic hue or fades somewhat toward a lemon-yellow.

After all, the kinds of structures installed in State park areas are few in variety, and so our problem of architectural control is not so complex as it may at first appear. Roughly, park structures may be divided into two classes—those for administration and those for recreational use. Under the administrative group we have: headquarters units, caretaker's quarters, entrance ways, water towers, fire-lookouts, and fish-hatcheries. Under the recreational-use group we have: shelters and lookouts, pavilions and recreation buildings, concession buildings, boat- and bath-houses, comfort stations, lodges, cabins, and amphitheatres.

The principles of construction employed in our park architecture should be simple and direct. Our exteriors should carry no gingerbread, twig architecture, or peanut brittle. A common type of architecture or form of construction should prevail in a given park so the visitor will not be everlastingly conscious of architectural disharmony.

In designing park buildings it should be remembered that all four elevations will in reality be front elevations

The Ahwahnee Hotel, Yosemite National Park, CA, 2007

and that the public will usually circulate about on all sides. On major park buildings, one side will always be the service entrance, and while fences in park areas are to be deplored and only installed where absolutely necessary, an adequate palisade on this side of the building should completely screen all service operations.

It is difficult, as a rule, to incorporate large sheets of glass in the design of a rustic building. Glass is somewhat out of harmony with rough rock and logwork, since the frontiersman had little or none of it and his window-openings were small. It may be desirable to break up larger windows into smaller lights by the introduction of wood muntins or division strips. In such

132

cases it will be found that stock muntins are too delicate in appearance in a wilderness setting and special heavier ones must be designed.

Giant Forest Lodge Historic District, Cabin No. 6, Sequoia & Kings Canyon National Parks, Three Rivers, CA, 1983

Heavy rustic buildings are suitable only to mountainous areas where forests abound, and in such cases the various structural elements, such as logs, timbers, and rocks, must be considerably oversized to be in scale with the near-by trees, boulders, and slopes. The same type should be lighter in scale in less mountainous regions. But every effort should be made to steer clear of the "twig" type of architecture which flourishes under the name of rustic.

As a rule, park structures are less conspicuous and may be more readily screened when the silhouette is low and horizontal lines predominate. Wherever possible, verticality in park buildings should be avoided. This usually calls for a roof low in pitch. It too frequently occurs that the roofs of park buildings unnecessarily dominate the entire design and are conspicuous from a long distance.

Our park buildings should be well built so as to require as little maintenance as possible. Like fraternity houses, they should be foolproof, since vandalism is common in public areas. In most areas the type of park architecture which combines rough rockwork with logs or hewn timbers and heavy shake roofs is preferable.

In planning a building which is to have an attendant, the possibility of one-man control is sometimes of value. The attendant, be he naturalist in a museum or salesman in a concession building, should be so located that his eye can readily sweep the entire interior and observe any vandalism or improper conduct.

Fireplaces for cooking are usually oversized and homely in our parks. It does not require much cooking surface to provide for the heating of food for one family. A chimney is by no means necessary to a picnic fireplace.

One of the principal phases of park development which may be an indicator of appreciation of good installations is rockwork in general. The rock selected should first of all be proper in scale. That is, the average size of the rocks should be sufficiently large to justify the use of masonry. Whether in retaining walls or in buildings or bridges it is usually better to employ rough rockwork or rubble than to use cut stone. The weather faces of rock should be exposed. Rock should be selected for its color and for the lichens and mosses that abound on its surface as well as its hardness. Above everything else, rocks should be laid geologically correct, that is, they should be placed on their natural beds.

Dams for swimming, fishing, and smaller recreational lakes should be treated in a naturalistic manner.

The planning, designing, and execution of park structures is a specialty in itself. We would advise park officials, wherever possible, to seek the aid of the landscape and architectural professions. While the National Park Service under this program assists to a major extent in furnishing landscape architects and architects as inspectors and technical foremen, it also welcomes and encourages the States to secure competent professional service from private practice. We should strive for a sound and appropriate architecture but we are not interested in individual architectural masterpieces.

Originally published in Harlean James ed. *American Planning and Civic Annual*, Washington: American Planning and Civic Association, 1935.

Initially printed on a home press in 1943, Conrad E. Meinecke's *Your Cabin in the Woods* publishes a collection of hand-drawn cabin plans accompanied by detailed instructions that even the least experienced builder could follow. Annotated with anecdotes and advice that reflect faith in the restorative power of nature, hard work and manual labour—a "cure for restlessness"—the book upholds the mainstream American values of the early twentieth century. It reflects the nation's burgeoning nostalgia for modest living, surrounded by nature. Advocating for the social, financial and psychological benefits of building things, Meinecke focuses on the cabin—with its links to the self-reliance, ingenuity and resilience of the pioneer spirit—as an ideal outlet for amateur building enthusiasts. *Your Cabin in the Woods* also includes an early example of an A-frame cabin design, "The Squatter," which Meinecke encourages readers to use as a temporary shelter while building more elaborate accommodations. A classic in the DIY tradition, *Your Cabin in the Woods* has been in print for more than seventy years and was recently rereleased by Hachette in 2016. [SR]

Conrad E. Meinecke
Your Cabin in the Woods

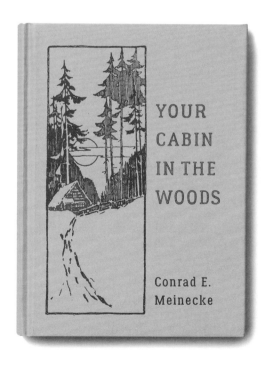

Conrad E. Meinecke, *Your Cabin in the Woods*, 2016 [reprint edition]

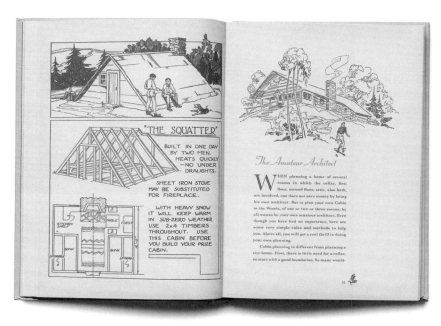

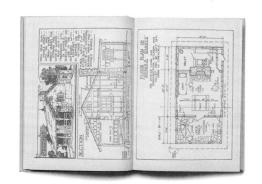

Everything Cold is New Again: Culture, the Circumpolar, and Identity in Canadian Design, 1964 to the Present

Michael Prokopow

Anyone browsing the August 1964 issue of *Canadian Interiors* would likely have noticed the considerable coverage of the XIII Milan Triennale and its theme of leisure. The design fair, established in 1923, was arguably the world's most important summary of current trends in industrial design and a platform for the promotion of the design cultures of participating nations. The magazine's reporting of the event took two forms: a harsh critique of the organization of the international fair—labelled a "fiasco" by reporter Madge Phillips—and a lavishly illustrated, highly complimentary photo essay about Canada's two official entries, a "northern cottage" and a formally curated display of industrial products.[1] The juxtaposition of the editor's criticism of the state of international design at the fair and enthusiastic praise of Canada's contributions was striking. Although some degree of favouritism could rightly be expected from the leading national design magazine reporting about Canadian design at an international fair, the significance of the report was that it adjudged the country's official design installation to be first rate and the aesthetic and material vocabulary of the pavillion to be a brilliant embodiment of the country.

Designed by Ottawa architects Paul Schoeler and Brian Barkham, the pavillion was unabashedly modern. A rectangular box that was completely glazed on two sides, it captured the quintessentially progressive and modest character of Canada and the important role that its northern geography played in the fashioning of the national temperament. Comprised of a large living room, a compact kitchen, a screened-in porch at the front and two bedrooms, the cabin attempted to evoke, in the densely wooded gardens of the Milan fair site, the idea of Canada. In similar ways, the interiors—the furnishings

and their arrangement—presented an appealing tableau of national domesticity. The vision of Jacques St-Cyr (a designer with the Government of Canada's exhibition committee), the cabin was both stylish and comfortable. As the reviewer for *Canadian Interiors* explained, the character of the cabin was "a perfect combination of Canadiana and leisure."[2]

Indeed, much was made about how the cabin's architecture and its decoration captured the character of the country. Significantly, however, the furnishings in the cottage were, in large part, created by Danish emigrants to Canada, and other items, broadly modernist in form, likewise exhibited characteristics of contemporary design from Denmark, Sweden, Norway, and Finland. There was both ideological and cultural logic in the aesthetic language on display in the cottage, and the transposition of Nordic design sensibilities to a Canadian setting (even one staged for commercial and advertising sake) made sense. The vast popularity of what had, since the mid-1950s, been branded as "Scandinavian design," and the meanings attached to the idea of Scandinavian society and its design culture, were viewed empathetically in Canada.

In these ways, Canada's cottage in Milan represented a potent study in the semiotic operations of material culture. The objects on display—the work of skilled artisans and designers—encapsulated and exemplified the traditions

137

"Canada Weekend House," XIII
Milan Triennale, 1964

of making that were closely associated with the histories and practices of
Scandinavian craft and design, and at the same time, evinced a reflexively
benevolent Canadian interpretation of the same. The published photographs
of the furnishings in the cottage's living room reveal a tonal and material
character that is referentially Nordic.

A pair of tall "simple modern" lamps—one light in colour and the other
dark—each with tapering shades of spun nylon by ceramist Lotte Bostlund
sit on tables at either end of the pair of low sofa beds against a wall of cedar
panelling. Floor to ceiling "webby woven beige drapes" by Karen Bulow
cover the cottage's expansive glass windows. Two upholstered adjustable
teak folding deck chairs designed by Kai Stonor Poulsen and produced by the
Canadian firm Scandia sit facing the sofa. Distinguished by their curvilinear
armrests and small fixed neck pillows, they balance practicality with elegance.
Near the window is one of two folding tables in teak by Poulsen. Designed
with X bases they share certain stylistic motifs with the lounge chairs, and
are reminiscent, for example, of the work of Danish furniture designers Knud
Andersen and Poul Hundevad.

In the middle of the room on a circular floor plate filled with crushed white
rocks stands Court Noxon's free-standing conical and rotating enamelled
fireplace from his family firm Metalsmiths in Toronto. Against the interior
window overlooking the porch sits Hugh Spencer's Clairtone Project G stereo
designed in 1963. In both cases, the objects evoke a mood that hovers between
the casual and the chic: the distinctive shape of Noxon's fireplace as much

138

embodies current trends in Swedish and Danish metal fireplace design (take, for example, Stig Lindberg's remarkable enamelled stoves for Gustavsberg) as the excitement of the Apollo missions and the lure of Southern Californian living. As for Spencer's radically innovative stereo—its elegant coffin-like rosewood veneered central volume and its projecting chrome-plated arms holding fixed orb speakers—although deemed "a little citified" by the commentator for *Canadian Interiors* and "expensive for a cottage" was likewise singled out as "good Canadian design." And "as such," the reviewer noted, "belongs in a design exhibition."[3]

Thus the Canadian cottage in Milan demonstrated the confidence of the nation. The aesthetic language of the wood and glass structure and its simultaneously casual, thoughtful, and Scandinavian-inspired contents communicated much about the nation's character and self-awareness at a particularly significant and optimistic point in its history as preparations for its centennial anniversary in 1967 were well under way. In looking to advertise Canada as a particular type of country, the organizers of the Canadian cottage purposely linked the nation to Scandinavia and its topographical, social, and cultural affinities. As much authentically earnest as idealistically staged, the presentation of contemporary Canada as a legatee of Nordic-Scandinavian design sensibilities constituted a powerful declaration of identity—aesthetic and otherwise.

It makes sense, therefore, that the conditions of Canada's northern and modest character could be understood as being Scandinavian in character, or at least owing a considerable debt to the Nordic world. Notwithstanding the fact of the dominant Danish-Canadian design presence at the Canadian cottage in Milan, it is fair to say that the tangible articulation of Canadian character as Scandinavian was much more than simply the stylistic preferences of the exhibition's organizers or a participation in prevailing

trends. Rather, for reasons well considered and well understood, there existed in Canadian design culture an awareness of and affinity for the achievements and implications of Scandinavian design in the context of contemporary Canadian life and a determined, consequential exploration of Scandinavian aesthetics on the part of Canadian designers.

—

1. "Triennale Canadian Exhibit," *Canadian Interiors* 1, no. 5 (August 1964): 13.

2. Ibid., 16–18.

3. Ibid., 16.

Excerpt from Michael Prokopow, "Everything Cold is New Again: Culture, the Circumpolar, and Identity in Canadian Design, 1964 to the Present," in Rachel Gotlieb and Michael Prokopow eds. *True Nordic: How Scandinavia Influenced Design in Canada*, London: Black Dog Publishing, 2016, pp. 25–27.

Ideas of North: Glenn Gould and the Aesthetic of the Sublime

Anyssa Neumann

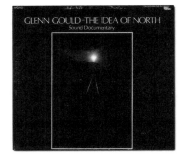

Glenn Gould, *The Idea of North*, Sound Documentary (LP dust jacket), 1971. Glenn Gould, *The Idea of North* (production still), 1967

In 1965, one year after his startling retirement from the international concert stage at age thirty-one, the Canadian pianist Glenn Gould took a train deep into the northern regions of his native country, to the western shore of Hudson Bay. There, in subarctic solitude, he began to work on his first radio documentary, *The Idea of North*, a quiet, contrapuntal meditation on the mentality and metaphor of North[1] in Canadian consciousness. Wielding a portable tape-recorder, Gould interviewed five people who had "a remarkable experience of the north"[2] and wove together their impressions of both physical and psychological contact with its elemental force, reflections on "isolation, on absence, stillness, remoteness, and the absence of alternatives."[3] Upon return to the recording studios in Toronto, Gould cut, edited, spliced, and layered these interviews into a complex vocal fugue, creating an hour-long "docudrama" broadcast on CBC radio in 1967. *The Idea of North* became the first installment of what Gould later called *The Solitude Trilogy*, which included two more docudramas, one observing a remote settlement in Newfoundland, the other offering a glimpse into Mennonite enclaves in Manitoba. No longer occupied by the demands of a concert career, Gould was free to devote himself to the recording studio both as pianist and as creator of radio documentaries, which were, he admitted, less "factual documentary" than "metaphoric comment."[4] In the womb-like security of the recording studio, released from the musical and social demands of a live audience, he began to cultivate a new aesthetic of limitless technological creation. Central to Gould's ideal of creative possibility, I contend, was his lifelong captivation with the idea of North, a metaphor for the sheer physical profundity of the northern land, "an escape from the limitations of civilization,"[5] a state of mind. In this paper I argue that by using this metaphor of North, Gould developed a conception of the sublime that linked metaphysical philosophy with artistic invention.

Gould's fascination with the north did not develop from his freed-up, post-concert-career schedule but rather began in his early childhood. A lifelong resident of Toronto, he first encountered the imagery of the Canadian wilderness through Group of Seven paintings, reproductions of which hung in many Canadian schoolrooms, and later through regional maps, aerial photographs, and geological surveys.[6] His sense of the north as something "other," separate, away from society, stemmed from the weekend trips his family took to their summer house on Lake Simcoe, an hour north of Toronto. Gould was fond of disappearing into the woods with his dog, visiting cows in the fields, and motor-boating on the lake; his preference for seclusion emerged early in life. At Simcoe, he could practice the piano in peace, listen to the radio, and fiddle with recording equipment on his own schedule, developing a lifelong love affair with the microphone.[7] In Toronto, he often retreated to the refuge of the organ at the Presbyterian church his family attended, playing Bach, alone, in a spiritual dimension of solitude: "Those moments of evening sanctuary became very special to me. They meant one could find a certain tranquility, even in the city, but only if one opted not to be part of it...."[8] Gould also opted out of mainstream romantic piano repertoire, favoring Bach foremost, followed by the Second Viennese School. At age fifteen, he wrote that "the aim of these men...is to recapture the pure subjectivity of the Renaissance, Baroque, and early classical era...this return to bygone days has been...a spiritual refreshner [sic] and aesthetic directive...."[9] Also spiritually refreshing were Rosalyn Tureck's recordings of Bach. In her playing, Gould found an aesthetic direction that mirrored his own attempts: "It was playing of such uprightness, to put it in the moral sphere. There was such a sense of repose that had nothing to do with languor, but rather with moral rectitude in the liturgical sense."[10] His emphasis on the link between spiritual, moral, and aesthetic concerns in music is reflected in his perception of the Canadian north as a place of spiritual purification and distance, a place where a "neo-Thoreauvian way of life"[11] is possible.

* * *

The rhetoric of musical ecstasy parallels Gould's own description of the experience of social isolation, "a sense of exaltation...the only word that really applies to that particular kind of aloneness...an experience that most people don't permit themselves to know."[12] Solitude is the prerequisite for an ecstasy that frees one from self and transcends the physical and temporal limitations that prevent him from approaching the sublime, an ideal realm. In Gould's final installment of *The Solitude Trilogy*, a portrait of Mennonite life called *Quiet in the Land*, a character says that "we need to learn...to get on in this world of ours without becoming tainted by it."[13] Gould frequently equated separation from the world with latitude, but, I propose, being unable to abandon the material and physical reality of his art, he internalized this geographical distance by transforming his inner life into an idea of North, an unlimited expanse of creative possibilities.[14]

Just as the Group of Seven painters had seemingly discovered "a new aesthetic based on Canada itself" in the early twentieth century, expressing "the spirituality and essential Canadian-ness of untouched northern landscapes,"[15] so did Glenn Gould discover a musical aesthetic of purity, order, contemplation, and endless wonder based on the idea of the Canadian North as "a place of spiritual cleansing and healing, a powerful antidote to the greed and decadence of modernity."[16] And though the Group of Seven had painted a *terra nullius* that Gould and other artists, writers, and thinkers accepted without question—expediently presenting a land devoid of human life and history—Gould's own idealized projection of what this space should be, or could be, resulted in such a virtuosic melding of ancient ideas, past music, and contemporary technologies that his artistic vision and influence has indeed been "made inescapable," as philosopher Mark Kingwell writes: "He cannot be ignored."[17] This staggering legacy was not merely captured by recording equipment but was in fact realized as the recordings themselves, auditory reifications of his lifelong search for wonder and serenity. Inherent in Glenn Gould's art—his playing, recording, writing, and radio work—was a moral reckoning of beauty and virtue, a belief in the transformation of the soul, a desire for transcendence and meaning, and a trust in the afterlife over its alternative: oblivion. In the introduction to *The Idea of North*, Gould wrote: "Something really does happen to most people who go into the north—they become at least aware of the creative opportunity which the physical fact of the country represents and—quite often, I think—come to measure their own work and life against that rather staggering creative possibility: they become, in effect, philosophers."[18]

—

1. In this essay, I will differentiate between "north" as a geographical location and "North" as the mythical, mystical, or metaphysical associations evoked by the geographical north.

2. Glenn Gould, "'The Idea of North': An Introduction," in *The Glenn Gould Reader*, ed. Tim Page (London: Faber and Faber Limited, 1987), 392.

3. Peter Davidson, *The Idea of North* (London: Reaktion Books, 2005), 18.

4. Gould, "Glenn Gould Interviews Glenn Gould About Glenn Gould," in *The Glenn Gould Reader*, 325.

5. Davidson, *The Idea of North*, 21.

6. Gould, "'The Idea of North': An Introduction," 391. The early twentieth century Canadian landscape painters known as the Group of Seven, active from 1913 until the 1930s, sought to express the spirituality, purity, and magnitude of the untouched northern wilderness of Canada. Influenced by Post-Impressionism and Scandinavian art, the Group of Seven broke away from conservative, traditional portrayals of landscape to pursue discovery of an expression based on Canada itself, its rugged geography and its mystical spirit.

7. Peter F. Ostwald, *Glenn Gould: The Ecstasy and Tragedy of Genius* (New York: W. W. Norton & Company, 1997), 90.

8. Gould, quoted in Ostwald, *Ecstasy and Tragedy*, 69.

9. Gould, quoted ibid., 86.

10. Gould, quoted ibid., 101.

11. Gould, from a letter dated August 3, 1971, *Glenn Gould: Selected Letters*, ed. John Roberts and Ghyslaine Guertin (Toronto: Oxford University Press, 1992), 150.

12. Gould, quoted in Jonathan Cott, *Conversations with Glenn Gould* (Chicago: University of Chicago Press, 1984), 106.

13. Gould, quoted in Elizabeth Angilette, *Glenn Gould: Philosopher at the Keyboard* (New Jersey: Scarecrow Press, Inc., 1992), 145.

14. In the words of Kant, "To be sufficient for oneself, and consequently to have no need of society, without at the same time being unsociable...is something bordering on the sublime." Quoted in Geoffrey Payzant, *Glenn Gould: Music and Mind* (Toronto: Key Porter, 1992), 57.

15. Davidson, *The Idea of North*, 194.

16. Ibid., 191.

17. Mark Kingwell, *Glenn Gould* (Toronto: Penguin Canada, 2009), 59.

18. Gould, "'The Idea of North': An Introduction," 392.

Opposite: Kenneth Lind Cabin, location unknown, 1947

Anyssa Neumann, "Ideas of North: Glenn Gould and the Aesthetic of the Sublime," *voiceXchange* 5, no. 1 (2010): 35–46.

In the mid-twentieth century, architectural photography assumed a position of considerable cultural importance, documenting significant building projects and communicating a specific, utopian, vision of modern living to a broad audience. Photographers Julius Shulman, Ezra Stoller, Balthazar Korab and Maynard Parker, among others, worked on assignment for architectural firms and mass-market publications such as *Life*, *Sunset* and *Good Housekeeping*, depicting post-war living in aspirational, romantic images. Shulman in particular captured the essence of the post-war American dream in his photographs of residential spaces, amassing an extensive catalogue of California's modern design aesthetic. Second-home ownership boomed in the post-war period, particularly on the West Coast, reflected in the number of cabins and vacation homes Shulman photographed for publication in the seductive spreads of *Sunset*, *Better Homes and Gardens* and similar magazines. Cabin design appealed to many of modern architecture's most influential figures, as it offered an opportunity for site responsiveness, and for material and formal experimentation often impossible with primary residences. The cabins in Shulman's pictures are far removed from their log and pioneer origins, and represent new approaches that apply the utopian language of Modernist architecture—with its emphasis on simplicity and purity of form—to the traditional form.

More than architectural documentation, Shulman's pictures offer glimpses into the lives and predilections of his subjects' inhabitants—his attention to interior design equalled his attention to external form. By focusing his lens on the seamless integration of architecture and landscape, on interior details (exposed brick, stone fireplaces, bear skin rugs), and on a structure's human presence, Shulman articulated the role of modern architecture and design in constructing a new leisure culture. In each series of photographs, shot on black and white film and colour transparency, Shulman presents a compelling narrative—one that shaped the desires and aspirations of millions of readers, and reconfigured the simple retreat in nature. [SR]

Photographs by Julius Shulman

The Modern Cabin

Davis Pavilion, Lake Arrowhead,
CA, 1961

146

Hansen House, Lake Arrowhead,
CA, 1958

147

Liddle Cabin, Mount Ranier
National Park, WA, 1969

David Hill

Mail-Order Modern: Supermarket Magazines, Vacation Cabins, and Modular Measure in the 1950s

In August 1958, shoppers at the local A&P supermarket could pick up the latest 10-cent copy of *Woman's Day* magazine with cover stories befitting the culture and season: "Summer Reading Issue" and "Frankfurter Cook Book." Along with these articles, the table of contents introduced another summer-themed story with equal enthusiasm. In what would become the first in a yearly series, the magazine presented a low-cost, do-it-yourself vacation cabin, "the answer to everybody's dream: a place to get away from it all for as little money as possible."[1] Just $1,500, to be exact. While homemaking magazines of this time routinely filled pages with glossy images illustrating decorating tips, dinnertime fare, and inventive recipes, it was not common for them to feature houses designed by well-known architects, much less offer the plans by mail-order.

Between 1958 and 1963, *Woman's Day* commissioned seven different architects to design cabins for summer issue feature. This was not exactly a novel concept. John Entenza's *Arts and Architecture* magazine had already initiated the Case Study House Program to promote modern residential design, industrialization, new materials, and prefabrication.[2] And by the 1930s, well-known architects such as Albert Frey had built designs for low-cost weekend houses.[3] A couple of important factors, however, distinguished the *Woman's Day* program: the magazine, owned and marketed by one of the largest grocery retailers in the U.S., had broad popular appeal; and readers could purchase fully detailed plans for less than one dollar.[4] The cabins were not just models, and unlike the Case Study Houses, they were designs that were within the financial reach of the average homeowner.

Viewed simplistically, the *Woman's Day* vacation cabin articles offer a nostalgic glimpse of 1950s lifestyle, but a more careful appraisal of the series reveals several important social and technological developments that influenced the cabins—and re-shaped professional architectural practice—several years to follow. In the decade following the war, a record number of houses were built to meet the demand of returning soldiers and their growing families. By the late 1950s, the suburban single-family house had become a symbol of improved social standing and financial stability. At the same time, architects were challenged with designing not just one-off house solutions, but affordable, functional, and aesthetically appealing prototypes that would provide models for modern living. These attempts to address a massive housing crisis were socially responsible, but they challenged standard architectural practice that valued traditional architect-client relations and looked disapprovingly at mass-produced, repetitive designs. New materials and technologies which relied on mass production and prefabrication also drastically increased the speed of construction, and many architects were eager to propose new schemes based on modular building systems.

150

Increased house construction allowed huge numbers of people to settle rapidly in the city peripheries. By 1957, nearly 30% of the U.S. population lived in the suburbs (up from 15.3% in 1940).[5] Levittown and Lustron were nearly a decade old, and the *Woman's Day* cabin articles shifted the discussion from high-volume starter homes for GI's to affordable leisure time retreats marketed directly to an ascending middle class.

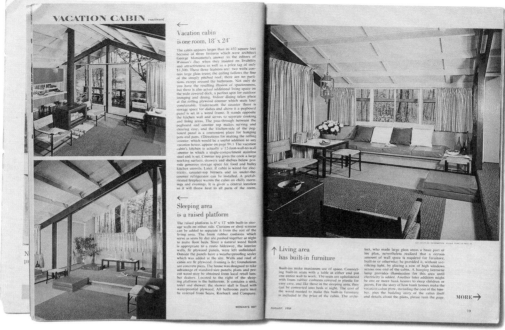

"Vacation Cabin," *Woman's Day* (interior spread), August 1958

The term "cabin" implies romantic connotations, and *Woman's Day* clearly marketed the designs in woodsy settings. But instead of touting rustic lean-tos, the magazine commissioned designs from architects who relied on new materials and employed novel techniques including modular coordination and prefabrication. War-born technologies had come to influence housing construction, and while automation offered a practical approach for developers like the Levitts and inventors like Strandlund, licensed architects were still discussing the broader technical ramifications of factory production while debating the ethical points of client-less design projects. In a time when advertising architectural services was considered taboo, the cabins were provocative, in small measure because of their designs, but more importantly because professional services were offered for sale in popular press magazines with tens of thousands of readers.

1. "Vacation Cabin," *Woman's Day*, August 1958, 17.

2. Elizabeth A.T. Smith, *Case Study Houses* (New York: Taschen, 2002).

3. Joseph Rosa, *Albert Frey, Architect* (New York: Princeton Architectural Press, 1999), 60–61.

4. "Vacation Cabin," *Woman's Day*, August 1958, 21.

5. Frank Hobbs and Stoops, Nicole, "Demographic Trends in the 20th Century—Census 2000 Special Reports," United States Census Bureau, accessed July 12, 2012, http://www.census.gov/prod/2002pubs/censr4.pdf

Excerpt from Hill, David, "Mail-Order Modern: Supermarket Magazines, Vacation Cabins, and Modular Measure in the 1950s," in *Offsite: Theory and Practice of Architectural Production*, eds. Smith, Ryan E., et. al. (Washington: ACSA, 2012), 40–45.

A-Frame

Chad Randl

The A-frame was the right shape at the right time. It was the era of the "second everything," when postwar prosperity made second televisions, second bathrooms, and second cars expected accoutrements of middle-class American life. Next, signs at the hardware store and ads in popular magazines declared, "Every family needs two homes! ... one for the work-week, one for pure pleasure." In the 1950s and 1960s, more Americans than ever before found a vacation home (once limited to the wealthy) within their reach. The increase in disposable income and free time, an economy driven by individual consumption, and a new cultural emphasis on recreation redefined leisure as a middle-class prerogative and contributed to the democratization of the vacation home.

Many of these homes were based upon forms traditional to wilderness settings—the log cabin and the clapboard cottage. On the opposite side were high-style boxes with flat roofs and glass facades, standing brazen against the landscape. But for those wanting a place that was innovative and exciting, modern yet warm, a place wholly suited to the informality of the new recreation lifestyle, a third alternative emerged.

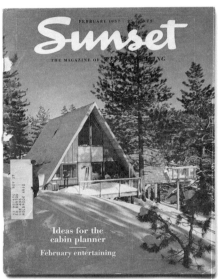

Sunset (cover), February 1957

Starting in the 1950s, the A-frame gained prominence as a popular vacation home type. Its appeal transcended geography and class in part because its form defied categorization. Was it the embodiment of contemporary geometric invention or a steadfast, timeless form, suggesting rustic survival? From grand versions overlooking Big Sur to the small plywood shacks advertised in *Field* and *Stream,* there was an A-frame for almost every budget. It was sturdy, easy to build, and seemed appropriate to any setting. Perhaps its greatest appeal was that it was different, an expression of individuality that meant relaxation and escape from the everyday, workaday world.

After the war, a succession of architects found the A-frame to be an appropriately whimsical and informal stage on which to play out the still nebulous leisure lifestyle. Through their designs, the postwar A-frame, in all its myriad variations, took shape. The excitement aroused by these early designs attracted the attention of a building industry that had grown

Top to bottom: Henrik Bull,
Flender Residence, Stowe,
VT, 1953. George T. Rockrise,
Perlman Residence, Squaw
Valley, CA, 1954. A-Frame Cabin
(Plan No. 381), 1967

153

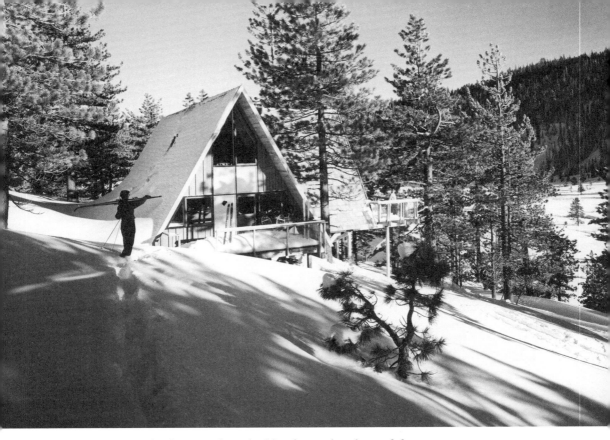

fat on the postwar housing boom and was looking for markets beyond the suburbs. National timber corporations and local lumberyards and contractors recognized the profits to be had in vacation homes. Partnering with mass-market magazines and home-design services, they promoted second homes in hundreds of articles, plan books, and do-it-yourself guidebooks. Because A-frames were instantly recognizable and appealed to a variety of demographic groups, they were often at the forefront of these initiatives. The appearance of prepackaged A-frame kits made an already simple structure even easier and cheaper to build, furthering its appeal and hastening its spread from coast to coast.

Soon, the A-frame was a national phenomenon. It dotted ski slopes from Stowe, Vermont, to Squaw Valley, California, and was a common sight in resort communities and forests and on back roads in between. Triangular pool cabanas, garden sheds, and playhouses brought a touch of the leisure lifestyle to the suburban backyard. By the early 1960s, the A-frame became a cultural icon, a geometric representation of the good life. Hoping to capitalize on this connotation, a variety of companies made A frames the centerpiece of their advertising and promotional campaigns. Restaurants, gas stations, liquor stores, and a range of other businesses set up shop in triangular buildings, relying on the prominent shape to lure customers. A-frames were also adapted for hundreds of the new religious structures that accompanied the postwar move to the suburbs. Triangular restaurants and churches illustrated how the A-frame made its way beyond the lakeshore and the ski slope to influence wider architectural circles. At the same time they were indicative of the A-frame's increasing prominence in American culture.

George T. Rockrise, Perlman Residence, Squaw Valley, CA, 1954

Excerpt from Chad Randl, *A-Frame* (Hudson, NY: Princeton Architectural Press, 2004), 10–11. Reprinted by permission of Princeton Architectural Press.

Drop City

Peter Rabbit

Droppers have learned how to build beautiful houses out of cartops for less than 200 dollars, less than 100 dollars. We know how to use solar heating; we're hip to windpower.

Drop City, Trinidad, CO, 1968

***

Luke Cool taught Droppers to design domes, build solar heaters, make dwellings in which a family can live in comfort and beauty. Luke Cool is the king of the junkheap, teaching Droppers and the world how to USE things. Jump up on top of the car with an axe and chop 'um out, all around the edges just like a can opener, stomp, pop out the back glass, use it for a window, slip off the mirrors, use them for a solar cooker, pull out the insulation, use it, USE IT; make a honeycomb sandwich out of beer cans and plywood—fantastic strength—and USE IT.

Luke Cool says: "We are the victims of outmoded traditions and building codes. Living space and heat can be made available to *all* at a fraction of the present cost through the application of advanced building techniques, such as solar heated domes. Directly tied to my work with these new structures and Drop City is my belief that we have all been part of a nightmare perversion of our technology and wealth, leading our country to spend billions of dollars on a criminal war and preparations for other wars while so many people live in miserable surrounding and work at unrewarding jobs."

155

Domes use materials in the most reasonable and efficient way. Bucky Fuller gave Drop City the 1966 Dymaxion Award for poetically economic structural accomplishments. Soon domed cities will spread across the world, anywhere land is cheap—on the deserts, in the swamps, on mountains, tundras, ice caps. The tribes are moving, building completely free and open way-stations, each a warm and beautiful conscious environment. We are winning.

***

I think Lard first turned Luke on to Drop City. Lard was in graduate school in Albuquerque, Luke was designing and building modular structures. Lard told Luke about the domes the Droppers were building and he came up to see for himself. His mind was blown by Curley and Clard and the beautiful-funky domes. For two years Drop City became the focus for Luke Cool's considerable energy.

The first structure he put up at Drop City was the Cartop Dome, a dome about 27' by 14' made entirely of cartops. It was an incredible material

Drop City, Trinidad, CO, 1968. Peter Rabbit, *Drop City* (cover), 1971

breakthrough for the Droppers. The entire Cartop Dome cost $15, mostly for sheet metal screws.

Luke had all the panels ready to be put together when he arrived at Drop City. He had cut the tops from junk cars with an axe. If you cut carefully around the edge, you can get a 3 12' by 7' sheet of 27-guage steel with a baked-on enamel surface from each car, 3 12' by 9' from station wagons. Droppers loved station wagons.

After the tops were chopped out, Luke put a template of a given module on the top and outlined it with chalk. There was a 1" lip on each side of each panel. The module was then cut out with heavy-duty electric sheet metal shears. It takes 10 to 15 minutes to cut out each panel. After the modules are out, the lips are bent over at 90° with a sheet metal break, holes are drilled in the bent-over lips and the panels are fastened together with sheet metal screws. Fast, efficient, cheap. We also used the insulation from the cars. The inside skin was made from old paintings of Clard and Lard and the Wop.

Luke brought three people with him to help put up the Cartop Dome. It took the Droppers and Luke's crew two and a half days to put in the foundation and get the entire dome up. Clard and Lard put in a floor and some windows. One was a broken plate glass masterpiece from Jennie's Lounge in Trinidad; it had half a funky Hawaiian hula chick painted on it. Next was a potbelly stove, and then they moved in.

After we built the Cartop we realized that everyone in the world can have a beautiful comfortable dwelling unit for less than $1,000. Low-cost housing units that are being built now cost at least ten times that much. What incredible waste and stupidity.

Excerpt from Peter Rabbit, *Drop City*, New York: Olympia Press, 1971.

Left to right: "Mrs. Oleo Margarine" with daughter "Melissa," Drop City, Trinidad, CO, 1965. Clard Svenson inside Theater Dome, Drop City, Trinidad, CO, 1967. Drop City, Trinidad, CO, 1966

157

Drop City Revisited

Simon Sadler

Drop City, Trinidad, CO, from the
Environmental Communications
Slide Set "Survey on Domes,"
c. 1967

Revisited with a fresh eye, Drop City appears more than utilitarian. Drop City
constructions were intellectually engaging, formally memorable, communally
involving, and endowed a powerful sense of place to the seasonal mud and
dust of southeastern Colorado. Drop City's architectural style was suggestive
of the explosive shards of Droppers' early art projects at the University of
Kansas, of prismatic LSD visions, of stained glass, of petals opening, and of
the sun rising.[1] Drop City affected a manner bestriding form and *informe*.
Unlike the derided paisley swirl usually associated with psychedelia, it exerted
architectonic appeal, full of abrupt nodes, edges, and disjunctions. Drop City's
architectural notoriety was attributable to its "bricolage" of materials and
ideas, which made the geometric design principles of Richard Buckminster
Fuller (1895–1983) into a countercultural language and then metamorphosed
them. In 1966, Drop City was pioneering the amateur geodesic dome and its
variant the "Zome"; it soon hosted passive solar energy systems as well. Drop
City was to the counterculture as Constructivism was to the early Soviet state.

158

FULLER AND DROP CITY

The most outstanding exemplar suggested by Drop City to the outside world was of a grassroots application for Richard Buckminster Fuller's geodesic design principles, upon which he had been working since 1948. During his long life, few figures so polarized opinion in cultural and scientific fields (particularly architecture) as did this free-ranging engineer. Following Fuller's reassessment of his life during his early thirties, he dedicated his energy to the eradication of human suffering through what he termed "design science." Outraged at what he considered to be the architectural profession's prodigal indulgence in "art" rather than reason, Fuller fashioned a series of (in)famous models for ultraefficient inhabitation, culminating with the geodesic dome, which Fuller successfully patented in 1954. Geodesic domes were three-way grids (derived by subdividing the faces of triangular polyhedra) that approximated to great circle arcs plotting hemispherical volumes. Usually metallic, and highly structurally efficient, the domes could be enclosed with skins of wood, metal, glass, plastic, and fabric. Some 300,000 geodesic domes were constructed between the 1950s and the 1970s.[2] In the mid-1960s, and relatively late in his life, Fuller was approaching the peak of his popularity and influence, his face broken into a triangulated geodesic skin for the January 10 cover of *Time* magazine (1964).

The geodesic dome quickly found favor as an industrial and exhibition structure, but its everyday habitability was only rudimentarily tested, experienced mainly by those with the institutional support of the armed forces, Peace Corps, and universities. It was not until 1966 that Mr. and Mrs. Fuller themselves received the keys to their own dome home, built using a plywood kit in Carbondale, near Fuller's offices at Southern Illinois University.[3] Drop City residents were now performing a geodesic experiment remarkable in at least three respects: first, by volunteering as guinea pigs for the private civilian deployment of the geodesic dome; second, by attempting to build domes without access to blueprints, let alone kits; and third, doing so with virtually no resources bar their personal energy and ingenuity.

Drop City had originally been conceived as a collection of A-frame buildings (a typology that remained attached to the back of Drop City's Kitchen Dome), and its commitment to the geodesic principle was decided only after Droppers heard Fuller speaking at the University of Colorado, Boulder, in 1965,

159

where Dropper Clark Richert was in graduate school and Fuller's design for a new Fine Arts building was under consideration. Fuller took an immediate and paternal interest in the new Drop City settlement, with artist John McHale, Fuller's distinguished assistant formerly of London's Independent Group, acting as intermediary. Droppers kept Fuller and his research team at Carbondale informed of progress on the Drop City site, and sought advice, cultivating a familiarity aided by the use of real names rather than the pseudonyms that otherwise helped Droppers disaffiliate from the outside world and confound journalists.

During new year, 1966, Droppers received notice that Fuller had created the "Dymaxion Award" in recognition of their achievement, and the legend of Drop City was set instantly on the strength of its six "Fuller-style" domes. The award was accompanied by a gift from Fuller of $500, a vast sum for the Droppers greater than the original purchase price of their land.[4] There was a trade-off for Fuller too since his association with Drop City bolstered his reputation among the swelling countercultural opponents to the very military and federal institutions in which many of Fuller's connections had been earlier forged. "First Hippie Commune Wins the Buckminster Fuller Cymaxion Award!" exclaimed a line of blurb on the cover of Rabbit's *Drop City*, the publisher confused about the spelling of the Dymaxion name but well aware of the crew cut benefactor's gathering celebrity amongst a long-haired audience.

Fuller's award seemingly confirmed the presence at Drop City of design science, and Drop City remained famous as a showcase for the geodesic dome principle. But there are hitches to this reading, of which Fuller himself was surely aware as he guardedly applauded nothing more specific than the Dropper's "poetically economic architecture."[5] Certainly, Drop City was a revelatory collective act, but in this it was no more than "analogous" to Fuller's vision of the world. Drop City sprang from negotiations, mysticism, drugs, and serendipity, whereas Fuller pronounced collective salvation from a lone mind cleared of distraction and pursuing fixed, rational objectives. The mismatch was not only ideological, but structural, since only three of the six structures present at Drop City in 1966 were true Fuller geodesics.[6] It can be stated that to varying degrees, all the domes were "deviations" from, or "mutations" of, the techniques familiar at Carbondale and that it is this that makes them architecturally significant, formally and methodologically.

The Fullerine inspiration was dramatically apparent in the first building to be erected at Drop City, the "Great Pumpkin" (1965), an eighteen-foot-diameter dome made with two-by-four timber members joined with plywood plate. Straightaway, though, the geodesic principle had gone awry: "The chord measurements for our first dome were taken from a model a farmer happened to have in his yard. We thought we were building a geodesic dome; it turned out to be a [truncated] dodecahedron."[7] The eccentricity of the structure was accentuated by its observation of local rustic building techniques—tarpaper was arduously bonded with wire and bottle caps (donated by local bars) to chicken wire and coated with stucco, a method found in the wall of a nearby farmhouse. Then these vernacular elements were in turn disrupted by a "potlatch" mentality, the building's frame built with timber scrapped by a local lumber yard, and its pentagonal windows fabricated from auto windshields and sealed (to the degree to which any of the hippie domes were ever sealed) with stolen cement, tar, and fibered aluminum paint.[8] Drop City provided the

Drop City, Trinidad, CO, 1967.
Drop City, Trinidad, CO, 1967

perfect illustration of bricolage, an emergent cultural paradigm quite different to design science. According to anthropologist Claude Lévi-Strauss, bricolage was the tendency of so-called primitive peoples to appropriate and reorder existing resources, especially those of the industrial world.[9] A double reading of the Drop City structures was possible, at once the by-product of industrial modernity and of a primitivist remove from it (reminiscent of Kurt Schwitters' dadaist Merzbau and the funk aesthetic of Bruce Goff and Herb Greene).

Drop City was making an expanded "architectural" language out of Fuller's "scientific" precepts. What one finds at Drop City is a succession of iterations developing like variants upon the classical orders. The "Drop aesthetic" of the first dome was retained even when Bernofsky, Richert, and Richard Kallweit succeeded in making the second structure on site, the Kitchen Block (1965), as a true two-frequency, twenty-foot geodesic dome. Again, the timber frame (this time joined by three-inch pipe and covered in plywood) was illuminated by the wildly unconventional module of auto windshields, and the combinations of materials, including stolen items and garbage, altered the erstwhile technocratic cool of geodesics. Droppers were unable to tar and coat the Kitchen Block before rains came, and the plywood warped permanently, so that weathering, too, had intervened into the timeless truths of Platonic geometry. The transition at Drop City from geometric abstraction to viscerality continued: "there were prisms in some of the little windows, and sunspectrums moved across the floor and walls, each minute in a different place."[10]

Observation of such phenomena demanded limitless attention. Aided by drugs, Drop City's laissez-faire time management allowed access to the "temporality" of architecture and not at all in the strategic manner demanded by Fuller. When the first acid trip at Drop City was taken in Douthit's newly completed twenty-three-foot geodesic, material, technical, and constructional errors conjured architectural "events" from Fuller's perfected forms.[11] The geodesic dome, it is believed, was a by-product discovered as Fuller was modeling his Cartesian mental processes.[12] Drop City's wonky domes were more fitting to the alogical thought process of the Aquarian mind.

—

1. On Dropper art, see Peter Rabbit, *Drop City* (New York: Olympia Press, 1971), p. 26, p. 54; Timothy Miller, "The Sixties-Era Communes," in Peter Braunstein and Michael William Doyle, eds., *Imagine Nation: The American Counterculture of the 1960s and '70s* (New York: Routledge, 2002), pp. 327–351, p. 332; Timothy Miller, *The 60s Communes: Hippies and Beyond* (Syracuse, NY: Syracuse University Press, 1999), p. 32, p. 36.

2. See Martin Pawley, *Buckminster Fuller* (London: Grafton, 1992), p. 14.

3. See Pawley, *Buckminster Fuller*, p. 41 (noting a conflict in dating p. 141).

4. See Miller, *The 60s Communes*, p. 33, p. 35.

5. Ibid.

6. Douthit counts a total of ten structures by decade's end. Rabbit, *Drop City*, p. 26. Smaller and more temporary installations were also present on the site.

7. Voyd, "Funk Architecture," p. 156.

8. See Rabbit, *Drop City*, p. 21; Voyd, "Funk Architecture," p. 156; Miller, *The 60s Communes*, p. 33.

9. See Claude Lévi-Strauss, *La Penseé sauvage* (Paris: Plon, 1962), trans. *The Savage Mind* (Chicago: University of Chicago Press, 1966).

10. Rabbit, *Drop City*, pp. 21–22.

11. Ibid., p. 49.

12. See Pawley, Buckminster Fuller, p. 121, citing Lloyd Steven Sieden, *Buckminster Fuller's Universe* (New York: Plenum, 1989).

Excerpt from Simon Sadler, "Drop City Revisited," *Journal of Architectural Education*, Vol. 59, No. 3 (Feb. 2006), pp. 5–14 Reprinted with permission of Taylor and Francis Ltd. http://www.informaworld.com

Understanding Whole Systems: Countercultural Publications

Inspired by the writing and design practice of Buckminster Fuller, Stewart Brand founded the *Whole Earth Catalog* in 1968 to address the interests of the countercultural and back to the land movements that were flourishing at the time. Emphasizing green building practices, sustainability and a DIY ethos, the *Whole Earth Catalog* became a cultural mainstay and shaped a generation's approach to creative, sustainable living—while presciently anticipating the open source culture that would come to define the twenty-first century. A component of the *Catalog* was devoted to reviews of books, magazines and instruction manuals that proposed alternative, often experimental forms of shelter and ways to live. These how-to manuals were "cookbooks" for new models of modern life that starkly contrasted those popularized in the pages of *House and Garden* and *House Beautiful*. By providing step-by-step building instructions, and encouraging resourcefulness and innovation, these publications addressed a fervent alternative subculture—interested in a return to the handmade and using recycled or sustainable materials in opposition to the rampant consumerism and mass production that characterized the post-war period. Manual publication proved to be an effective avenue for disseminating and promoting new conceptions of living, and they remain important records of larger artistic and political expressions.

Publications such as Ant Farm's *Inflatocookbook*, Steve Baer's *Dome Cookbook* and Ken Isaacs' *Culture Breakers, Alternatives, and Other Numbers* included plans, drawings and material lists that enabled readers to build their own alternative living structures (in the same vein as Conrad Meinecke's *Your Cabin in the Woods*). Lloyd Kahn, editor of the Shelter section of *Whole Earth*, published a number of compilations of built structures, such as *Domebook 1* and *Domebook 2*, to document the emergence of a new vernacular architecture. While the designers' reinventions of form, space and aesthetic were undeniably radical, their domes, inflatables and other alternative living structures can be viewed as reconfigurations of the romantic log cabin tradition epitomized by Henry David Thoreau's embrace of simple living at Walden pond. [SR]

Stuart Brand ed., *The Last Whole Earth Catalog: Access to Tools* (cover and interior spreads), September 1971

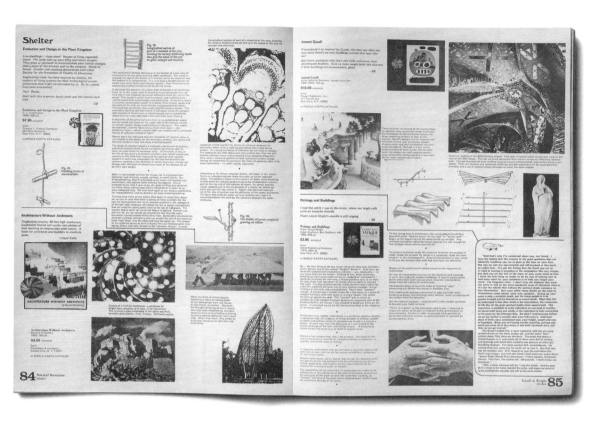

Ant Farm, *Inflatocookbook*
(interior page), 1973

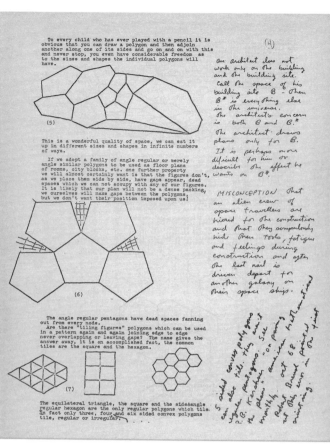

To every child who has ever played with a pencil it is obvious that you can draw a polygon and then adjoin another along one of its sides and go on and on with this and never stop, you even have considerable freedom as to the sizes and shapes the individual polygons will have.

(5)

This is a wonderful quality of space, we can eat it up in different sizes and shapes in infinite numbers of ways.

If we adopt a family of angle regular or merely angle similar polygons to be used as floor plans of rooms, city blocks, etc. one further property we will almost certainly want is that the figures don't, as we place them side by side, have gaps appear, dead spaces which we can not occupy with any of our figures. It is likely that our plan will not be a dense packing, we ourselves will make gaps between the polygons, but we don't want their position imposed upon us!

(6)

The angle regular pentagons have dead spaces fanning out from every node.
Are there "tiling figures" polygons which can be used in a pattern again and again joining edge to edge never overlapping or leaving gaps? The name gives the answer away, it is an accomplished fact, the common tiles are the square and the hexagon.

(7)

The equilateral triangle, the square and the side&angle regular hexagon are the only regular polygons which tile. In fact only three, four and six sided convex polygons tile, regular or irregular.

(4)

an architect does not work only on the building and the building site. call the space of his building site B - then B* is everything else in the universe. the architect's concern is both B and B*. The architect draws plans only for B. It is perhaps more difficult for him to describe the effect he wants on B*.

MISCONCEPTION that an alien crew of space travellers are hired for the construction and that they scrupulously hide their tools, fatigue and feelings during construction and after the last nail is driven depart for another galaxy on their space ship.

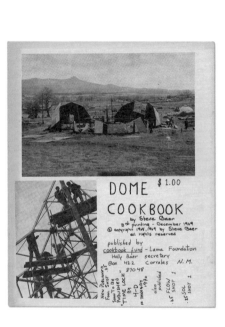

DOME COOKBOOK
by Steve Baer
3rd printing - December 1969
© copyright 1968,1969 by Steve Baer
all rights reserved

$1.00

published by
cookbook fund - Lama Foundation
Holly Baer secretary
Box 422 Corrales N. M.
87048

Steve Baer, *Dome Cookbook*
(cover and interior pages), 1969

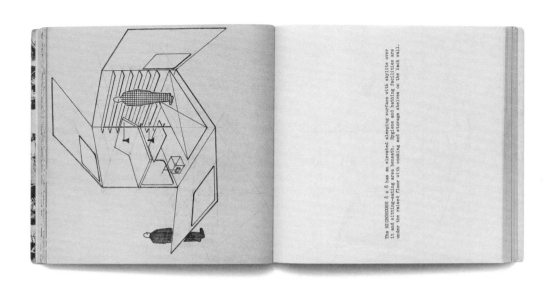

The MICROHOUSE 8 x 8 has an elevated sleeping surface with daylite over it and sitting-eating area beneath. Hygiene and bathing facilities are under the raised floor with cooking and storage shelves on the back wall.

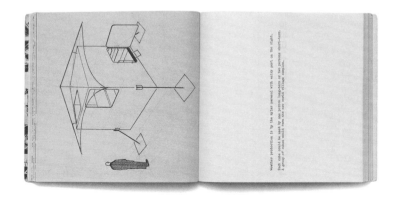

Weather protection is by the mylar panels with entry port on the right.

Such cube could be used by one person long-term or two persons short-term. A group of cubes would form the new world village complex.

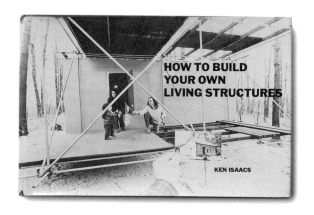

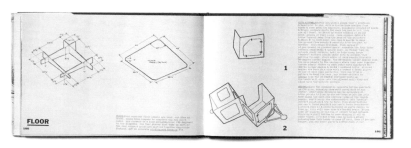

<u>Opposite:</u> Ken Isaacs, *Culture Breakers, Alternatives & Other Numbers* (cover and interior spreads), 1969

<u>Above:</u> Ken Isaacs, *How to Build Your Own Living Structures* (cover and interior spreads), 1974

Scott Watson

Urban Renewal:
Ghost Traps, Collage,
Condos, and Squats

In 1971, most of a squatter community on the Maplewood "intertidal" Mud Flats, near where Malcolm Lowry had written *Under the Volcano*, was burned to the ground by civic authorities, ostensibly to clear the way for private development. Squatting in the intertidal zone is as old as Vancouver and is an important part of the history of the city. (Finn Slough on the Fraser River is a squatting community still present in 2005; it was established in the 1890s.) Intertidal squats have been established and last largely due to the ambiguity of jurisdiction over the intertidal area. In Canada, private property, regulated by cities and their zoning laws, can extend no further than the mean high tide mark. The intertidal zone is the jurisdiction of the federal government. The 1971 official arson marked a turning point, or point of no return, in the transformation of metropolitan Vancouver. The Maplewood intertidal squat was constructed not just alternately to new condominium living, but in active polemical opposition to it—indeed, not only that but even in opposition to humanist modernism of the 1950s. The hippie aesthetics of the Maplewood squat derived entirely from the crumbling civic inventory. The Maplewood squat was a highly symbolic episode in a dynamic tension between values still active today. It was both urban and rural: it was a bit of country ringed by the city. Backed by a liminal forest that separated it from the growing bedroom suburb of North Vancouver, it faced the Shell Oil refinery located across the Burrard Inlet.

168

Squatting became symbolic of everything that was slated for demolition and for the possibility of protest. This was authentic uncommodifiable human habitation, the polar opposite of the condo. Squatting was deployed to prevent the building of a hotel at the entrance to Stanley Park. (The site is today an extension of Stanley Park.) And squatting became a utopian model for self-determined "village," self-sustaining communities in a city whose neighbourhoods were being razed for condo high-rises. The intertidal location was ruled by diurnal rhythms and lunar cycles, so available for parables of the rightness of living in harmony with nature.

Tom Burrows, who built and lived at the Maplewood Mud Flats, produced an important body of "intertidal" sculpture there, and later embarked on a world-wide project, in 1976, to document squatting. Burrows' house and his sculptures were, in the early 1970s, published in *artscanada* (February/March 1972) in the context of other artists such as Dean Ellis, who also made "Smithson-inspired" ephemeral constructivist works in the intertidal zone. Burrows' photographs of his mud flat sculptures stand as among the most eloquent documents of the period. Bricolage constructions inspired by the drawings of Kasimir Malevich

and meditations on mirroring and symmetry involved him in a pursuit of formal questions.[1] But subject also to the action of the tides and the incomprehension of the hippie squatters, who would salvage material from them, they were liminal in every sense, most importantly in the meeting of the organic and the inorganic. Having been a student in London in 1968, Burrows was among the most informed about Situationist anti-aesthetics of all Vancouver artists (as were Wall and Wallace, who also lived in London during this time). The title of his article on his work at Maplewood, "only take for granted the things you can touch," vouches for the distinction to be made between the image industry and the hand-built house.[2]

—

1. Dennis Wheeler (Burrows' friend) wrote his M.A. thesis on Malevich. Dennis Wheeler, *Kasimir Malevich and Suprematism: art in the context of the revolution* (master's thesis, The University of British Columbia, 1971).

2. Tom Burrows, "only take for granted the things you can touch," *artscanada* 29:1 (February/March, 1972), 41–45.

Excerpt from "Urban Renewal: Ghost Traps, Collage, Condos, and Squats—Vancouver Art in the Sixties," in *Intertidal: Vancouver Art and Artists*, ed. Dieter Roelstraete and Scott Watson (Antwerp & Vancouver: Museum van Hedendaagse Kunst Antwerpen and the Morris and Helen Belkin Art Gallery, The University of British Columbia, 2005), 30–49.

For many writers, a cabin has not only served as a place to work, but also as a source of inspiration. It allows for escape from the demands of society, communion with nature and a simpler existence. Often this engenders a very specific type of reflection, where the cabin itself or what the cabin experience offers becomes central to the narrative—from observations of the natural landscape and the demands of physical labour to recollections of childhood and meditations on life. [JMV]

The Writer's Cabin

Annie Dillard at her cabin, 1987.
Gary Snyder and Allen Ginsberg,
Glacier Park, WA, 1965. Margaret
Atwood, location unknown, 1972.
Anne LaBastille at her cabin, n.d.,
Courtesy of Adirondack Experience

170

The Small Cabin

Margaret Atwood

The house we built gradually
from the ground up when we were young
(three rooms, the walls
raw trees) burned down
last year   they said

I didn't see it, and so
the house is still there in me

among branches as always   I stand
inside it looking out
at the rain moving across the lake

but when I go back
to the empty place in the forest
the house will blaze and crumple
suddenly in my mind

collapsing like a cardboard carton
thrown on a bonfire, summers
crackling, my earlier
selves outlined in flame.

Left in my head will be
the blackened earth: the truth.

Where did the house go?

Where do the words go
when we have said them?

Pilgrim at Tinker Creek

Annie Dillard

Seeing is of course very much a matter of verbalization. Unless I call my attention to what passes before my eyes, I simply won't see it. It is, as Ruskin says, "not merely unnoticed, but in the full clear sense of the word, unseen." My eyes alone can't solve analogy tests using figures, the ones which show, with increasing elaborations, a big square, then a small square in a big square, then a big triangle, and expect me to find a small triangle in a big triangle. I have to say the words, describe what I'm seeing. If Tinker Mountain erupted, I'd be likely to notice. But if I want to notice the lesser cataclysms of valley life, I have to maintain in my head a running description of the present. It's not that I'm observant; it's just that I talk too much. Otherwise, especially in a strange place, I'll never know what's happening. Like a blind man at the ball game, I need a radio.

When I see this way I analyze and pry. I hurl over logs and roll away stones; I study the bank a square foot at a time, probing and tilting my head. Some days when a mist covers the mountains when the muskrats won't show and the microscope's mirror shatters, I want to climb up the blank blue dome as a man would storm the inside of a circus tent, wildly, dangling, and with a steel knife claw a rent in the top, peep, and, if I must, fall.

But there is another kind of seeing that involves a letting go. When I see this way I sway transfixed and emptied. The difference between the two ways of seeing is the difference between walking with and without a camera. When I walk with a camera I walk from shot to shot, reading the light on a calibrated meter. When I walk without a camera, my own shutter opens, and the moment's light prints on my own silver gut. When I see this second way I am above all an unscrupulous observer.

***

It was sunny one evening last summer at Tinker Creek; the sun was low in the sky, upstream. I was sitting on the sycamore log bridge with the sunset at my back, watching the shiners the size of minnows who were feeding over the muddy sand in skittery schools. Again and again, one fish, then another, turned for a split second across the current and flash! the sun shot out from its silver side. I couldn't watch for it. It was always just happening somewhere else, and it drew my vision just as it disappeared: flash, like a sudden dazzle of the thinnest blade, a sparking over a dun and olive ground at chance intervals from every direction. Then I noticed white specks, some sort of pale petals, small, floating from under my feet on the creek's surface, very slow and steady. So I blurred my eyes and gazed towards the brim of my hat and saw a new world. I saw the pale white circles roll up, roll up, like the world's turning, mute and perfect, and I saw the linear flashes, gleaming silver, like stars being born at random down a rolling scroll of time. Something broke and something opened. I filled up like a new wineskin. I breathed an air like light; I saw a light like water. I was the lip of a fountain the creek filled forever; I was ether, the leaf in the zephyr; I was flesh-flake, feather, bone.

When I see this way I see truly. As Thoreau says, I return to my senses. I am the man who watches the baseball game in silence in an empty stadium. I see the game purely; I'm abstracted and dazed. When it's all over and the white-suited players lope off the green field to their shadowed dugouts, I leap to my feet; I cheer and cheer.

* * *

But I can't go out and try to see this way. I'll fail, I'll go mad. All I can do is try to gag the commentator, to hush the noise of useless interior babble that keeps me from seeing just as surely as a newspaper dangled before my eyes. The effort is really a discipline requiring a lifetime of dedicated struggle; it marks the literature of saints and monks of every order East and West, under every rule and no rule, discalced and shod. The world's spiritual geniuses seem to discover universally that the mind's muddy river, this ceaseless flow of trivia and trash, cannot be dammed, and that trying to dam it is a waste of effort that might lead to madness. Instead you must allow the muddy river to flow unheeded in the dim channels of consciousness; you raise your sights; you look along it, mildly, acknowledging its presence without interest and gazing beyond it into the realm of the real where subjects and objects act and rest purely, without utterance. "Launch into the deep," says Jacques Ellul, "and you shall see."

The secret of seeing is, then, the pearl of great price. If I thought he could teach me to find it and keep it forever I would stagger barefoot across a hundred deserts after any lunatic at all. But although the pearl may be found, it may not be sought. The literature of illumination reveals this above all: although it comes to those who wait for it, it is always, even to the most practiced and adept, a gift and a total surprise. I return from one walk knowing where the killdeer nests in the field by the creek and the hour the laurel blooms. I return from the same walk a day later scarcely knowing my own name. Litanies hum in my ears; my tongue flaps in my mouth Ailinon, alleluia! I cannot cause light; the most I can do is try to put myself in the path of its beam. It is possible, in deep space, to sail on solar wind. Light, be it particle or wave, has force: you rig a giant sail and go. The secret of seeing is to sail on solar wind. Hone and spread your spirit till you yourself are a sail, whetted, translucent, broadside to the merest puff.

* * *

Living this way by the creek, where the light appears and vanishes on the water, where muskrats surface and dive, and redwings scatter, I have come to know a special side of nature. I look to the mountains, and the mountains still slumber, blue and mute and rapt. I say, it gathers; the world abides. But I look to the creek, and I say: it scatters, it comes and goes. When I leave the house the sparrows flee and hush; on the banks of the creek jays scream in alarm, squirrels race for cover, tadpoles dive, frogs leap, snakes freeze, warblers vanish. Why do they hide? I will not hurt them. They simply do not want to be seen. "Nature," said Heraclitus, "is wont to hide herself." A fleeing mockingbird unfurls for a second a dazzling array of white fans ... and disappears in the leaves. Shane! ... Shane! Nature flashes the old mighty glance—the come-hither look—drops the handkerchief, turns tail, and is gone. The nature I know is old touch-and-go.

I wonder whether what I see and seem to understand about nature is merely one of the accidents of freedom, repeated by chance before my eyes, or whether it has any counterpart in the worlds beyond Tinker Creek. I find in quantum mechanics a world symbolically similar to my world at the creek.

To Louis Ginsberg [Paterson, NJ] July 10, 1974

Allen Ginsberg

Dear Louis:

Hard work for me potbellied city-lax,
pushing wheelbarrows empty up hill, shoveling red dirt
into a sieve, shaking out fine Mexican-red dust,
lifting iron spoons full w/clay into flat-bed jeep,
mixing gravel from old gold mines with measures of grey concrete
with red clay dust, to color kitchen floor, then
watering hardened concrete with hose so it won't crack
And logs, draw knives strip bark, chisels smooth out branch holes,
tumbling round posts over each other a bed of two pine laid parallel,
helping dig foot deep holes for porch stone foundation
all work done in a month—then unseasonable rain—
days under apartment—high ponderosa's dripping water
onto lean-to roofed with black and white plastic rolls,
sleeping bags muddy wet at dawn, squirrels scampering away from our apples,
deer at Gary Snyder's pond-edge in garden—
Unexpected rain ending sweaty labor, a few days
sheltered indoors, reading Zen koans or Lu Yu's
eleventh century laughter about his drunken white hair—
Now sun's out, Wednesday sky's blue,
Cool wind in pines dries housetops and grass fields—
Trail to re-stack wet lumber to dry in sunlight,
Load the truck with second hand windows to take to Marysville
to dip in vats of chemical paint remover, and on to Frisco
to poetry reading this Friday w/ McClure & Snyder,
Benefit small island attacked by Yamaha Industries tourism—
Small sample of great natural world eaten by human cancer—
I read your friend Bluefarb's letter but could not make head or tail of it—
Yes he reasons well, but poems my stepmother likes he thinks are off track,
He doesn't believe in Jahweh but he wants me to believe,
He doesn't practice religion but wants me to practice what he rejected—
He doesn't respect my learning but wants me to respect his bookishness—
He takes things personally and denounces my vanity—
It's too confusing to argue when neither of us know what we're discussing
and meanwhile pseudo-peace in mid-east makes all previous reasons vain—
assertions of sovereignty yesteryear today are bargained away today—
Meanwhile lumber must be piled properly or it'll warp
And what I'm learning is not history or Kabbalah
but bruises on my hands and knees, splinters from rough cut wood
and how difficult it is to master the "primitive"
the old story, how I lost track of shelter and food, given them in cities,
and how hard and beautiful both seem when worked for by hand.
I'll write in a few days when returned from the white-hilled city—
Meanwhile we have each other's love while still alive—

Son, Allen

Woodswoman

Anne LaBastille

The cabin never had seemed so beautiful. I found my energy returning, my responses to the environment quickening, my reflexes sharpening, my muscles hardening, and my body slimming again. Packing away my heels, I stretched my toes luxuriously again in moccasins and lumberjack boots. Corns which had appeared in Washington, gradually diminished. My streak of aggressive driving passed. I slept well. How contenting to spend summer mornings again at my desk or on the sun deck, writing, typing, answering correspondence, then dashing into the lake for a swim. How relaxing to rock by the crackling Franklin stove, reading or gazing out the picture windows at an autumn stained-glass sunset. How comforting to burrow into the soft blankets of my sleeping loft on those awesome, frigid winter nights. And how inspiring to wake at dawn to the smell of spring and trill of peepers.

Yet to be completely honest, my sojourn in the city had been profitable. I came home flushed with success, having done a good job, earned a handsome salary, and made excellent contacts. Although I knew that I could never stand to live in a city again, I also realized that a small connection with it had become necessary to bring a balance into my life. The city (regardless which one it is) *does* provide a certain degree of sophistication and intellectualism. It offers the challenge of professional matters. It throws new and interesting people in one's path. There is a dynamic and an energy in cities which is diametric to the life-forces of the forest.

Still the cabin is the wellspring, the source, the hub of my existence. It gives me tranquility, a closeness to nature and wildlife, good health and fitness, a sense of security, the opportunity for resourcefulness, reflection, and creative thinking. Yet my existence here has not been, and never will be, idyllic. Nature is too demanding for that. It requires a constant response to the environment. I must adapt to its changes—the seasons, the vagaries of weather, wear and tear on house and land, the physical demands on my body, the sensuous pulls on my senses. Despite these demands, I share a feeling of continuity, contentment, and oneness with the natural world, with life itself, in my surroundings of tall pines, clear lakes, flying squirrels, trailless peaks, shy deer, clean air, bullfrogs, black flies, and trilliums.

The Terror and Tedium of Living Like Thoreau

Diana Saverin

I first went to Alaska during a college summer. Although the scale of the landscape often made me feel tiny and insignificant as a willow, its beauty and bigness also made its way into my own life. Just living and walking and feeding on that land became a way to participate in its grandeur.

I kept going back. More than once, I considered dropping out of college to stay. After graduation, the idea of moving to a city and getting an office job scared me much more than, say, bears. I could see the days soaring by there: a fluorescent-lit routine repeating itself for years.

So I rented a small cabin on a hill, where I was planning to live some version of the American dream, following a template laid out by Thoreau. He'd gone to the woods, as he put it, to live deliberately: "to front only the essential facts of life, and see if I could not learn what it had to teach, and not, when I came to die, discover that I had not lived." He'd gone there to "suck out all the marrow of life." That's what solitude in the wilderness was all about: living life close to the bone, where it's sweetest. In my own cabin, I imagined, I'd think in sentences, notice the breeze, leave behind the frivolities of society and technology—everything that wasn't life raw and vivid and real.

My cabin was near Denali National Park, and I occasionally hitchhiked south to that huge park, trading in my cabin shelter for the bivouac. A few days after encountering the barking birds, I hiked back to the park road, rode the camper bus to the highway, and then hitchhiked and walked back to mile marker 253 on the George Parks Highway in the Alaskan interior.

John and Joyce Elmore, my landlords, had homesteaded the property there some 40 years before. They'd walked its perimeter in snowshoes one February, and in the months that followed, they'd built the one-room A-frame cabin that became their home. Eventually, they'd upgraded to a house John built with a kitchen, a living room, a bedroom, a spiral staircase, a porch, running water, electricity, wi-fi. They rented me their old cabin because, Joyce told, they didn't want it to collapse into the earth, as many vacated cabins in the north do.

***

Deliberate living wasn't coming easily. I rarely knew what to do. Much of the time, I slept through the three alarms I set each morning, then put a pot of hot water for oatmeal and coffee on the propane stove. I ate a leisurely breakfast, read magazines dated from months before, watched branches sway through the windows.

It was challenging even to read, or enjoy the view. The mosquitos were *bad*. Outside, they were intolerable. Walking in the woods was no good: running, full speed, was my only option. Inside, they could be just as oppressive. Especially at night. It took only one little sneak to fill the room where I slept and ate and read with a boisterous, twangy buzz. At such times, no thought other than one about the death of that insect could survive. I'd always thought I was a calm person. I'd always thought I could overcome such fleeting and insignificant distractions. I'd always thought I enjoyed being in nature.

In June, the days were hot, too. I walked around the cabin in my underwear and a t-shirt murdering skeeters with the swatter John had given me as a welcome-to-Alaska present. I relied only on myself to fill days, and with nothing siphoning those twenty-four hours into tame, comprehensible pieces, each day grew into a wild expanse of time—unruly, long, and quiet.

It wasn't all bugs and heat. I sometimes helped John cut, chop, and stack wood, and always tried to keep the cabin clean. When the weather was warm

and the breeze kept the bugs at bay, I walked down to the creek to wash, or sat naked in a sunny patch of the hill with a bucket of cold water, a bottle of soap, and a mug I used as a showerhead, pouring cup after cup over my head.

The Elmores' big house was a short walk along the ridge from my little cabin. I sometimes walked there to visit them: filling jugs of water from their hose, checking my

email and looking up bird names with their wi-fi, catching a ride in the bucket of John's tractor. The trips yielded chatter about the weather or the bugs or the roadwork or John's diabetes. Sometimes, I had visitors in the little cabin: the man I was dating who lived in California, backpackers I'd met while hiking a nearby trail. Most of the time, though, I lived alone. My outhouse had no door, my view had no roads, my faucet had no water, and my power outlets had no electricity.

***

A whole crew of our men have chased reality in cabins, tents, trailers, abandoned buses: Thoreau in Walden Pond, Join Muir in the Sierras, Aldo Leopold in Sand County, Edward Abbey in the Utah Desert, Chris McCandless in Alaska. In my cabin, I read their stories, and the stories, too, of the few women like them: Annie Dillard, Gretel Ehrlich, Cheryl Strayed.

I lined the windowsill of the little cabin with these books, and looked at them as often as I did the landscape the window framed. The words urged me to get a sense for life before I got too comfortable in it. The writers told me to wake up, to see.

As much as I loved the books, there were times when these stories made me question my own project. Was I living a cliché? Walking a trail others had walked before me, giving this whole solitude thing a superficial and stereotyped trial? My friend Ray called me one afternoon from Sitka, a town in southeast Alaska. (I didn't have electricity or water in the cabin, sure, but I did have cell service—3G, in fact.) She was working as an environmental activist, at the same organization where I'd met her the year before. She pressed me: "What good are you doing for the world from there? Why do you want to be alone?"

It was selfish in some ways, I knew. But I justified it to myself in lofty terms: I was living out an old and familiar American ritual, enacting some secular rite of passage, awaiting some insight about the world we live in and this one life I've got to spend.

But then I'd hang up, and remember how, before arriving, I'd dreamed of the insights, of the days I'd spend watching woodchucks and waterbugs, of the wind sweeping me up in its warm embrace and the whole world breathing into my ear alone air full of secrets. Then I'd look around. It was still hot and buggy, windier some days than I could believe, and a lot of the time, I was bored. I had no idea how to spend a day.

Cabin Fever

Mark Wigley

Theodore Kaczynski's cabin,
Lincoln, MT, 1996

December 2nd 1997. A small hut that had been hidden in the sparsely
populated woods of Montana is lifted onto a flatbed truck, covered with a black
tarpaulin and transported 1100 miles to Sacramento, California. Shadowed
by a caravan of photographers and a swarm of helicopters, it takes three days
for the 10 by 12 foot wooden box to make the epic journey from isolation to
metropolitan center. For the first time, a whole building is to be presented as
evidence in a court case. Architecture is brought to trial. A seemingly innocent
structure is accused of sheltering the target of the biggest manhunt ever, the
infamous Unabomber who had terrorized the nation for eighteen years.

Not much for the jurors to look at though. Everyone can picture the
building before seeing it. Any child could draw it. Indeed, people are always
drawing it, dreaming about it. The simple form plays a key role in the
American imagination. The cabin in the woods is the generic retreat that is
meant to tame restless city dwellers and has long been institutionalized in
the camp hut, the holiday house, the fishing lodge. In fact, the unabomber's
building is a copy of the cabin to which Thoreau so famously withdrew from
the city between 1845 and 1847. It self-consciously participates in a long
cultural tradition.

179

Yet the unique power of this form is precisely that it is not seen as a cultural artifact. It is understood to be the form that precedes the arrival of culture. The retreat is always a retreat in time, a withdrawal to a lost simplicity, purity, immediacy, harmony...a lost beginning. In the romanticized national mythology of the immigrant pioneer, the domestication of the wild by the independent settler begins with the construction of a simple domestic space using primitive means. The wooden box with a pitched roof symbolizes the moment of settling down, the erection of an isolated house in the wilderness that precedes collective settlement. The cabin is that which precedes pattern, a solitary point in an unmapped terrain. Indeed, it is the pattern of the house itself, the newly defined limits of an interior carved within an unlimited and threateningly mysterious space, that makes possible the domestication of territory and the eventual rise of settlements.

The Unabomber's view, Lincoln, MT, 2008

This is not simply an American fantasy. It is a generic fantasy about a generic form. Each culture dreams of the mythical isolated hut, and each has its symbolic retreats, its designated sites of withdrawal from the dominant patterns. It may not even be possible to think about the patterns without thinking of these sites. Settlement is always conceived in terms of its other.

The unabomber used his settler's cabin to unsettle the dominant pattern. His carefully written manifesto on the horrors of industrialized life condemns the modern city for its stressful, crowded existence in which people are kept prisoner under constant surveillance by police, cameras, and the manipulations of social programming. The enemy is technology, as exemplified by the computer that has united the world into a single social and spatial organization. The solution is to go back to the purity of "wild nature" in the age of the humble log cabin. Everyone should withdraw from the computer to the cabin. Within such a retreat, sixteen bombs were built and targeted with deadly effect against symbols of the technological order: computer scientists, airline executives, biogeneticists, electrical engineers. The point of the violence, said the ex-professor of mathematics, was to break society down into small units, to break the pattern.

The cabin itself is a manifesto, a puritanical polemic. No electricity or water softens the bomber's life or connects it to the national infrastructure. The only furniture is a single chair, a small table and a bed made of a sheet of plywood covered with a thin layer of foam. There are two tiny windows. Neither provides a scenic view. One is at the top of a wall and offers a square of sky. The other, a little lower on the facing wall, monitors the access path.

180

There is a single door at the center and a storage loft suspended under the roof. Built by its occupant with simple tools and reused wood from an abandoned cabin, the house is immaculately constructed. The dark stained wallboards are neatly matched. Roof joists are rhythmically arranged. Windows, door and air vent are triumphs of minimalist anti-detailing. Every nail pinning down the green tar paper on the roof is exactly spaced. The house is a display of control—even if it was never meant to be seen by anyone other than its reclusive occupant.

***

The cabin in the woods is actually at the center of the city. Far from disconnected, the terrorist ruthlessly exploited the ever-present intimate ties between isolated cell and dense urbanization. His frightening talent was the ability to hide his points of connection. While refusing to attach himself to the telephone, water and electricity lines that were only a quarter of a mile away, he kept his rural mail box on the roadside nearby, using the mail network to distribute his terror and get his manifesto published in national newspapers. This is why a seemingly isolated hut could exemplify one of the greatest fears of urban life. The cabin has always belonged to the downtown to which it was eventually brought.

***

The rigorous aesthetic of simplicity, natural materials, craftsmanship, and geometric purity has become an unsettling agent of horror.

Excerpt from Mark Wigley, "Cabin Fever," *Perspecta*, vol. 30, 1999, 122–25. Reprinted with the permission of *Perspecta*, Yale School of Architecture.

The Cabin on the Screen: Defining the "Cabin Horror" Film

Matthew Grant

Through a close examination of Sam Raimi's *The Evil Dead* (1981) and its sequel, *Evil Dead 2: Dead by Dawn* (1987), as well as Drew Goddard's *The Cabin in the Woods* (2012), it is possible to attain a more unified understanding of the "cabin horror" film, its defining features, and its ability to accurately encompass the experience of viewing horror. Each of these three films skillfully uses the cabin as an isolated site of release for repressed desires. The cabin manifests these unsanctioned violent or sexual urges through its physical layout (a creepy, yet initially safe main floor juxtaposed against a hidden, mayhem-inducing basement) and inherent purpose (a place to transgress by partying, drinking, and having sex). In every film, the cabin and the surrounding wilderness gain a malevolent agency through their almost sentient role as obstacle and isolating influence. Doors slam shut, floorboards trip, and tree branches come to life with a vengeance in the cabin horror film, imbuing the landscape itself with a vindictive spirit and secluding power. Finally, the cabin functions effectively as a microcosm in which horror film tropes and conventions can be tested, upheld, or revised over time. This is especially evident when considering all three films together, as the pure horror aesthetic of *The Evil Dead* shifts into comedy and self-reflexivity with *Evil Dead 2* and *The Cabin in the Woods*. Through its function as a site of release for repressed desire, its hostile isolationist agency and its playful adaptability as a genre-spanning setting, the cabin is revealed to be a unique, enduring landscape of horror and the cabin horror film a distinct subgenre with its own conventions and modes, functioning perfectly as an evocation and microcosm of the horror genre itself.

Before defining the specific attributes and conventions which make up the cabin horror film, it is necessary to first establish it as a valid subgenre, rather than a simple cycle or trend in horror. There are three specific pieces of evidence which substantiate this claim. The first is the cabin's longevity in contemporary horror film, from its birth in the 1980s to its resurgence in the 2000s. The cabin horror genre surfaced in the 1980s with slashers and slasher-inspired films, such as

The Evil Dead, *Evil Dead 2*, Sean Cunningham's *Friday the 13th* (1980), and Stan Winston's *Pumpkinhead* (1988). Its oversaturation and decline in the late 1980s and 1990s might have signalled its end if it were a simple cycle or finite trend, but in the 2000s cabin horror experienced a renaissance with films such as Daniel Myrick and Eduardo Sánchez's *The Blair Witch Project* (1999), Eli Roth's *Cabin Fever* (2002), Rob Schmidt's *Wrong Turn* (2003), David Koepp's *Secret Window* (2004), Lars von Trier's *Antichrist* (2009), Eli Craig's *Tucker and Dale vs. Evil* (2010), and *The Cabin in the Woods*. The length of its presence in the horror film landscape, as well as its return from oversaturation and obscurity, suggests that the cabin horror film is a durable, distinct subgenre on its own.

The second piece of evidence lies in the cabin horror film's adaptability and fluidity with other subgenres and genres proper. From its slasher origins and influences, to its forays into comedy (*Evil Dead 2*, *Tucker and Dale*), pseudo-documentary (*The Blair Witch Project*) and the art film (*Antichrist*), the cabin is not bound by horror conventions and modes. Able to meld itself to other, disparate genres while retaining its essential qualities, the cabin horror film is both highly adaptable and tightly structured. This adaptability signals both its power as a symbol of horror and its enduring identity in the face of competing genre conventions—attributes which again suggest the cabin horror film's status as subgenre over cycle.

Finally, the uniqueness of the cabin horror film's setting contributes to its attainment of subgenre status. An isolated cabin, removed from society and any meddling institutions, represents not only the American Dream and its fulfillment, but also horror film's divergence from traditional Gothic settings. As Robin Wood suggests, "the process whereby horror becomes associated with its true milieu, the family, is reflected in its steady geographical progress toward America" (18). The cabin represents the slow culmination of that progress. It is completely removed from the Gothic connotations of the European mansion or haunted house, emphatically denying the traditional settings and class systems of earlier horror films. Entirely contemporary and reflective of the American middle class, the cabin functions as a more relatable, realistic site of horror and violence. For these reasons, cabin horror must be defined as a distinct subgenre in modern horror film.

—

Works Cited

Arnzen, Michael A. "Who's Laughing Now? ... the Postmodern Splatter Film." *Journal of Popular Film & Television* 21.4 (1994): 176-84. Print.

Cwik, Gregory. "Cabin in the Woods: Slasher-Films, and Meta-Horror." *Academic Journal of Film and Media* 8.1 (2012): n. pag. Web. 25 February 2013.

Hockenhull, Stella. "Sublime Landscapes in Contemporary British Horror: *The Last Great Wilderness and Eden Lake*." *Horror Studies* 1.2 (2010): 207-24. Print.

Royer, Carl, and Diana Royer. "Horror, Humor, Poetry: Sam Raimi's *Evil Dead* Trilogy." *The Spectacle of Isolation in Horror Films: Dark Parades*. New York: Haworth Press, 2005. 39-51. Print.

Smith, Paul Julian. "Scare Quotes." *Film Quarterly* 65.4 (2012): 8-9. Print.

Wood, Robin. "An Introduction to the American Horror Film." *The American Nightmare: Essays on the Horror Film*. Ed. Richard Lippe and Robin Wood. Toronto: Festival of Festivals, 1979. 7-28. Print.

Excerpt from Matthew Grant, "The Cabin on the Screen: Defining the 'Cabin Horror' Film", *Film Matters* 5, no. 1 (2014): 5-12. Reproduced with permission of the Licensor through PLSclear.

Marcel Breuer and Walter
Gropius, Chamberlain Cottage,
Wayland, MA (front elevation),
1941

Chamberlain Cottage

One of Marcel Breuer's first American commissions, and his final collaboration with Walter Gropius, the Chamberlain Cottage exemplifies his innovative approach to cottage design. The six-hundred-square-foot weekend cottage was built in a densely wooded area adjacent to a river, and reveals the architect's deep sensitivity to site. It features what would become known as his longhouse style: residences organized by a suspended, wood-framed rectangular structure. Experimenting with the possibilities of wood framing, Breuer left the fir siding unpainted; instead, he applied a clear stain to emphasize the natural grain of the wood. The cottage evidences Breuer and Gropius' interest in simple, geometric construction, with a large, screened porch extending from the main volume of the house.

Breuer's work in Cape Cod, which contributed to the development of a collection of experimental vacation homes in the popular East Coast locale, reflects explicit rejection of the traditional New England style popular at the time. Although the modestly sized home is essentially a one-room cabin, it was among the most innovative examples of residential architecture in the United States at the time of its construction. By applying the utopian language of Modernist architecture—its emphasis on simplicity and purity of form—to this traditional building type, Breuer contributed to a fundamental shift in popular conceptions of the cabin: what was once considered a pragmatic response to need for shelter became a manifestation of romantic desire for a simpler life, surrounded by nature.

Architect: Marcel Breuer and Walter Gropius
Location: Wayland, Massachusetts
Year: 1940

Type: Modern
Dimensions: 2.9 × 11.3 × 10.3 m
Materials: fieldstone, glass, metal, wood

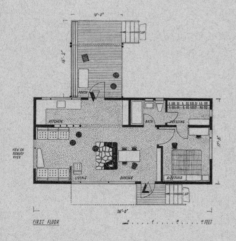

FIRST FLOOR

Other Examples:
Marcel Breuer, Kepes House, Wellfleet, MA, 1949
Marcel Breuer, Scott House, Dennis, MA, 1949
Roy Johnson and Stanley Torkelson, The Wood House, Westchester, NY, 1950
Jack Hall, Hatch House, Wellfleet, MA, 1960

Leisure House

John Campbell's Leisure House was developed during the post-war boom in construction of modest, affordable vacation homes. Renewed interest in leisure combined with fervent DIY spirit to produce a popular appetite for architectural design that exploited the possibilities of new materials, such as plywood, and allowed for construction without professional assistance. Launched at the San Francisco Arts Festival in 1951, the Leisure House catered to this cultural enthusiasm for the all-roof, A-frame form—and this simple, inexpensive design contributed to its widespread popularity. While Campbell was not the first architect to propose the geometric structure, he was among the most effective at mass-marketing A-frames to a wide demographic, by selling prefabricated kits in popular magazines and at trade shows nationwide. The charming, economical design could be modified to accommodate a variety of sites and climates, and it appealed to Americans looking for stylish, open plan designs for their second homes. After exhibiting his prototype to great acclaim in 1951, Campbell advertised his plans as a simple, DIY project that could be assembled in three to five days with limited building experience. Campbell would go on to design other prefab cabins, including the 1961 Woman's Day Low-Cost Vacation Home, but none would capture the cultural zeitgeist as much as his original A-frame.

Architect: Campbell & Wong
Location: Various
Year: 1951

Type: A-frame; Prefab
Dimensions: 5.5 × 7.3 m
Materials: glass, plywood

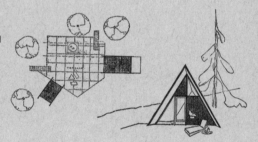

Left to right: John Campbell, John Campbell's Leisure House (rendering), published in *Interiors,* January 1951. John Campbell, John Campbell's Leisure House, San Francisco Arts Festival, 1951. John Campbell, John Campbell's Leisure House, San Francisco Arts Festival (under construction), 1951. John Campbell, John Campbell's Leisure House, San Francisco Arts Festival, 1951. John Campbell, John Campbell's Leisure House (rendering), published in *Interiors,* January 1951

Other Examples:
Henrik Bull, Flender A-frame, Stowe, VT, 1954
Andrew Geller, Reese House, Sagaponack, NY, 1955
Hellyer A-frame, Tacoma, WA, 1958
Nathaniel Owings, Wild Bird House, Big Sur, CA, 1958
Scott & Scott Architects, Whistler Cabin, Whistler, BC, 2016

Seth Peterson Cottage

One of the final commissions completed before his death, Frank Lloyd Wright's Seth Peterson Cottage is considered the culmination of the Usonian vision that he refined in over sixty residential projects throughout his career. With its open plan, built-in furnishings and horizontal composition, the two-room cottage—his smallest domestic design—is a catalogue of his design philosophy, which champions architecture developed in harmony with the natural landscape. The large chimney, slanted roof (that appears almost suspended in air) and living area constructed entirely of glass also reflect Wright's persistent interest in the relationships between interior and exterior, architecture and nature. Wright tiled the cottage floor in the same flagstone he used for the exterior terrace, creating a seamless transition between inside and outside, and allowing the natural landscape to determine how the interior space is conceived and experienced. The efficient design, which wastes no square footage on hallways or entrances, celebrates the materials of its making. Regrettably, both Wright and Seth Peterson passed away before the cottage was completed, and the structure was left uninhabited and neglected for decades. It was rehabilitated in the late 1980s and is now rented for overnight stays.

Architect: Frank Lloyd Wright
Location: Mirror Lake State Park, Wisconsin
Year: 1958

Type: Modernist
Dimensions: 268.2 m²
Materials: cedar shingles, Douglas fir, flagstone, glass, sandstone

Other Examples:
The Robert Lamp Cottage, Lake Medota, Madison, WI, 1893
Edward H. Pitkin Summer cottage, Sapper Island, ON, 1900
The Henry Wallis Summer Cottage, Lake Delavan WI, 1900
Ocotillo Desert Camp, South Mountain, AZ, 1929
A.K. Chahroudi Summer Cottage, Massaro House, Lake Mahopac, NY, 1951
Donald E. and Virginia Lovness House, Stillwater, MN, 1956

Frank Lloyd Wright, Seth Peterson
Cottage, Mirror Lake, WI, c. 1960

191

John Campbell, John Campbell's Leisure House, San Francisco Arts Festival, 1951

Porn

In 2009, Zach Klein, co-founder of Vimeo, and a group of friends created a Tumblr with photos of cabins and simple captions: Cabin Porn. The inspiration board for a building project on fifty-five acres of forest in upstate New York struck a nerve with young urbanites who dreamt of their own refuge in nature. In our hyperconnected world, the simple cabin (when artfully appointed) was heralded as antidote to the endemic stress and alienation of twenty-first century life. By invoking the word "Porn,"—an allusion to how the internet facilitates circulation and consumption of images that satisfy specific desires—they demonstrated that the idea of the cabin can trigger strong collective emotion.

The cabin, in both material and symbolic form, is ubiquitous in contemporary society. It has moved from production to consumption, from fringe to mainstream and from "authentic" to "inauthentic." It is part of a long tradition of appropriation. Early politicians evoked the log cabin as a symbol of simpler times—the Whigs' William Henry Harrison used it to gain votes during his campaign of 1840. Log Cabin Syrup—named by its creator in homage to President Abraham Lincoln, who spent his childhood living in a log cabin—was introduced in 1887. And in 1916, John Lloyd Wright (son of Frank Lloyd Wright) invented Lincoln Logs, a children's toy consisting of notched wooden logs for building miniature versions of cabins, corrals, forts and other dwellings. They were an instant success, capitalizing on a distinctly North American building tradition and capturing the imagination of a new generation. The popularity of Lincoln Logs reached its peak in the mid-1950s, coinciding with the broadcast of the Davy Crockett television miniseries.

So it was that the cabin became integrated into North American visual culture—first through printed material and objects, later through mass media. This aesthetics of ruggedness has reached its apex, with companies (Pendleton, Roots, Hershel Supply) referencing the cabin in their marketing materials and product design—to sell not only their wares, but also a certain lifestyle. Living history sites (Upper Canada Village, Colonial Williamsburg, Black Creek Pioneer Village) highlight how enduring is the popular fantasy of participating in frontier life to escape the excesses of contemporary culture.

Architecturally speaking, the cabin typology has inspired large-scale building projects, residential commissions and even tourist attractions. BIG's unrealized proposal for the Kimball Art Center in Park City, Utah, inspired by the area's mining heritage, appropriates aged structures for contemporary use—the proposal was essentially for a "highly evolved log cabin." Tech companies (such as Twitter, Hootsuite) have used cabin design and imagery in their headquarters to redefine office culture by fusing technological innovation with a more rustic tradition. Contemporary vacation homes reference traditional cabins while integrating sustainability, new materials and formal experimentation. The cabin has come far from its pragmatic origin; it's become a platform from which to observe and understand contemporary life.

Olson Kundig, Delta Shelter, Mazama, WA, 2005

Top to bottom: Studio Padron, Hemmelig Rom [Secret Room], Ellenville, NY, 2015. John Lloyd Wright, Lincoln Logs, c. 1923. Cabin, Walden, TN, 2016

Why Look
at Cabin Porn?

Finn Arne Jørgensen

THE BIG ALLURE OF A SMALL HOUSE IN NATURE

Once upon a place there was a cabin. It doesn't matter where or when; all we need to know is that it was somewhere else. It is dusk, or possibly dawn, with a dark blue light that just barely manages to illuminate the landscape. The cabin is hidden in a snow-covered copse; we can barely see the darker outline of the cabin against the trees. The scene looks to be on a tiny, frozen island, surrounded by flat, snowy ice. A warm orange glow streams out of the large cabin window, marking it as a refuge from the wintry cold outside and pulling the viewer's attention to the cabin. The slightly asymmetric composition of the trees and the placement of the cabin create an aesthetically pleasing image. The island and the trees help define the cabin, at the same time as the human presence implied by the cabin helps define the island as a *place*. We—as viewers and observers—feel a yearning to experience and to possess such a place of our own. Here we can *belong*.

This is cabin porn. It is a heartbreakingly beautiful and surprisingly popular Internet phenomenon. The photograph above appeared on the Cabin Porn website that gave a name to the phenomenon in July 2012.[1] It is one of more than a thousand images on just this one website, each of them "liked" and reposted hundreds or thousands of times. The images circulate online on other sites as well, creating a visual and often very enthusiastic public discourse on architecture and authenticity in the modern world.

The title Cabin Porn is used quite tongue in cheek, but it is also rather profound. It is intended as a reference to the somewhat guilty pleasure of looking at a particular kind of picture—in this case, cabins or, more specifically, a subset of the buildings we call cabins. It can be compared to the broader genre of contemporary visual culture known as "ruin porn," visually appealing pictures of a decaying built environment (e.g., Millington 2013). Ruin porn has been extensively criticized for aestheticizing poverty and decay without discussing its causes or otherwise engaging with significant related debates over social and environmental justice. Many of the images on Cabin Porn do indeed border on ruin porn, showing cabins that have moved beyond rustic and into the realm of the broken, abandoned, and discarded. And, as in ruin porn, there are few, if any, explicit attempts at critical discussion of underlying social or economic issues in cabin porn.

The actual buildings depicted on the Cabin Porn website range widely. We find examples of everything from the whimsical to the deeply serious, from the very old to the brand-new, and from the handmade and organic to modern concrete, steel, and glass. Geographically, the cabins span the world, but they display a strong emphasis on the temperate band of the North. The posts identify the country or state the cabin is located in, choosing to treat the United States and Canada not as whole countries but as a collection of states with individual identities. If we break down the collected posts this way, Scandinavia is strongly represented. Sweden tops the list with sixty-nine posts, followed by California with fifty-nine, and Norway with forty-seven. New York, Washington, and Maine follow closely, though most US states are represented. More exotic locations (at least in this context) like Antarctica, Nagano in Japan, and Chogoria in Kenya demonstrate the global character of cabin porn.

Cabin above Chesières, Switzerland, 2013

The Cabin Porn website operates as a blog built on the Tumblr platform, currently one of the leading social networks for sharing images and other multimedia material. "Follow the world's creators," Tumblr encourages its users, thereby implying not only that this is where you can find the most creative people in the world but also that the world is, in a sense, created here, online. The Cabin Porn account started posting entries in 2009 but took a while to find its formula. At the end of 2013, the site had close to eleven hundred posts. The website was started by Zach Klein, cofounder of the online video service Vimeo and a "proselytizer of country living" (Tiku 2011).

Posts generally have very few words, often just indicating the general location of the depicted cabin. In the Tumblr format, people generally don't comment on the pictures. They can "like" the pictures, and they can share or repost them on their own Tumblr blogs. Cabin Porn functions as a central seeder site—from here the images spread to other social networks such as Facebook and Twitter. The act of viewing and appreciating cabin porn thus becomes a silently communal thing, a global community of cabin pornographers. Still, we can't say much about the audience of Cabin Porn: exactly how many they are, who they are, and why they look at cabin porn.

Why should we, as scholars interested in the cultural forms of the public sphere, look at cabin porn? We can find a first clue in John Berger's *Why Look at Animals?* (2009), which the title and opening of this essay paraphrase. In this brief book of essays, Berger argues that animals, once central to the daily existence of our lives, have been reduced to mere spectacle. Berger's claim is that in becoming something we only look at, animals have lost some of their essence. Animals no longer do any real work for most of us—we no longer depend on them for transportation, clothing, or labor. Real, live animals have even become invisible as sources of food, instead appearing as prepackaged, almost abstract pieces of meat or processed into a million other products in grocery stores. The live, productive animals have faded away from our consciousness, instead becoming part of visual culture—ubiquitously present in zoos, in books, and in moving images of any kind. Jon Mooallem (2013) argues that it is through such images that we now work out our relationship to the natural world, making nature as much a place of the imagination as something "out there," away from people and civilization. This observation was also at the core of environmental historian William Cronon's influential and controversial essay "The Trouble with Wilderness" (1995).

An initial reading of the visual culture of cabin porn as a cultural phenomenon suggests that cabin porn follows a similar downward trajectory. The images seem to say that we once lived in simpler conditions, in architecture closer to nature. We lived more productive and more honest lives. In the peace and quiet away from the distractions of modern life, we could listen to ourselves. The images of cabin porn whisper to us of this lost state of grace, of an age of wood and earth and things that were real and true. The cabins of cabin porn are as much ideas as actual places; they are observation points outside of time and space from which we can observe not just nature but also ourselves and the world we live in. These sensations are not articulated, only experienced as a feeling. Cabin porn thus presents us with insights into how we use digital media to think about nature, technology, and modern society. The mediated images of cabin porn not only articulate broader social trends but also shape them and give them direction. In drawing our attention to the visual appearance of a good life in nature, cabin porn tells us something too about the undesired elements of modern society. In other words, what we don't see in cabin porn can be just as revealing as what we do see.

The rise of cabin porn as a visual genre reflects a growing international interest in cabins, shedworking, and rustic, exurban living off the grid—most of it romanticizing rural and low-tech lifestyles (see Grey 2012; Montgomery-Fate 2012; Pollan 2008 [1997]; Powers 2010; Ureneck 2012). On the surface, the disembodied architecture of cabin porn seems to be a form of nostalgia, where the dream of the cabin becomes an arena for resolving an ambivalent relationship to technology and all the bothersome things of modern life. To understand cabin porn as visual culture and as a form of media, we need to situate it within a historical context.

As noted above, Scandinavian cabins feature frequently on the Cabin Porn website. It would not be incorrect to assume that some of the international cultural templates for cabin architecture and cabin living emerged out of Scandinavian history and the generations of emigrants that settled across North America in the 1800s. We need to recognize, however, that the different Scandinavian countries do not have the same cabin traditions. In Denmark, the summer beach house reigns supreme. In Sweden, the summer cabin dominates, followed by some simpler and older sport cabins. Finland and Norway compete over the dubious honor of being the nation most obsessed with cabins, all year round (Müller 2007; Pihl Atmer 1998; Tress 2002). As a Norwegian, I am hardly a neutral observer, even though I do not personally own or use a cabin; yet I would still argue that Norwegian cabins provide us with some of the most interesting insights into the paradoxes and contradictions of cabin living in the modern world. By actively comparing the visual nostalgia of cabin porn with the historical development of Norwegian cabin culture, this essay investigates how authenticity and technology are both contested and coconstructed in new global media centered on the cabin.

"I KNOW IT WHEN I SEE IT"—DEFINING AUTHENTICITY IN A DIGITAL WORLD

Images—whether posted online or elsewhere—do something for us, and we need to examine what this "something" is. We are all familiar with the saying that a picture is worth a thousand words; a picture is a kind of shortcut to meaning. One critical implication is that a picture does not say the equivalent of a thousand words or more, but bypasses words altogether. The picture triggers a form of recognition in the viewer—in the case of cabin porn, the recognition of something as representative of historical or natural authenticity. It is evocative rather than exhaustive, allowing viewers to fill in the gaps with their own values, experiences, and associations. Such visual shortcuts do not appear only in digital media. In fact, cabins are often filled with similar historical markers. We can find in them examples of artifacts from family history, such as great-grandmother's loom or a wooden bowl the owner found at a yard sale. This is a very concrete form of history. But we can also find examples of a much more abstract sense of history. If something looks old, or uses visual elements from traditional folk craft, such as traditional Norwegian rose painting, it becomes a marker of authenticity. Architects and cabin owners consciously use these visual elements to create a sense of historical authenticity in cabins, which inspired the statement that "the older a cabin looks, the newer it actually is" (Holm 2008).

Ideas of nature are thoroughly embedded in our definitions of authenticity. "Nature writing" in the footsteps of Aldo Leopold and Henry David Thoreau is a well-established genre, where people write about their experience of nature, very often lamenting the loss of something natural and authentic in the modern, technological age or worrying about impending loss. Thoreau's cabin, as it appears in *Walden Pond*, has much in common with cabin porn as a genre. "Yesterday I came here to live," he wrote in his journal after he began building his cabin on July 5, 1845 (Thoreau 2009: 21). Thoreau uses his cabin at Walden Pond as a means to discuss whether technology has improved us as human beings. "While civilization has been improving our houses, it has not equally improved the men who are to inhabit them," he argued (Thoreau 2004 [1854]: 33). Comfort, convenience, and luxury had become a hindrance to the elevation of mankind. Thoreau's call for a life contemplatively centered on the absolute necessities resonates with the search for financial and technological independence in the modern "off the grid" movement.

Norway has its own nature writing tradition, often connected to traveling, trekking, hunting, and cabin living—the philosopher Arne Næss is perhaps the most internationally well known, and he did much of his thinking at his very rustic cabin Tvergastein, high up in the Hallingskarvet mountains. At the cabin, in his view, "two buckets of water make you a rich man"; simplicity was the essence of cabin living (Næss 1999: 30). Here he hints at a lived tradition of nature philosophy that manifests itself in the physical cabin structure and the way people use it as a way of experiencing nature. The cabin, then, becomes a form of vernacular nature philosophy, lived and enacted by ordinary people who don't necessarily write about it. This gives a sense of the longer historical tradition that cabin porn shows us glimpses of.

In the end, it all comes down to the slippery subject of authenticity. Cabin porn is a phenomenon that holds the key to one of the big research problems I have struggled with as a historian writing about Norwegian cabin culture. How do we define what is a cabin? And what is not a cabin? In my own research, I am concerned not so much with technical definitions of what cabins are but with the changing cultural conceptions of generations of Norwegians building, using, and dreaming about cabins. Cabins, after all, are not just private buildings out in the wilderness somewhere—they are part of a shared public culture, a distributed idea that has developed over time, in dialogue with ideas of the nation-state, of leisure, and of nature and technology (Gansmo, Berker, and Jørgensen 2011; Rye and Berg 2011). Many Norwegians have some kind of inner moral-aesthetic compass that allows them to look at a cabin and pass judgment over it—is it "authentic" or is it not? It has been surprisingly hard to get people to put words to this feeling and to spell out the specific features and characteristics a building needs to have, or not have, to qualify as a cabin. If an old cabin is upgraded with different technological features, at what point does it stop being an "authentic cabin" and become something else?

This cultural judgment is a great example of how visual culture bypasses words and the need to spell out exact definitions. While people have a hard time articulating authenticity, they know it when they see it. Fascinatingly, this provides us with an obvious link between cabins and porn, perhaps making the phrase *cabin porn* less flippant than it initially seems. The statement "I know it when I see it" is one of the most famous phrases in the history of the US Supreme Court, stated by Justice Potter Stewart in 1964 when judging possible obscenity in the movie *The Lovers*.[2] Stewart refused to provide an exhaustive definition of pornography, but claimed that he knew it when he saw it. According to *Wikipedia* (2013), the phrase has become a colloquial expression, used when "a speaker attempts to categorize an observable fact or event, although the category is subjective or lacks clearly defined parameters."

I think this is an appropriate way of describing the relationship many have to cabins. So where does this leave us with cabin porn? There is some process going on here between the visual images we see online and the mental idea we have, the thing we observe, and the set of often vaguely defined ideas we have about the object. We are talking not about objective standards but rather about a shared set of subjective values about cabins. However, we can't properly understand the value of looking at cabin porn unless we know what we are looking for. Interpreted as simply an act of passive consumption, cabin porn is an empty spectacle; yet, when interpreted as an act of meaning-creation, cabin porn is also a sincere form of engagement with nature.

—

1. I will hereafter refer to the phenomenon in general as "cabin porn" and the website as Cabin Porn.

2. The full statement reads: "I shall not today attempt further to define the kinds of material I understand to be embraced within that shorthand description [hard-core pornography']; and perhaps I could never succeed in intelligibly doing so. But I know it when I see it, and the motion picture involved in this case is not that." Justice Potter Stewart, concurring opinion in Jacobellis v. Ohio 378 U.S. 184 (1964), regarding possibly obscenity in *The Lovers*.

References

Berger, John. 2009. *Why Look at Animals?* New York: Penguin Books.

Cabin Porn. Home page. cabinporn.com (accessed April 7, 2015).

Cronon, William. 1995. "The Trouble with Wilderness; or, Getting Back to the Wrong Nature." In *Uncommon Ground: Rethinking the Human Place in Nature*, edited by William Cronon, 69-90. New York: Norton.

Gansmo, Helen Jøsok, Thomas Berker, and Finn Arne Jørgensen, eds. 2011. *Norske hytter i endring: Om bærekraft og behag* (*Norwegian Cabins in Change: Sustainability and Comfort*) Trondheim, Norway: Tapir Akademisk.

Grey, C. T. 2012. *Fifty Sheds of Grey: Erotica for the Not-Too-Modern Male*. London: Boxtree.

Holm, Erling Dokk. 2008. "Slik blir morgendagens hytte" ("This Is Tomorrow's Cabin"). *E24*, February 17. e24.no/eiendom/slik-blir-morgendagens-hytte/2258157.

Millington, Nate. 2013. "Post-Industrial Imaginaries: Nature, Representation, and Ruin in Detroit, Michigan." *International Journal of Urban and Regional Research* 37, no. 1: 279-96.

Montgomery-Fate, Tom. 2012. *Cabin Fever: A Suburban Father's Search for the Wild*. Boston: Beacon.

Mooallem, Jon. 2013. *Wild Ones: A Sometimes Dismaying, Weirdly Reassuring Story about Looking at People Looking at Animals in America*. New York: Penguin.

Müller, Dieter K. 2007. "Second Homes in the Nordic Countries: Between Common Heritage and Exclusive Commodity." *Scandinavian Journal of Hospitality and Tourism* 7, no. 3: 193-201.

Næss, Arne. 1999. *Livsfilosofi* (*Life Philosophy*). Oslo: Universitetsforlaget.

Pihl Atmer, Ann Katrin. 1998. *Livet som leves där måste smaka vildmark: Sportstugor och friluftsliv 1900-1945* (*The Life That Is Lived There Must Taste of Wilderness: Sport Cabins and Outdoor Life, 1900-1945*). Stockholm: Stockholmia förlag.

Pollan, Michael. 2008 [1997]. *A Place of My Own: The Architecture of Daydreams*. New York: Penguin.

Powers, William. 2010. *Twelve by Twelve: A One-Room Cabin off the Grid and beyond the American Dream*. Novato, CA: New World Library.

Rye, Johan Fredrik, and Nina Gunnerud Berg. 2011. "The Second Home Phenomenon and Norwegian Rurality." *Norsk geografisk tidsskrift* (*Norwegian Journal of Geography*) 65, no. 3: 126-36.

Thoreau, Henry David. 2004 [1854]. *Walden: A Fully Annotated Edition*. Edited by Jeffrey S. Cramer. New Haven, CT: Yale University Press.

———. 2009. *The Journal, 1837-1861*. Edited by Damion Searls. New York: New York Review Books.

Tiku, Nitasha. 2011. "Zach Klein: Investor, Entrepreneur, Cabin-Loving 'Proselytizer of Country Living.' " *BetaBeat*, November 21. observer.com/2011/11/zach-klein-investor-entrepreneur-cabin-loving-proselytizer-of-country-living.

Tress, Gunther. 2002. "Development of Second-Home Tourism in Denmark." *Scandinavian Journal of Hospitality and Tourism* 2, no. 2: 109-22.

Ureneck, Lou. 2012. *Cabin: Two Brothers, a Dream, and Five Acres in Maine*. New York: Penguin.

Wikipedia. 2013. "I Know It When I See It." en.wikipedia.org/wiki/I_know_it_when_I_see_it (accessed September 18, 2013).

The Log Cabin Campaign: Image Deception in 1840

Steven Seidman

Log Cabin Anecdotes: Illustrated Incidents in the Life of Gen. William Henry Harrison, 1840

The Whig Party's campaign in the United States in 1840 for William Henry Harrison can be called the first great political marketing campaign that mythologized a candidate. The campaign, called "The Log Cabin Campaign," targeted the so-called "common man"—previously a main source of support for Andrew Jackson (and his successor, Martin Van Buren) and the Democrats.

The Whigs in 1840 introduced three ideas to election campaigns: one was to use a potent symbol—the log cabin (often combined with soldiers and a jug of hard cider)—for candidate Harrison, typically depicted as a rough-and-ready farmer and military hero; another was the creation of silk flag banners, which frequently added a portrait of Harrison and the phrases "Old Tip" and "The Hero of Tippecanoe" (a battle during the War of 1812) to the American flag; the party also introduced effective slogans into politics, with "Tippecanoe and Tyler Too," which referred to the Whig's ticket, headed by Harrison, with John Tyler as his running mate.

Some of the Whig rallies, with banners unfurled, drew an estimated 100,000 people, perhaps attracted by the seemingly endless supplies of hard cider. It mattered little to most partisans that the "common man" image concocted for Harrison was false. The log cabin was used to represent Harrison's "poor" and "humble" background. His background was neither; rather, he was born in a mansion on a Virginia plantation and lived in a fancy house in Indiana when nominated for the presidency. Regardless of the truth, the imagery and the hard cider that was distributed at the gigantic rallies undoubtedly excited voters and boosted the Harrison campaign. This is evident in the voter turnout that increased from 54 percent in 1836 to 77 percent in 1840; the Harrison-Tyler ticket won by a 6 percent margin in the popular vote and claimed 80 percent of the electoral votes. The Democrats were thrown out of power—after holding it for a dozen years—and the Whigs gained their first president.

The log-cabin imagery, along with emphasis on Harrison's military leadership, was accompanied by pageantry. The Whigs borrowed most of the Democratic Party's past publicity ideas and took them to new heights. They published their own newspapers (one of which became the *New York Herald Tribune*); wrote campaign songs; organized rallies and parades; printed broadsides and banners; and produced goods such as hairbrushes adorned with portraits of Harrison, ceramic dishes with his "modest" farm on them, "Tippecanoe Shaving Soap or Log-Cabin Emollient," and, above all, miniature log cabins. One observer counted one thousand banners in a Baltimore parade for Harrison.

At present, Heritage Auctions, Inc. has a rare silk campaign flag banner from the 1840 campaign up for auction. Most of these flags, as Heritage's Web site points out, "feature merely a campaign slogan or a central portrait of the candidate," but this banner shows the candidate in front of a log cabin, with a barrel of hard cider being tapped alongside it. Heritage estimates that this campaign banner will sell for between $20,000 and $25,000.

Harrison & Tyler Campaign Emblem, 1840

—

Sources: Paul F. Boller, Jr., *Presidential Campaigns: From George Washington to George W. Bush*, 2nd rev. ed. (New York: Oxford University Press, 2004); Robert Gray Gunderson, *The Log-Cabin Campaign* (Lexington, Ky: University of Kentucky Press, 1957); Keith Melder, *Hail to the Candidate: Presidential Campaigns from Banners to Broadcasts* (Washington, D.C.: Smithsonian Institution, 1992); Peter F. Nardulli, Jon K. Dalager, and Donald E. Greco, "Voter Turnout in U.S. Presidential Elections: An Historical View and Some Speculation," *PS: Political Science and Politics* 29 (1996): 480–490.

Steven A. Seidman, "The Log Cabin Campaign: Image Deception in 1840", *Blog: Posters and Election Propaganda* (blog), May 10, 2010.

Lincoln Logs—Toying with the Frontier Myth

Erin Cho

A father and his children playing with Lincoln Logs, 1953

Interesting playthings typifying "the spirit of America" was the slogan John Lloyd Wright used in 1918 to market and sell his new toy, 'Lincoln Logs'. To this date few have written about this famous toy and its creator. Perhaps this is because in 1939 a fire destroyed many of the documents from Wright's early career. An architect by profession, Wright has remained somewhat anonymous, possibly because his accomplishments seem slight compared to the works of his father, Frank Lloyd Wright, one of America's foremost architects of the twentieth century. Yet this paucity of research is most likely a result of the current embryonic stage of material cultural history.

According to the historian John Brewer, the attention devoted to 'high' culture has not been given to such things as costume, the tools of a trade, household utensils and furniture, and playthings. Often over-looked, toys invariably reveal assumptions made by adults about the culture in which they live or the values they think desirable. In revisiting and analysing the period between 1900–20, the years of Wright's youth, it is possible to capture the influences which led him to invent this historic toy in 1918.

Born on December 12th, 1892, in Oak Park, Illinois, John Lloyd Wright was the second son in a family that would come to number four boys and two girls. The Wright children's activities were centred on the playroom that their father added to their house in 1895. The long, high vaulted room was full of building blocks of all shapes and sizes. A firm believer in Friedrich Froebel's 'Kindergarten' methods, Frank Lloyd Wright and his wife, Catherine, educated their children according to Froebel's theories. This training, which was directed towards the development of analytical thinking, assumed that for the child who observed, took to pieces, and reassembled things, the desire to create shape and form was a natural instinct. This was the basis of Frank's own childhood education. Emphasising learning from nature, it reinforced knowledge Frank had gleaned from his early experiences on his uncle's farm

204

in Wisconsin and introduced him to the formative geometrics that became the basis for his architecture.

Similarly, Froebel's methods influenced John's system of design of both his buildings and his toys. His experimenting with the design of toy construction blocks reflected an education which emphasised rhythmic pattern, prefabrication, and construction from interchangeable elements. Lincoln Logs required special care to repack and came in a much greater variety of sizes than today's version. This compelled children to work out what was to be built through trial and error, forcing them to observe, take to pieces and to reassemble.

Lincoln Logs are significantly distinct from the other abstract construction block toys Wright created later in his toymaking career. This difference stems from America's mentality preceding and surrounding Wright's creation of the toy. John Lloyd Wright grew up in a period of reform, now referred to as the 'Progressive Era'. There was concern among civic-minded members of the middle classes about what the urbanisation of life would do to national virility and traditional American values. These fears were embraced by President Theodore Roosevelt who, along with historian, Frederick Jackson Turner, questioned whether American ideals and institutions could survive the closing of the frontier.

While progressives were busily improving the political and economic environment through institutional and legislative means, they were also advocating the ethic of simple living. Crying out for discriminating consumption, social service, aesthetic simplicity, and a renewed contact with nature, activists believed that Jeffersonian simplicity was of profound relevance to modern urban industrial life. Consequently, as the wild became increasingly remote to urban dwellers in the twentieth-century, they tried to surround themselves with its symbols. Companies such as L. L. Bean which marketed sporting, outdoor, and hunting gear rose to success while popular magazines of the day promoted ideas such as 'if you cannot build a "cabin in the woods", it may be the next best thing to tuck one away somewhere in your home. It will at least help you imagine that you have escaped from the rigors of everyday life'.

America's nature-lovers lost no time in adapting this ideology to their children's minds. Fictionalised accounts of the Adventures of the 'Bobbsey Twins' and 'Camp Fire Girls' soon seeped into children's literature, reviving America's heritage of outdoor adventure. John and his siblings were representative of the audience these books were geared towards: American children who had the time and money to make a virtue of outdoor life. John describes the books they had access to in their Oak Park home:

> Long, thick, big, little books. Covers without books, books without covers; colored, patterned, and textured papers in large folios, all piled up and pushed on wide ledges on either side of a long window. John would have been familiar with these heroes and heroines who spent their free time from school in field or forest, displaying the type of childhood middle-class parents saw as healthy and admirable.

During high school, John made a conscious decision to spend his summer vacations at his great-uncle's farm in Wisconsin as his father had. Perhaps John's regard for nature had increased as the camping movement became a major activity among middle-class youth. The message that camps would foster healthy bodies, simplicity and a love for and knowledge of nature was appealing to early twentieth-century Americans who were worried about the degenerative effects of urban life. Organisations such as the 'Woodcraft Indians', 'The Boy Scouts of America', and 'Camp Fire Girls' were founded during the early 1900s upon the premise of teaching woodcraft, natural history, Indian-lore, and, above all, democratic values.

John Lloyd Wright, *Toy-cabin Construction*, US Patent 1351086 A, 1920

John found himself further influenced by these trends because his father was a fervent believer in the Progressive notions about outdoor life and simple living. An articulate champion for the social role of architecture, Frank Lloyd Wright expressed his sentiments in his works. Disgusted with the 'General Grant Gothic' style that dominated neighbourhoods in the late Victorian America, Wright embraced as his guiding design concepts a union of simplicity with an organic aesthetic and settled in the Chicago area to work with Louis Sullivan, an architect who once announced 'the intellectual trend of the hour is toward simplification'.

When Edward Bok of *Ladies' Home Journal* led a highly publicised campaign in the early twentieth-century for inexpensive, simplified domestic architecture, Frank Lloyd Wright submitted designs of his 'prairie house'. The main rooms of these 'prairie houses', which Wright introduced to the magazine's readers as a 'simple mode of living in keeping with a high ideal of family life together', flowed together in uninterrupted space that, in effect, continued outside. Wright enhanced these efforts to harmonise his buildings with the natural environment not only by implementing earthy colours and rich textures, but also by using wood. Declaring that 'wood is the most humanly intimate of all materials', Wright often stated that it was the Japanese who best understood the uses of wood:

> *In Japanese architecture may be seen what a sensitive material alone for its own sake can do for human sensibilities, as beauty, for the human spirit. Whether pole, beam, plank, board, slat, or rod, the Japanese architect got the forms and treatments of his architecture out of tree nature, wood wise, and heightened the natural beauty of the material by cunning peculiar to himself.*

In 1915, Japan's imperial household invited Wright to build the Imperial Hotel at Tokyo. Frank took his son, John, with him when he went to oversee the project two years later. In the hotel's construction, Frank implemented a revolutionary technique referred to as 'floating cantilever construction', where projecting beams were joined or locked into beams extending from opposite piers. According to John, it was this construction technique which inspired him to create Lincoln Logs, miniature hardwood logs notched on the sides to fit into each other, in Japan one year later. The esteem his father had for wood as a building material no doubt influenced John's decision to choose it as a material for his blocks.

Many have claimed, however, that John Lloyd Wright's Lincoln Logs were simply a modified version of Joel Ellis' 'Log Cabin Playhouse', invented in 1866. They support this contention with the speculation that John probably played with such a toy as a child. Whether or not this is true, there is evidence that other forces may have inspired him to create this log cabin toy and break conventional marketing techniques (rather than including a photograph of children playing with logs, John packaged his toy in colourful boxes with a simple drawing of a log cabin on the front). Even though the log cabin was a Swedish import and had not been adopted by English settlers until well into the eighteenth century, between 1840 and 1918, writers and illustrators had mythologised log cabin living. Dramatised in the presidential campaigns of 1840 and 1860, the log cabin came to be identified with democracy and the frontier spirit as Americans began to marvel at their own progress and to make a virtue of their early struggles with the wilderness. These sentiments were confirmed with the publication of Mary Newton Standard's widely read Colonial Virginia in 1917, which erroneously concluded that Virginian settlements consisted of log cabins. It was during this period when the log cabin 'myth' was at its full height, and when the virtues it carried appeared to be under threat that, Wright developed his toy—a toy which reinforced the myth, and reminded American children of their proud heritage.

Finally, we must ask why John Lloyd Wright named his toy after Abraham Lincoln? At the turn of the century, Lincoln had already become a symbol of unity, hope, and inspiration for all citizens. There were a great number of celebrations and commemorations of Lincoln while John was growing up: in 1909, the nation celebrated his 100th birthday; in 1911, the log cabin where Lincoln was born was dedicated by President Taft; and in 1916, President Wilson delivered the acceptance speech when this log cabin was presented to the United States by the Lincoln Farm Association. Moreover, from 1901 plans for a Lincoln Memorial were being debated in Congress. During this period when Americans felt the ideals and institutions from its frontier past were being threatened by increased industrialisation and urbanisation, the values Lincoln represented were extremely potent. Lincoln reminded Americans that their country was a unique place where 'every door is open ... for the ruler to emerge when he will and claim his leadership in the free life'. Lincoln's log cabin birthplace emerged as a powerful symbol demonstrating that every individual, no matter how humble his origins, could achieve greatness. John Lloyd Wright, like any American, probably encountered a barrage of such images deifying Lincoln. His toy's simple title captures the sentiments of this period, reaffirming a sense of patriotism to Progressive America as it found itself entering the Great War. Contributing to the spirit of the times, Wright included two portraits of Lincoln on the covers of his sets of Lincoln Logs.

Never able to give himself over completely to toys, John Lloyd Wright resumed his career in architecture shortly after inventing Lincoln Logs. Because he believed in his father's guiding principles of design, emphasising an intimate relationship between interior and exterior space partly through the use of natural materials, John continued to struggle between his father's dominating personality and style and his own creative development. Despite this conflict, he produced original works such as 'The Holden House', or 'House of Wood', and 'Shangri-La', or 'House of Seven Levels', which reflected his affection and remarkable skill with wood. Although his interest turned away from toys, other toy-makers tried to capitalise on Wright's success. Lincoln Bricks and Lincoln Stones both made brief appearances on toyshop shelves. When Halsam's American Logs were produced in 1934, toy-makers expected them to be a success, for the logs' notched indentations looked far more realistic than Wright's. But although Halsam's logs were marketed for years, they were always in the shadow of Lincoln Logs; children even referred to these so-called 'improved' logs by their predecessor's name. Today, up to a million American consumers buy a set of Lincoln Logs for their children every year, suggesting that the values and ideals this toy represents are still important in an increasingly technological world.

Perhaps our needs are not so distant from Progressive Americans. Though the issue of urbanisation is no longer new and the spectre of world war does not haunt us, the growing sentiment that America is in decline perhaps sparks a desire among American parents to provide their children with toys that evoke their country's unique heritage. Finally, although conditions no longer exist wherein one in every seven Americans is a slave, because one in every seven Americans lives in poverty, the name Lincoln represents values and ideals as important to us now as they were a century ago. Thus, although as an architect John Lloyd Wright found himself in the shadow of his father, as a toy-maker he cast a unique and lasting light on an institution called childhood; here, Frank Lloyd Wright could never compete.

Erin Cho, "Lincoln Logs—Toying with the Frontier Myth", *History Today* 43, no. 4 (1993). Reprinted by permission of *History Today Ltd*.

Living history museums are designed to transport visitors back in time. They take an interactive approach to facilitating understanding of the past, and often feature a collection of restored or reconstructed buildings in an open-air setting, with costumed interpreters portraying life and performing activities reminiscent of a given period. In North America, many of these types of museums focus on the stories of early immigrants and of frontier settlement; unsurprisingly, the log cabin is a recurring feature. [JMV]

Living History Sites

Left to right: Upper Canada Village, Morrisburg, ON, 1961. Black Creek Pioneer Village, North York, ON, c. 1960. Black Creek Pioneer Village, North York, ON, c. 1960s. Black Creek Pioneer Village, North York, ON, 1975

How to Build a Community

Zach Klein

BARRYVILLE, NEW YORK

I needed a remote piece of land where anything was possible. I'd spent six years in the city building online communities and now I wanted to build one offline. Specifically, a place for a bunch of friends to be outdoors, somewhere we could be less preoccupied by our professions and more reliant on each other as we practice new skills together. I imagined a landscape nested with shelters we would make ourselves without any previous experience. My search began in upstate New York. I was looking for a place where the locals wouldn't mind our experiments with architecture, assembling what would surely look like a commune...After a year driving wider and wider circles around New York City, I got a tip on a barn and some property for rent in the hills above the majestic Upper Delaware Valley, a part of the state I had never visited before.

***

The barn didn't work out; too many rooms lacked floorboards for the price. But I fell for the area. We stopped for BLTs at a motel restaurant, and I took out my phone to swipe through real estate listings. When I saw the thumbnails on the realtor's page, I just knew it. Two and a half miles upriver, 50 acres of forest were for sale. The property had a dirt road cutting through a stand of shagbark hickories, leading to a simple shed-style cabin with no electricity or plumbing that sat high above a brook feeding back down to the Delaware.

***

A few months later, in August, I headed up with my wife, Court, and two dozen friends to camp on our new land...That weekend touched off what have become the happiest years of my life.

    A bunch of us still share Beaver Brook, which is now named after the tributary running through it. It's our camp, where we experience splendid nature; make architecture, art, and food; practice community-building; learn new skills; and maintain a place where we—a diaspora of friends and family—can enjoy each other's company. It's a place of remarkable haves and have-nots: trout just big enough to eat; an international convention of fireflies every summer; in the winter, countless tracks of squirrels and snowshoes over

Beaver Brook, Sullivan County, NY, c. 2013

211

the frozen brook. There's also no plumbing or electricity or insulation in most of the buildings. A total lack of cell service (a few of us will admit to seeking out the one spot on the top of the hill with some reception). Deafening quiet on some days, on others it's howling. And always plenty of mouse poop on anything you leave out overnight. We wouldn't have it any other way.

***

Today, five years into our stay at Beaver Brook, we have an official process for residency, with dues and a few rules. The gist is that you come and do a lot of hard labor in exchange for good food and, once we're certain you have a good heart and a strong work ethic, an invitation to join. There are months when we visit only on weekends; then we take advantage with long summertime binges. Usually at least one person lives here year-round. We've collaborated to design and build various amenities. There are five shelters, a bunkhouse for large gatherings, a wood-fired sauna, all sorts of toolsheds, several outhouses, and a paddock for dumping our humanure, though we never really get around to it and mostly store firewood there.

***

Beaver Brook, Sullivan County, NY, c. 2013

Not long after I founded Beaver Brook, I made a Web page called Cabin Porn. A few of my friends and I collected photos of buildings that had shaped our ideas of what homes could be: the kind of buildings that are made by hand, fashioned with imagination and easy-to-find materials made interesting by ingenuity and craftsmanship. The kind of buildings built by bold people who learned as they went along and never wavered in their determination. Nearly ten million people have visited the site since 2010, and twelve thousand people have shared their cabins with us.

It doesn't surprise me that Cabin Porn appeals to such a large audience. The more we migrate to a technical world, the more sublime nature is to behold. Pictures of cabins, for their part, often have an effect of recasting wilderness as move-in ready. While that's rarely ever true, what these photos do consistently—the part that interests me most—is remind each of us that we have a home inside us ready to be built if we try. It's a wonderful kind of confidence to discover that you can provide yourself shelter and offer warm hospitality with such simple construction. I hope more and more people realize the joy of the challenge and take it. The tools have never been cheaper, the know-how never more free. And online and offline communities are helping to connect us with mentors and models that show us what we are capable of making for ourselves.

The hospitality phenomenon Airbnb has exploited—and intensified—the cabin porn culture so pervasive in our contemporary moment; it makes the cabin experience available without the financial and logistic burdens of building and owning one. Founded in 2008, only a year before Zach Klein and Steven Leckart began posting dreamy cabin images on their Tumblr blog, Airbnb has participated in the commodification of wilderness living through its emphasis on remote hideaways and raw natural beauty—only a click away. From the beginning, cabins, cottages, domes and treehouses have consistently been among the site's most popular properties, revealing that the desire to escape to nature remains a significant cultural phenomenon. By exploiting the sharing economy, Airbnb takes the Cabin Porn phenomenon to its logical conclusion: not only can you ogle seductive cabin photos online, you can experience the fantasy in real life, if only temporarily. As with Cabin Porn, photography is the lure on Airbnb—notably so since the company revamped its web design to mimic the image and discovery-based browsing model of Tumblr and Instagram. The photographs—wide angle shots at dusk, sunsets glistening over bodies of water, interior close-ups of log beams, exposed brick, artfully positioned telescopes—would not be out of place on an Instagram feed. In fact, a number of properties have been featured on Cabin Porn itself, complete with a link to the Airbnb listing. [SR]

Airbnb and Cabin Mania

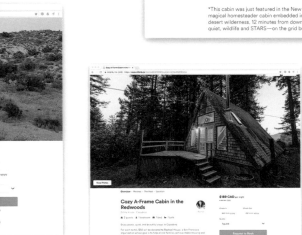

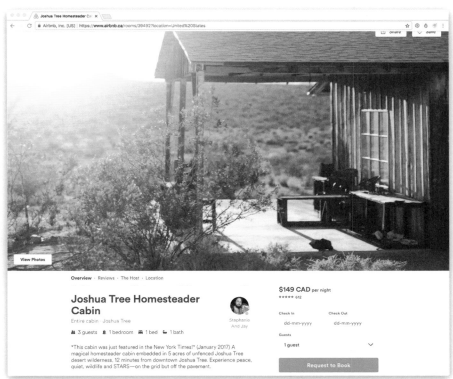

Overview · Reviews · The Host · Location

Joshua Tree Homesteader Cabin

Entire cabin · Joshua Tree

👥 3 guests 🛏 1 bedroom 🛏 1 bed 🛁 1 bath

"This cabin was just featured in the New York Times!" (January 2017) A magical homesteader cabin embedded in 5 acres of unfenced Joshua Tree desert wilderness, 12 minutes from downtown Joshua Tree. Experience peace, quiet, wildlife and STARS—on the grid but off the pavement.

Stephanie
And Jay

$149 CAD per night
★★★★★ 612

Check In | Check Out
dd-mm-yyyy | dd-mm-yyyy

Guests
1 guest ⌄

Request to Book

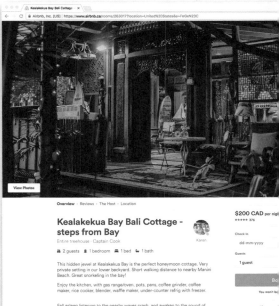

Overview · Reviews · The Host · Location

Kealakekua Bay Bali Cottage - steps from Bay

Entire treehouse · Captain Cook

👥 2 guests 🛏 1 bedroom 🛏 1 bed 🛁 1 bath

This hidden jewel at Kealakekua Bay is the perfect honeymoon cottage. Very private setting in our lower backyard. Short walking distance to nearby Manini Beach. Great snorkeling in the bay!

Enjoy the kitchen, with gas range/oven, pots, pans, coffee grinder, coffee maker, rice cooker, blender, waffle maker, under-counter refrig with freezer.

Fall asleep listening to the nearby waves crash, and awaken to the sound of birds. Surrounded by tropical landscape and pond. Magical Hideaway!!

Karen

$200 CAD per nigh
★★★★★ 376

Check In
dd-mm-yyyy

Guests
1 guest

The Sinister Truth Behind Cabin Porn

Akiva Blander

Tiny living is now touted as an innovative and responsible residential choice. A recent preoccupation with cabins has inevitably followed. Perhaps comparable to last year's trendy obsession with Nordic hygge culture, which emphasized a certain comfort and domestic splendor, the cabin phenomenon has suffused many aspects of the design world. (There seems, in any case, no escape from the cottage industry of cabin-themed coffee-table books and stylish but useless manuals.)

Snøhetta, Gapahuk Cabin, Norway, 2017

The fascination is easily explained, at least in part. Enduring cultural notions see in the cabin not just the promise of a getaway but also restoration, primarily through rarefied contact with nature. Indeed, the cabin's smallness can act to "limit the imprint of form on the natural context," says Neeraj Bhatia, cocurator of the recent *Ways of Life* exhibition in Kassel, Germany, which displayed prototype cabin-esque dwellings that examined the changing relationships between work and domestic life, the individual and nature. These relationships, Bhatia adds, "need to be negotiated through architecture."

For architects, the allure is in the clarity of the program. The univocal purpose of a cabin—basic, temporary shelter—and its small scale invite experimentation with concept, siting, and materials. Further, it offers designers complete control. "There is the possibility to be present in all decisions and get hands-on experience on a complete project," explains Anne Cecilie Haug, a senior architect at Snøhetta who was involved in the design of the firm's Gapahuk cabin project.

A ready-made "social cabin" that "fits into nearly any scenery," Gapahuk illustrates how the typology is being reexamined by more established architectural offices. The design gives particular attention to common areas, such as a spacious living room, a kitchen, and outdoor patios. The move, says Haug, is subtle but intentional, borne out of the observation that cabin dwellers often feel a more magnetic connection to their surroundings than to each other.

But this plea for familial well-being cannot hide the fact that cabins have become a new form of naturalized luxury for the well-off, where social and environmental consciousness comes built in. The Summit Powder Mountain development in Utah, for example, was founded by progressive elites looking to both brainstorm solutions to global problems and preserve the mountain's calm and beauty. Although the development may be in harmony with nature, its structure betrays certain exclusionary and antidemocratic tendencies: "Thought leaders"—often quite wealthy, with often quite similar thoughts—band together to steer humanity toward brighter horizons, literally from above.

Walden Monterey in California, a self-described "forward-thinking enclave" set in another nirvana, markets rustic charm to Silicon Valley's ultrarich shopping around for a second or third home. The 600-acre development on the Monterey Peninsula comprises 22 lots costing $5 million each (three have been reserved so far), on which future residents can build their own custom homes. They must, however, conform to two "cultural rules": Houses must be powered by renewable energy, and cutting down trees is forbidden.

As the name suggests, Walden Monterey is about "finding a place where you can disconnect from the world, and reconnect with nature," says Nick Jekogian, the developer behind the complex. Shared amenities like yoga platforms (facing both the sunrise and sunset, naturally), a kids' playground, a trail network, and a Zen garden are meant to aid in this reconnection. Walden's emphasis on sustainability and repose, coupled with its recruitment of well-known firms such as MAD Architects, mirrors a contemporary mode of consumption, favoring simplicity and sparseness over excess and grandiosity, not unlike the "minimalism" trend of recent years. As Jekogian puts it, "You don't need a massive mansion anymore to live luxuriously."

Working with humbler aims (and smaller budgets) than these affluent enclaves are emerging architects producing cabins that are tailored to specific geographic settings or personal circumstances. For example, the 1,100-square-foot Little House, designed by the young Seattle-based firm MW Works, frames precise views of the surrounding forest and Washington's Hood Canal. The design of Garden House in Eindhoven, the Netherlands, by Caspar Schols, is structured according

Left to right: Scott & Scott Architects, Whistler Cabin, Whistler, BC, 2016. mwlworks architecture+design, Little House, Hood Canal, WA, 2015. MINI Living and Bureau V, *Urban Cabin*, Brooklyn, NY, 2017

to a long list of programmatic requirements (for instance, a place for grandchildren to stay over, or a space for hosting up to 30 people) given to the Dutch architect by his mother. The cabin's sliding wood frame and shell help accommodate a broad range of activities.

On the one hand, the contemporary reinvention of the cabin type represents a backlash against a technology-obsessed and work-oriented culture. Also, it advances an alternative lifestyle that allows those fortunate enough to retreat from the spontaneity and risks of urban living and public life. "I think people are very attracted to that—getting away from the complexities that we have," says Jekogian. Occasionally, as in the case of Urban Cabin, which went on display at Brooklyn's A/D/O, the cabin repackages a messy metropolitan environment rather than a rural and pristine one—although here, too, the cabin's appeal lies in the quietude it offers.

In many of these cases, the cabins amount to an ecoconscious and bucolic gated community, where residents enjoy picturesque vistas and the wonders of living "close to the land," minus its more threatening aspects. This is an idyllic vision of luxury, simultaneously embedded within and detached from its surroundings. Today, the public sphere continues to be eroded, while self-sufficiency and individual valorization are trumpeted as social virtues more than ever. Could there be a better metaphor?

Akiva Blander, "Not Your Grandfather's Cabin," *Metropolis Magazine*, November/December 2017.

The last five years have seen a spate of books about cabins. They run the gamut in content, covering everything from DIY projects to innovative, technological approaches to a centuries-old architectural typology. But one of the commonalities they share is attention to presentation: beautiful imagery tends to highlight unique relationships between geographic location and structure. Like shelter magazines, they invite readers in, offering more than just a way to escape; these books advocate a way of life. [JMV]

Eye Candy: Recent Publications on Cabins

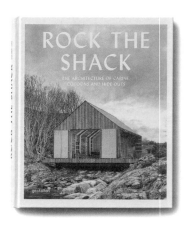

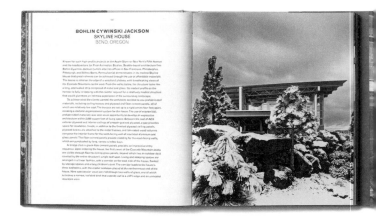

Left to right: *Retreat: The Modern House in Nature* (cover and interior spread), 2015, published by Rizzoli. *Hide and Seek: The Architecture of Cabins and Hide-Outs* (cover), 2014, published by Gestalten. *Rock the Shack: The Architecture of Cabins, Cocoons and Hide-Outs* (cover), 2013, published by Gestalten

JUNIPER HOUSE
MURMAN ARKITEKTER
GOTLAND, SWEDEN

TIMBERLAND

Top to bottom: *Rock the Shack: The Architecture of Cabins, Cocoons and Hide-Outs* (interior spread), 2013, published by Gestalten
Cabins (cover and interior spread), 2014, published by TASCHEN

A Place of My Own:
The Architecture
of Daydreams

Michael Pollan

A room of one's own: Is there anybody who hasn't at one time or another wished for such a place, hasn't turned those soft words over until they'd assumed a habitable shape? What they propose, to anyone who admits them into the space of a day-dream, is a place of solitude a few steps off the beaten track of everyday life. Beyond that, though, the form the dream takes seems to vary with the dreamer. Generally the imagined room has a fixed terrestrial address, whether located deep within the family house or out in the woods under its own roof. For some people, though, the same dream can just as easily assume a vehicular form. I'm thinking of the one-person cockpit or cabin, a mobile room in which to journey some distance from the shore of one's usual cares. Fixed or mobile, a dream of escape is what this probably sounds like. But it's more like a wish for a slightly different angle on things—for the view from the tower, or tree line, or the bobbing point a couple hundred yards off the coast. It might be a view of the same old life, but from out here it will look different, the outlines of the self a little more distinct.

***

I don't want this to sound like some kind of vision, because though my building might have started out that way, a dreamy notion I'd once had, it was more literal than that now. Not just some metaphor or dream, the building I saw in front of me was a new and luminous fact. A new fact in this world, that was plain enough, but also a new fact in my life. That I had dreamt it and then had a hand in making it a fact was more gratifying than I can say, but now I was looking past that, or trying to, wondering, pointlessly perhaps, about how this building I'd helped to shape might come in time to shape me, where the two of us might be headed. Since the day Joe and I got it all closed in the building had reminded me of a wheelhouse, and now that it stood there all lit up on the wide night, a bright windshield gazing out from beneath its visor at some prospect up ahead, it certainly looked to be journeying *some*where.

But now I was dreaming.

I don't think there is a lighted house in the woods anywhere in this world that doesn't hint at a person inside and a story unfolding, and so, it seemed, did mine. As I walked with my crates up the hill toward my cabinet of light, the person that it hinted at was surely recognizable as me, or at least that part of me this room had been built to house. So this was the house for the self that stood a little apart and at an angle, the self that thought a good place to spend the day was between two walls of books in front of a big window overlooking life. The part of me that was willing to wager something worthwhile could come of being alone in the woods with one's thoughts, in a place of one's own, of one's own making. As for the story that this house hinted at, the first part of it you know already, the part about its making; the next wouldn't begin until tomorrow, on move-in day, a morning that from here held the bright promise of all beginnings, of departure, of once upon a time.

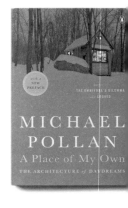

Michael Pollan, *A Place of My Own* (cover), 2008, published by Penguin Books, reprint edition

Allison Geller

Getting Off the Grid: A Re-Examination of the Writer's Cabin

The writer's cabin. You know the one—snow-crusted, pine-paneled, remote. You have to get there with chains on your tires. You are advised to bring copious amounts of rye whiskey, your best wood-chopping axe and fingerless gloves along with that manuscript you've been carrying around in your head. Also, the writing process works better if you've built the cabin yourself.

Ever since Henry David Thoreau, that original hipster, built his "airy and unplastered cabin" beside Walden Pond, detailing the subsequent improvements and additions to the 10-by-15-foot dwelling in Walden, male writers have been rushing to get off the grid—and tell you about it.

In his book "A Place Of My Own: The Education of an Amateur Builder," Michael Pollan points out that many architects throughout history have used the hut or cabin as a basis for expounding theories about their craft (Vitruvius, Frank Lloyd Wright, Le Corbusier), and many writers have done the same (Michel de Montaigne, George Bernard Shaw, and of course, Thoreau). Asceticism, loneliness and DIY are all principles that inform the cabin fantasy, and which seem to particularly draw men of letters. As Ken Gordon writes in his essay "Cabin Fever: My Own Private Walden Pond" about his own attempt to build a writer's cabin: "For the writers who can muster it, building the cabin is as important as inhabiting it. These are male writers, as far as I know, and they get great joy out of detailing the steps in the construction process. Fran Lebowitz once said that men 'have this sneaking suspicion that writing is not the most masculine profession.' So they relish the shop-class aspect because they know the disparity between describing something and actually doing it."

Nowadays, male writers tend to write about their cabin-building follies by first acknowledging, with self-deprecating good humor, their lack of experience, knowledge and manual dexterity. Then, they can't resist detailing all the steps involved, fascinated by what they're really doing. Pollan, for example, writes a whole book about making a not very nice cabin, not very well, at a not-at-all-modest cost. His reasons for building a cabin are threefold: to have a space of his own in which to write, to build that space in order to "add to the stock of reality," and because his wife is about to have a baby (in other words, very much adding to the stock of reality). He wants not only to get away, but also to make his own escape: "I wanted not only a room of my own, but a room of my own making. I wanted to build this place myself."

The book isn't supposed to teach the reader how to build a cabin, or place the cabin in a greater historical, literary or social context. It also doesn't do any deep self-reflection. With chapter titles like "Framing," "Windows," and "The Roof," Pollan wants to make sure we know that while this may be another book he's writing, he sure as hell did something.

***

"Why did men drink wine and women water?" asks the narrator of Virginia Woolf's famous lecture-turned-essay, "A Room of One's Own," as she reflects on the differences between the men's and women's colleges at a fictional university. "Why was one sex so prosperous and the other so poor? What effect has poverty on fiction? What conditions are necessary for the creation of works of art?" Woolf theorizes that only chance made it possible for the talents of, say, Jane Austen to bloom into literature: "her gift and her circumstance matched each other completely." Everyone else was beat by the common sitting room, with its constant interruptions and intrusions. Underneath Woolf's tempered voice is the desperation of all the women who didn't want to bang on nails to feel productive, but just to have a space to call theirs and the freedom to enclose themselves within it.

In the preface to "A Hut of One's Own: Life Outside The Circle of Architecture," architect and critic Ann Cline describes her book as "an essay that attempts to overturn Architecture's victory over Individual Experience." In her exploration of buildings on the fringes, she spends a sparse sentence dealing with the first phase of construction of her own hut: "To begin I built a simple platform—six feet by eight feet—with four corner columns supporting a pitched roof."

She continues in this vein to describe the hut's expansions and improvements, but always with an emphasis on the almost mystical practice of shaping the space, from both persuading the junkyard chief and his team to help her extract a pane of window from its steel I-beam to considering the sound of an overripe pomegranate splitting open on a tree outside. For her, hut improvements are about creating a space for her simple possessions to rest, a "poetry of pure experience." "As my dwelling took shape, it began to shape my life as well," she writes. "Like finding the firmness of scale through the placement of windows, I had found the commodity of my dwelling through the poetry of its use."

"A Hut of One's Own" is an architect's statement against architecture. Writing in the mid-1990s when mass media and consumerist culture were meeting with the information age, Cline's exploration is edged with social criticism. The primitive hut, particularly the one built with her own hands and molded to its environment, is a strike against that culture that replaces deeply personal experiences with designed ones. She references Woolf not just in the title, but also when she suggests that both men and women must create their own spaces in order to find their voices—to "experience the poetry of life (even before the issue of writing comes up)." Making a hut is not about pounding two-by-fours and saying, "Look what I made," but tapping into a level of experience that is cleared of distractions.

For women and cabins, individual experience—and making meaning out of it—is the victory. Even now, when the female artist is largely free of legal or social impingement, living out the cabin fantasy is only feasible if she has no other responsibilities (like kids, a household or a job), or that those can be easily shed. (Just a note on Thoreau: his delightful, hand-hewn cabin was a short walk away from his family home. During his experiment in radical self-reliance, his mother still did his laundry and made him pies.) It also bears noting that the idea of a woman retreating alone to a cabin evokes horror movie strings and friends murmuring, "I told her she should have at least brought a cell phone." Women who get off the grid are apt to be thought of as eccentric, cat lady-ish or just plain foolhardy. These less institutionalized constraints have led to the creation of all-women writers' retreats like Hedgebrook, a no-cost getaway on Whidbey Island north of Seattle, or foundations like A Room of Her Own, which gives female writers cash awards (including the $50,000 "Gift of Freedom" grant) and hosts yearly writers' retreats. Work and reflection are the aims here, not keeping the hands occupied.

And of course, if the tradition has been historically male, it's not because women don't escape to make art, too. For every Bon Iver, who produced his much-lauded debut album after retreating to a cabin in Wisconsin, there's an Annie Clark. Clark, known best by her stage name, St. Vincent, recorded

her album "Strange Mercy" over a month in October 2010, not in a cabin but in an Ace Hotel in Seattle. She describes the experience in an interview with *Vulture* magazine as a "technological detox" in which she had only the barest social contact. She calls it "a succinct process." The short storyist Amy Hempel and poet Rita Dove have declared their love of cabins (sometimes sheds) to pursue their literary lives, as has Annie Dillard, author of the most famous modern transcendental mash-up, "Pilgrim at Tinker Creek." Back in the 19th century, Mary Ann Evans (also protecting herself within the barriers of the male pseudonym George Eliot) lived away from the prying eyes of society with her married paramour, once writing in a letter that she had been "cut off from what is called the world" in order to live the creative and personal life she wanted.

My original idea was to write this essay in my own cabin, a place where I could experience being a woman alone, off the grid, with the sole goal of writing. That didn't work out. Instead, I'm cat-sitting for friends who are out of town. There is not less life in here; there is different life (feline instead of human). There are not fewer books, but different books (instead of Plath and memoirs, I read Lorca and noir). I still have the distraction of the phone and the screen, but at least here there is an opportunity for quietude. I've cracked a window but this far east, this far uptown, this late in the year, there's little noise save the occasional muffled horn or snatch of music unfurling from a passing car. There's a broken clock on the wall; the second hand twitches in time without ever moving forward a step.

For Woolf and the other women who were attempting to write fiction in Woolf's time, much was needed: money, freedom to experience, a place to examine that experience. These days, we have to be reigned in, to force a pause in our work, responsibilities, ambitions. Finding that place will never be simple, but it doesn't require a cabin in the wilderness or an education in draftsmanship. Magazines like this one are also a room of our own—as Cline calls it, a "deeply inhabited space"—in which we can examine the world and our place within it. As I write this, I'm in a room of my own—one that's temporary, not built by my hands, and not even my own. But I'm writing, and I'm drinking wine.

Excerpt from Allison Geller, "Getting Off the Grid: A Re-Examination of the Writer's Cabin," *A Women's Thing*, March 2015.

Cabin mythology has been integrated into visual and material culture since the late nineteenth century, when nostalgia for the pioneer and settler experience—a simpler life surrounded by nature—inspired log cabin mania; the architectural form was used to sell everything from maple syrup to children's building blocks. In our current moment, apparel and design companies actively participate in the enduring cultural obsession with cabins and outdoor experience by cultivating a cabin aesthetic—an attempt to capture, through design, the emotions, nostalgia and sense of escape experienced during a retreat to nature. This contemporary manifestation can be traced to the 1970s, when many companies began designing outdoor apparel and gear to capitalize on the popularity of back to the land movements and consumer longing for a more authentic existence in harmony with the natural world—commodifying what were considered alternative lifestyles. The North Face even pursued a geodesic dome tent design inspired by Buckminster Fuller, indicative of how counterculture was being absorbed and reconfigured by the mainstream. Iconic Canadian brand Roots began referencing cabin culture, and the relationship between the nation's identity and its natural landscape, in marketing, products and store design as early as the 1970s. Companies that have been operating for more than a century, such as Filson and L.L.Bean, have resurged in popularity; their traditional outdoor apparel resonates with our current cabin culture. Today it is common to see ad campaigns and lookbooks that explicitly evoke the cabin experience to entice young urbanites to purchase products—from apparel to vehicles to beer—revealing how cabin mythology has become inscribed in the North American imagination. The imagery borrows heavily from what has come to define the Instagram aesthetic—dreamy, washed out hues reminiscent of 1970s Polaroid film—to ignite desire for an antidote to the excesses of contemporary life. [SR]

The Aesthetics of Ruggedness

Left to right: Roots Canada, Lookbook, Spring/Summer, 2015. Camp Brand Goods, Lookbook, Fall/Winter, 2015. Herschel Supply Co., Lookbook: Fall Classic Collection, 2013. Herschel Supply Co., Lookbook, Spring/Summer, 2012. Herschel Supply Co., Lookbook: Fall Classic Collection, 2013

BIG (Bjarke Ingels Group) is a Danish architecture firm known for its iconic, sometimes controversial buildings that encourage dialogue with the local environment. In 2012, BIG won the bid to renovate and expand the Kimball Art Center in Park City, Utah. As a nod to the city's mining heritage—specifically the Silver King Coalition Building that burned down nearby in 1981—the firm proposed a heavy timber façade fashioned out of railroad trestles salvaged from the Great Salt Lake. The twisted five-story form mixes traditional materials with innovative design; it evokes what Ingels calls a "highly-evolved log cabin at an unprecedented scale." This playful abstraction of a vernacular architecture synonymous with ski towns demonstrates how steeped the Western psyche is in cabin imagery. But the design for the new building also proved polarizing. Public disapproval of the proposed project height resulted in the scheme being abandoned; BIG's 2014 revision, a wedge-shaped concrete structure that eliminated any reference to the log cabin, was rejected on the basis that it didn't relate either aesthetically or historically to the city centre. Unable to redevelop the property in a way that met its long-term needs, the Kimball Art Center sold the building to a developer. It moved to a temporary location to await a new home in the yet-to-be-built Arts and Culture District. [JMV]

Proposal for Kimball Art Center

Left to right: Silver King Coalition
Mines Building, Park City, UT, n.d.
Bjarke Ingels Group, Proposal for
Kimball Art Center, Park City, UT
(conceptual renderings), 2012

231

High-tech Companies, Low-tech Offices

Monica Kim

Twitter Headquarters, San Francisco, CA, c. 2014

Last summer, two nineteenth-century cabins were salvaged from remote ranch fields in Montana, to be moved to an Art Deco building in San Francisco. The houses were hewn from lodgepole pine and had adze marks on the beams. These relics once housed homesteaders as they worked the dry Montana soil; now they hold Twitter engineers.

The cabins could be just another example of startup culture's quirky opulence, but they might also illustrate the industry's odd love affair with "low technology." A concept associated with the natural world, and with old-school craftsmanship that long predates the Internet era, low technology is not virtual—so, to appropriate it, Internet companies have had to get creative. The reclaimed-wood cabins, fitted by hand in the late eighteen-hundreds, are an obvious example, but Twitter's designs lie on the extreme end of the spectrum. Other companies are using a more liberal, low-key interpretation of low technology that focusses on nature.

Samsung is constructing a new headquarters in San Jose with lush gardens on nearly every floor. In Seattle, Amazon is building three glass spheres filled with trees, so that employees can "work and socialize in a more natural, park-like setting." At Google's Dublin office, an entire floor is carpeted in grass. Facebook's second Menlo Park campus will have a rooftop park with a walking trail. One mile east of Apple's headquarters, the main structure of a second Silicon Valley campus, set to open in late 2016, will resemble a futuristic glass ring surrounded by greenery, like a spaceship that has landed in an Edenic orchard. David Muffly, the senior arborist on the project, is planting more than six thousand trees on the grounds, many of which will bear fruit; the courtyard is meant to "visually banish" cars and "replicate the original California landscape," the architect Norman Foster, who designed the campus, told *Architectural Record*.

Olle Lundberg, the founder and C.E.O. of Lundberg Design, has worked with many tech companies over the years, starting with Oracle, in 1990. "We have lost the visual connection to the maker in our lives, and our tech clients are the ones who feel most impoverished by it, because they're surrounded by the digital world," he says. "They're looking for a way to reestablish their individual identity, and we've found that introducing real crafts is one way to do that."

This craft-based theory is rooted in history. William Morris, the English artist and writer, and his friends turned back to pre-industrial arts in the eighteen-sixties, just after the Industrial Revolution. The Arts and Crafts movement defined itself against machines. "Without dignified, creative human occupation, people became disconnected from life," Morris said.

The digital revolution has had an even greater effect on our personal and professional lives. According to a Pew research report, eighty-seven per cent of American adults use the Internet today, up from fourteen per cent in 1995.

Research has shown that natural environments can restore our mental capacities. In Japan, medical patients are encouraged to "forest-bathe" (*shinrin-yoku*), taking extended walks through bamboo groves to lower their blood pressure, pulse rates, and cortisol levels.

These health benefits apply to the workplace as well, according to some studies. Rachel Kaplan, a professor of environmental psychology at the University of Michigan, has spent years researching the restorative effects of natural environments with her husband, Stephen Kaplan, who is also a professor at Michigan. Their Job Pressures Project found, in 1988, that workers with access to nature at the office—even simple views of trees and flowers—felt that their jobs were less stressful and more satisfying. In 2011, Ihab Elzeyadi, an architecture professor at the University of Oregon, performed a study at the college that found "architectural and design elements," specifically whether employees had ample lighting and natural views, could even influence the number of sick days people took. Workers with the best views—of wild, forest-like settings—took an average of about fifty-seven hours of sick leave per year, compared with nearly sixty-eight hours for employees with no view at all. If low-tech offices can potentially nourish the brains and improve the mental health of employees then, fine, bring on the log cabins.

Twitter Headquarters,
San Francisco, CA, c. 2014

The low-tech movement likely has to do with advancing the companies' own goals, too—and not only by getting people to take fewer sick days. For one thing, as Ben Mauk wrote, some research suggests that people who work in offices "enriched" by plants (or by other decorative elements, like art) are more productive. Also, companies like Lundberg's clients are searching for an aesthetic to attract workers in a competitive market—one more sophisticated than early approaches like Google's primary colors. They are looking, he says, for a non-traditional approach, perhaps seeking inspiration from the grungy coffee bars where they once wrote code. Above all, these companies want to hold on to the spirit of the small startups they once were. Five years ago, a designer named Sara Morishige Williams, working on behalf of Twitter (which her husband, Evan Williams, co-founded), asked Lundberg to help design one of the company's early offices. Twitter was then a startup of some thirty employees; by the time Lundberg began work on its current headquarters—cabins and all—there were more than three hundred and fifty. Lundberg also took planks from bowling lanes to build the reception desk, and carved hashtags into slabs of raw wood to fit the "handcrafted" aesthetic envisioned by Williams. Now that Twitter has more than twenty-three hundred employees and is publicly traded, a rooftop farmstead is no doubt on the horizon.

The Grotto Sauna designed by Canadian studio Partisans is intimately tied to the idea of the cabin in both scale and intent. Located on a large granite rock formation overlooking Lake Huron in Ontario, the 800-square-foot structure is a place of refuge. Inspired by an Italian grotto—a natural or artificial cave often located near water—the objective of this architectural intervention is to transport visitors into an otherworldly realm. For the Grotto Sauna, this experience begins with the exterior. It is a simple black box nestled unobtrusively in the landscape. Built from charred cedar using a traditional Japanese technique of wood preservation called Shou Sugi Ban, the structure appears as if it has been weathered by the elements. The interior, also fashioned from cedar, is more sensual. Computer-driven milling and fabrication allowed the designers to create a warm, womb-like space with curved wood walls and traditional stepped sauna seating. The sculptural forms reference the undulating surfaces of the surrounding land and the lapping waves of Lake Huron. In the tradition of selecting the ideal location for a cabin, Partisans gave careful consideration to site. The team digitally scanned the area and created three-dimensional models in an effort to balance optimal setting with impact on the land. Technology also played a role in the functionality of the sauna: double and triple glazed high-efficiency window panes frame the view; a layer of aluminum foil behind the wooden paneling provides insulation and a sealed space for timber expansion and contraction; and the cavity between the interior and exterior framework creates a convection current allowing the skin to breathe through pores in the seats and seams of the cedar panels. More than a mere shelter, or even an escape, the Grotto Sauna is a refined blending of science and craftsmanship. [JMV]

Partisans, Grotto Sauna

In effort to unite technology and nature, architecture firms have reinterpreted the log cabin tradition to develop a new functional aesthetic that prioritizes sustainability. Many of these projects were initiated by architecture departments at universities that embrace cabin design as an ideal form—for testing experimental sustainable architectural practices and for developing treatises on minimum spatial requirements for living. Responsiveness to site, innovative use of materials and formal experimentation characterize the cabins featured here. [SR]

College of Architecture, Texas Tech University, Sustainable Cabin, 2008–10

Sustainable Practices

Project: ARCHITECTURE, Girl Scouts of Utah Summer Cabins, Provo, UT, 2016

237

Cal Poly Pomona Architectural
Design Studio, The Wedge, Julia
Pfeiffer Burns State Park, Big Sur,
CA, 2015

University of Colorado, College
of Architecture and Planning,
Colorado Building Workshop,
Outward Bound Micro Cabins,
Leadville, CO, 2015

Clard Svenson inside Theater
Dome, Drop City, Trinidad, CO,
1967

Cartop Dome

Drop City—an artists' community formed in rural Colorado in 1965—was among the first and most well-known of the hippie communes established in the United States in the mid-twentieth century. Fusing art, architecture and ideals of utopian, back to the land living, Drop City was a laboratory for developing new models of intentional lifestyle and sustainable building practices. Inspired by the architectural ideas of Buckminster Fuller, residents embraced the dome as the ideal form for both living and social spaces; its radical form starkly contrasted the cookie-cutter suburban homes they renounced. Droppers sourced automobile roofs and other inexpensive

materials from the local dump to make the geometric panels that formed the domes' structure; in this light the domes can be viewed as reconfigurations of the DIY log cabin tradition so prevalent in American culture.

The Cartop Dome was the first of Steve Baer's contributions to the community and an early prototype of zome construction—an interpretation of Fuller's design that replaces his equilateral triangles with isosceles ones to create asymmetrical composition. Baer built the Cartop Dome for $15—most of the material was salvaged from the junkyard—and it took a group of residents two and a half days to assemble the structure. The dome

had no frame or internal supports, which droppers Clark Richert and Richard Kallweit took advantage of to paint the interior ceiling with a vibrant, geometric composition. With images of Drop City gracing the pages of mainstream magazines like *Life* and architectural journals *Architectural Forum* and *Domus*, the dome became synonymous with countercultural pursuits of the era, and was embraced as the multifaceted movement's vernacular architecture. While Drop City was abandoned by the mid-1970s, the commune's concern for sustainability and the use of found materials in architecture would continue to resonate with subsequent generations.

Location: Trinidad, Colorado
Year: 1967

Type: Alternative Living Structure; DIY
Dimensions: 4.3 × 4.9 × 7.3 m
Materials: found car parts, railroad tires, steel

To every child who has ever played with a pencil it is obvious that you can draw a polygon and then adjoin another along one of its sides and go on and on with this and never stop, you even have considerable freedom as to the sizes and shapes the individual polygons will have.

(5)

Other Examples:
Zome, Placita, NM, c. late 1960s
Dean and Linda Fleming Dome, Libre, CO, 1969
Pacific High School, CA, 1969
Jim the Bear's Commune Dome, VT, c. 1970
Red Rockers Dome, Farisita, CO, c. 1970
Bob Lander, Log Dome, BC, 1973

Left to right: Cartop Dome and Theater, Drop City, Trinidad, CO, c. 1966. Steve Baer, *Dome Cookbook* (detail), 1969. Drop City, Trinidad, CO, c. 1966. Cartop Dome, Graffiti Van and Kitchen Dome (in background), Drop City, Trinidad, CO, c. 1965–66. Cartop Dome, Drop City, Trinidad, CO, c. 1966

Leaf House

Built by two university professors seeking refuge on Hornby Island in the late 1960s, the Leaf House is part of a collection of experimental residences constructed during the period that reflect preference for the handmade—in opposition to mass production, which had come to define post-war society. During the mid-1960s and early 1970s Hornby Island was inundated with Canadians and Americans fleeing urban centres in search of a more organic, self-sufficient lifestyle, and architecture that could better reflect these ideals. Many communities gathered on the site; informed by the DIY and back to the land movements that were garnering considerable attention, they proposed unconventional forms of shelter and modes of living. The Leaf House was built within this climate and contributed to the emergence of a West Coast building style characterized by amateurism, use of locally sourced and repurposed materials, and DIY spirit. Assembled from materials salvaged from the local beach, the residence design is defined by a curved log that shapes the roof. While many contemporaneous Hornby Island residences embrace a collage aesthetic—largely due to reliance on found or repurposed materials—the Leaf House's more cohesive vision reveals deep reverence for the natural landscape that surrounds the structure. Intended to evoke the form of a leaf falling in the forest, the Leaf House represents an embrace of the unexpected, and a playful, whimsical approach to architecture.

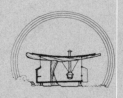

Architect: Lloyd House
Location: Hornby Island, British Columbia
Year: 1970

Type: DIY; Sustainable Design
Dimensions: 4.9 × 5.5 m
Materials: cedar, found logs, glass, metal

Bo Helliwell and Michael McNamara, Illustrations of Leaf House published in *Architectural Design*, 1978

245

La Petite Maison du Weekend

Commissioned for the Fabrications exhibition co-organized by MoMA, SFMOMA and the Wexner Center for the Arts in 1998, La Petite Maison du Weekend is a prototype of a mobile cottage that can be built for under $15,000. Nearly any off-the-grid site, regardless of climate or topography, will suit the prefabricated dwelling, which shelters two in a loft bedroom with a modest kitchen, a shower and a composting toilet. Completely self-sufficient, the dwelling generates electricity for lighting and refrigeration, collects rainwater, and composts waste. The sophisticated, minimalist design is a formal investigation of the minimum spatial requirements for living and an architecture that combines natural with technological systems.

Architect: Patkau Architects
Location: Wexner Center for the Arts, Columbus, Ohio
Year: 1998

Type: Minimum Requirements for Living; Prefab
Dimensions: 4.1 × 5.1 × 5.1 m
Materials: canvas, glass, metal, photovoltaic glass, plywood, timber

Patkau Architects, La Petite Maison du Weekend, Wexner Center for the Arts, Columbus, OH, 1998. Patkau Architects, La Petite Maison du Weekend, Wexner Center for the Arts, Columbus, OH (elevations and plans), 1998

Other Examples:
Henry David Thoreau, Walden Cottage, Concord, MA, 1845
Le Corbusier, Maison de week-end, La Celle-Saint-Cloud, France, 1934
Andrea Zittel, *A–Z Living Units*, 1994

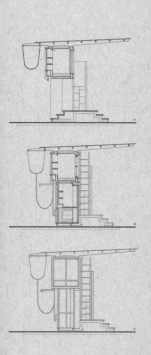

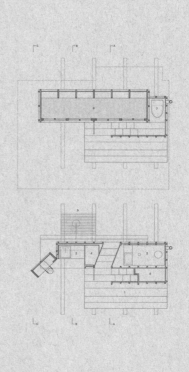

Art

The cabin is an iconic image in modern and contemporary art. It appears in virtually every artistic medium and across all modes of cultural production. The six artists whose works figure prominently in this exhibition each address the cabin from a very different perspective. For Mattie Gunterman the cabin was primarily a shelter from the formidable presence of the natural world. In her pictures it is a dense and stoic presence standing in spite of a distinctly inhospitable environment. Through her extraordinary photographs we gain a surprising insight into settler culture on the Northwest Coast during the late 19th century. For Walker Evans and Dorothea Lange, the cabin was the backdrop for the economic and social narratives that played out across the United States during the Great Depression. In their pictures the cabin is often the last remnant of a human presence in a depleted and devastated landscape. Fifty years later Vikky Alexander points to the cabin's complete disappearance and its replacement by an image. The image offered is not that of a cabin, but instead a simulacrum of nature that has come to stand for the cabin experience. Liz Magor invites us to consider the cabin's interior as the site of its meaning and signification. The cabin is a place of retreat and withdrawal, a storehouse of memory and a bulwark against invaders. In his films and constructed replicas James Benning circles back to the utopian roots of Henry David Thoreau's cabin at Walden Pond. The cabin is an idea, and nature is a real and persistent presence most effectively recognized from within the cabin's architecture. [BG]

Frederick Varley, *Forest Ranger's
Cabin, Lynn Valley*, c. 1932,
oil on board, Collection of the
Vancouver Art Gallery, Purchased
with funds from the Anne Eliza
Winn Trust

Mattie Gunterman was born Ida Madeline Warner in La Crosse, Wisconsin, in 1872. She learned photography from her uncle, Charles Warner, who was a commercial photographer in the town. After a brief sojourn in Seattle, Washington, Gunterman and her new family travelled (by foot) to the Kootenay region of British Columbia arriving in 1898. It was on this journey that Gunterman began using a newly acquired 4" × 5" plate camera to document her life and surroundings. Among these images are vivid documents of the cabins and shelters that made life possible in that rugged and remote landscape.

Gunterman's photograph of her family homestead is a carefully composed image that features a sturdy log cabin firmly wedged into the steep terrain. Other photographs show the distinct design of the cabin interiors that provided the strength and structural ingenuity to support the heavy snow that blanketed the region in the winter. Gunterman's elaborately staged compositions and delightful sense of humour are complimented by her technical rigour evident in the complex lighting solutions that must have been devised to produce her interior tableaus.

Gunterman's photograph of her son Henry and partner William Gunterman offers insight into the type of provisional cabin structures that were built to provide shelter for those in transit across the trails that criss-crossed the interior. The ready supply of clean and straight timber ensured that sturdy and durable cabins could be built for almost every need and purpose.

Mattie Gunterman documented her life with a 4" × 5" camera and glass plate negatives for twenty years before switching to a smaller film camera in the 1920s. She died at her home in 1945. [BG]

Mattie Gunterman

Above and following pages:
Gunterman's homestead in Beaton, 1900
Trail shelter with Henry, dog Nero and Bill, 1899
Group in front of snow covered cabin, 1902
Group of children in front of the Gunterman cabin, 1901
Women in rafters and man with brooms, 1902

Among the New Deal agencies established by the Franklin D. Roosevelt administration during the Great Depression, the Resettlement Administration (1935–37) and the Farm Security Administration (FSA) (1937–42) are notable for their commitment to documenting the farms, homesteads and migrations of rural Americans during the depths of the Depression. Among the hundreds of thousands of images produced by the twenty-two photographers deployed by Roy Stryker during his tenure as the head of the FSA's Historical Section, the photographs of Dorothea Lange and Walker Evans stand out as extraordinary documents of the cabins and simple built structures that housed sharecroppers, tenant farmers and migrant workers as they struggled to eke out a living on depleted land or migrated west in the hope of employment and shelter.

Born in 1895, Dorothea Lange studied photography at Columbia University before moving to Berkeley, California, to begin a career as a professional studio photographer. During the early years of the Depression, Lange, using a large Graflex camera, started to document the labour demonstrations, soup kitchens and homeless in the Bay Area. Hired by the FSA between 1935 and 1939, Lange travelled across the United States—from Washington, Utah and California in the West, to Georgia and North Carolina in the East, and Mississippi in the South—documenting the desperate conditions faced by many of the rural poor as they struggled to maintain their homes on devastated land or migrated to temporary jobs. The cabin plays a central role in much of Lange's photographs from this period. Families sit on cabin stoops or pose obligingly in their doorways, acknowledging the grave poverty of their condition while articulating the fundamental place of the home in any consideration of their plight.

Some photographs show sturdy log cabins—home to sharecroppers and tenant farmers—that were suffering from the neglect of absentee landowners who sought only to extract the maximum amount possible from the land. Other cabins became grave markers, abandoned as the land around them failed due to drought conditions and over-farming. In the West, new cabins were built to house migrant workers seeking employment or as homesteads built with FSA loans on unimproved lands as part of a rural rehabilitation effort. These cabins tended to be very rudimentary structures made from split-wood logs and often without windows or running water. They housed migrant workers, itinerant travellers and refugees in search of work. [BG]

Dorothea Lange

Born in 1903 in St. Louis, Missouri, Walker Evans turned to photography in the late 1920s inspired in part by the architectural photographs of Eugène Atget. Here he saw a role for the photograph as a document—direct, detailed and unsentimental, yet carefully constructed to establish a deep intimacy between the subject and its viewer.

Evans worked under contract to the American government's Resettlement Administration (RA) and the Farm Security Administration (FSA) from 1935 to 1938. In comparison to many of his colleagues in the FSA, Evans produced relatively few photographs. He often created multiple images of his FSA subjects documenting the people in their farms and homes with an intimacy and focus that defined a new model for documentary photography. Some of his most recognizable images are those taken in Hale County, Alabama, in 1936. There he took numerous photographs of the Burroughs, Tengle and Fields families in and around their sharecropper homesteads. Their cabins figure prominently in the photographs as they were the centre of family life and a clear symbol of their stark and impoverished existence.

As with much of Evans' work for the RA/FSA the photographs were connected to commercial assignments where he could submit the same material to both parties. Commissioned by *Fortune* magazine, which sent Evans and writer James Agee to document the living conditions of sharecroppers, the Hale county photographs are among Evans most famous. A few years later, in 1941, they were published as the book *Now Let Us Praise Famous Men*, a landmark publication in the emergent field of social documentary. Despite ethical questions regarding Evans and Agee's methodology, the photographs of the families and their cabin homes remain archetypal images of the Great Depression. [BG]

Walker Evans

Opposite and following pages:
Sharecropper Bud Fields and his family at home. Hale County, Alabama, 1936
Bedroom window of Bud Fields' home, Hale County, Alabama, 1936
Home of Bud Fields, Alabama sharecropper. Hale County, Alabama, 1936
Washstand in the dog run and kitchen of Floyd Burroughs' cabin. Hale County, Alabama, 1936

268

In the mid-1980s Vikky Alexander was one of a handful of young artists working with mass-produced images found in newspapers, magazines, television and advertising. Collectively identified as the "Pictures Generation" these New York–based artists sought to challenge conventional notions of authorship and originality and to produce new ways to think critically about consumer culture.

In contemporary life the cabin remains a preeminent symbol of a human place in nature. It represents the opportunity for a unique physical proximity to nature while at the same time ensuring a protected distance. This mediated and sheltered proximity to nature is often signalled in the form of a pleasing vista, ideally one that is offered through a large plate glass window overlooking a sweeping expanse of open water, a snow-capped mountain range, or a dense, virgin forest.

Alexander's *Lake in the Woods* (1986) was conceived as an installation at a commercial gallery in New York's East Village. The space was small and narrow, an attribute that Alexander exploited by covering one side of the gallery with a commercially available photomural depicting a northern lake at the edge of a wooded area. On the opposite wall the artist installed faux wood panelling topped by a row of mirrors. For the viewer entering this eccentric space, nature is reduced to a simulacrum—a substitute for the natural world that now precedes the original and comes to stand for nature. In Alexander's installation our experience of nature is determined in a series of reflections, faux surfaces and infinite repetitions, and in this way she invites us to consider if our access to the natural world can ever escape the rise of the simulacrum and the triumph of the image over the real. Certainly the preeminent place of the picture window in contemporary cabin design since the mid-century would suggest that nature is best experienced at a distance. [BG]

Vikky Alexander

Liz Magor is a Vancouver-based artist with a long and abiding interest in the woods as a site of escape, disappearance and resistance. Shelter is also a prominent subject of her art, especially those spaces that seem to blur the distinction between built and naturally occurring structures. A hollowed log with a sleeping bag tucked into it becomes a unique log cabin. A depression in the ground covered by underbrush and fallen branches suggests a readymade lean-to or a bolthole for someone on the run.

Magor's *Messenger* (1996–2002) is a rudimentary cabin in the woods. Its brightly lit interior draws the viewer forward to peer in the windows, trapping them in a voyeuristic impulse that unequivocally signals a breach of privacy,

a trespass, or, possibly, an invasion. And the impulse may be justified, for through the window on the bed we see a military helmet and a cluster of unexploded grenades, and inexplicably, a medieval helmet, gauntlets and a double-bladed axe. And yet, a dog sleeps peacefully on the bed and the shelves contain a well-ordered stockpile of provisions. This appears to be the cabin of a survivalist, built far from the influences and dangers of civilization. The sleeping dog is a sign of protection and domesticity, and the isolated cabin speaks to self-sufficiency and voluntary withdrawal. We, the viewers, are the invaders in this scenario, revealed by our own desire. [BG]

Liz Magor

Opposite and following pages:
Messenger, 1996–2002, wood, plaster, textile, found objects, Collection of the
  Vancouver Art Gallery, Gift of the Artist
Burrow, 1999, polymerized alpha gypsum, textile, stain, Collection of the Vancouver Art Gallery,
  Purchased with the financial support of the Canada Council for the Arts Acquisition Assistance
  Program and the Vancouver Art Gallery Acquisition Fund
Deep Woods Portfolio (detail), 1999, silver gelatin prints, Collection of the Vancouver Art Gallery,
  Gift of the Artist
Beaver Man, 1977, wood, asphalt shingles, metal, rubber, found objects, Collection of the
  Vancouver Art Gallery, Gift of the Artist

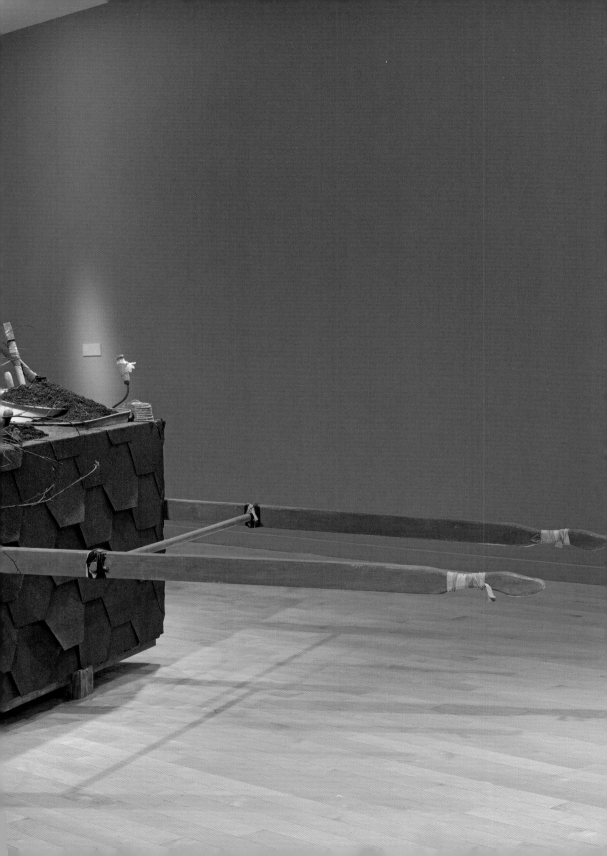

James Benning is an artist and filmmaker based in Southern California where he teaches at the California Institute of the Arts in Valencia and maintains an isolated property in the mountains of the Sierra Nevada. On that property he has built two cabins. One is a replica of Henry David Thoreau's cabin that he described in *Walden; or, Life the Woods* (1854). That cabin, designed and built by Thoreau, has become a symbol of introspection and transformation through submersion in nature. The second cabin is a reproduction of Theodore Kaczynski's cabin, based on Thoreau's design, but built with the purpose of a calculated withdrawal from society that he described in his manifesto, *Industrial Society and Its Future* (1995), written during his time at the cabin near Lincoln, Montana. These two cabins are both the object and the lens through which we see Benning's landscape.

In *Cabin Fever*, James Benning offers two more recent versions of the cabins. In this instance they are white abstracted reproductions, or 'architectural renderings' as Benning calls them: one (Kaczynski's cabin) sits at the entrance to the exhibition and the other (Thoreau's cabin) in the same space as his related film projections. The two films present static shots through the respective cabin windows on Benning's property; the sound is the ambient sounds of the landscape heard from within the cabin—the wind blows, a bird sings, a dog barks, a truck passes—little seems to happen and yet everything happens. Within this simple gesture time and space become real and concrete, their presence is dense, saturated and substantial. Architecture is an idea, nature is persistent. [BG]

James Benning

Opposite and following pages:
James Benning's replica of Henry David Thoreau's cabin, constructed in 2007
James Benning's replica of Theodore Kaczynski's cabin, constructed in 2008
Architectural Renderings (Two Cabins), 2014, Installation view of *James Benning: Decoding Fear*, Kunsthaus Graz, 2014, wood, plaster, metal
Two Cabins, 2011, Installation view of *James Benning: Decoding Fear*, Kunsthaus Graz, 2014, two-channel video installation, typewriter with wooden pedestal, wooden desk and pencil on wooden and plaster pedestal, Private Collection, Zurich

University of Colorado, College
of Architecture and Planning,
Colorado Building Workshop,
Outward Bound Micro Cabins,
Leadville, CO, 2015

Delta Shelter

Seattle-based Olson Kundig is well known for its innovative cabin designs that seamlessly fuse interest in technological processes with belief in the importance of the natural world. Inspired by tree houses and fire lookouts, the Delta Shelter—a three-storey, steel-clad structure—is an example of contemporary, sustainable design that thoughtfully responds to particularities of site. The cabin's miniscule, two-hundred foot footprint, as well as the materials used in its construction, harmonize with the surrounding wilderness and leave the landscape virtually untouched. The design is also notable for its verticality, which mimics trees in the adjacent forest and highlights the formal, geometric qualities of the architecture—essentially an elevated box. With a carport on the lower level, two bedrooms and bathrooms on the middle level and an open-plan living and dining area on the top, the Delta Shelter uses space extremely efficiently. The cabin features four 10' × 18' steel shutters operated by a hand-crank—a form of kinetic architecture that has become somewhat of a signature for the firm—to protect the structure from the elements when uninhabited. The functional, utilitarian aesthetic complements the natural beauty of the surroundings and minimizes the structure's visual impact, while the raw plywood interior components elevate the architectural experience of the space. A pinnacle of small house design, Olson Kundig's Delta Shelter was extremely influential in contemporary cabin architecture, particularly on the West Coast.

Architect: Olson Kundig
Location: Mazama, Washington
Year: 2005

Type: Porn; Prefab
Dimensions: 304.8 m²
Materials: glass, steel, wood

Olson Kundig, Delta Shelter, Mazama, WA, 2005. Olson Kundig, Delta Shelter, Mazuma, WA (sketches), 2005

Other Examples:
Olson Kundig, Rolling Huts, Mazama, WA, 2008
mwlworks, Little House, Puget Sound, WA, 2015
MUJI, MUJI Hut, 2017

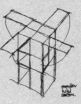

Cliff House

Nova Scotia–based MacKay-Lyons Sweetapple Architects are well known internationally for residential buildings that combine reverence for regional architectural vernacular with contemporary materials and building technologies. At 960 square feet, the Cliff House, which balances precariously over a rocky cliff, is a dramatic interpretation of the conventional, one-room cabin—a playful, poetic response to the majestic coastal landscape. Embracing mundane building materials (wood and steel) and a simple, geometric shape, the

Cliff House design introduces a striking relationship between built form and natural environment. Essentially a rectangular box clad in cedar shiplap, the main level contains the living spaces and a storage wall; the sleeping quarters are located above in an open loft. Despite the site's grandeur, the Cliff House is a humble, affordable cabin conceived as a prototype that could be refashioned for future projects. The cabin provides a dramatic, unimpeded experience of the landscape; with two-thirds suspended over the edge of

a bedrock cliff, anchored by a galvanized steel structure, the Cliff House gives inhabitants the sense they're floating above the vast expanse of the Atlantic Ocean. An exploration of opposites—traditional and contemporary, inhibited and orderly, natural and constructed—this sustainable, site-specific approach adds a decidedly twenty-first century sensibility to the traditional one-room cabin.

Architect: MacKay-Lyons Sweetapple Architects Ltd
Location: Tomlee Head, Nova Scotia
Year: 2010

Type: Porn
Dimensions: 4.9 × 13.4 m
Materials: glass, steel, wood

MacKay-Lyons Sweetapple Architects Limited, Cliff House, Tomlee Head, NS, 2010

Other Examples:
Castanes Architects, Tree House, Hood Canal, WA, 2002–03
Taylor Smyth Architects, Sunset Cabin, Lake Simcoe, ON, 2004
Olson Kundig, Gulf Islands Cabin, Gulf Islands, BC, 2010
bioi, Warburg House, Warburg, AB, 2012
superkül, Stealth Cabin, Bracebridge, ON, 2014

Outward Bound
Micro Cabins

Designed and completed by 28 graduate students during a semester at University of Colorado Denver, the Outward Bound Micro Cabins serve as housing and social space for Colorado Outward Bound School. While the cabins vary in size and plan, each one features a steel frame enclosing storage space and covered porches, and for living quarters, a prefabricated, rectangular box sits beneath the frame. Respectful of the forested landscape, the rustic, yet elegant structures harmonize with their surroundings; their vertical cladding and angular geometry mimic the neighbouring pine trees, and the interior is outfitted with built-in amenities constructed of birch plywood. To investigate possibilities for efficiency afforded by prefabrication, the walls and CNC'd plywood were prefabricated and trucked to the site; construction speed increased, and waste and site disruption were minimized.

Architect: University of Colorado Denver
Location: Leadville, Colorado
Year: 2015

Type: Worker; Prefab
Dimensions: 14 cabins—each smaller than 61m²
Materials: birch plywood, glass, steel, wood

Other Examples:
Olson Kundig, Rolling Huts, Mazama, WA, 2007–2008
Gensler, Eco Cabin, Camp Emerald Bay, Catalina Island, CA, 2010
Cal Poly College of Environmental Design, The Wedge, Santa Rosa, CA, 2014
Project:ARCHITECTURE, Girl Scout Cabins, Provo Canyon, UT, 2014

University of Colorado, College
of Architecture and Planning,
Colorado Building Workshop,
Outward Bound Micro Cabins,
Leadville, CO, 2015

303

MacKay-Lyons Sweetapple
Architects Limited, Cliff House,
Tomlee Head, NS, 2010

CABIN FEVER

A publication and exhibition of this magnitude requires years of research, conversations and intense, focused labour and would not have been possible without the immense contributions of many individuals. First and foremost we thank Kathleen S. Bartels, Director of the Vancouver Art Gallery, for her unwavering support of ambitious, interdisciplinary projects and for her commitment to an exhibition program that traces a history of visual culture. Her encouragement and support from the project's inception has been critical to our success. We extend our deepest appreciation to the Gallery staff who once again have approached a demanding and amorphous project with intelligence, ingenuity and enthusiasm. Curatorial Assistant Amy Luo expertly managed the many details required to mount an exhibition of this size and confronted every challenge with poise and savvy. Assistant Curator Zoë Chan entered the project as it neared its conclusion and remained unnerved by the frenetic pace and urgency of our requests. We are grateful to Manager of Curatorial Affairs Bruce Wiedrick for his assistance in navigating the exhibition's many details and budgetary challenges; his advice and support, as always, were critical. We thank our Curatorial colleagues Justina Bohach, Emma Conner, Ashlee Conery, Anh Le and Elaire Maund for their help throughout the development of this exhibition and publication. Our colleagues in the Education and Public Programs department, cheyanne turions and Stephanie Bokenfohr, crafted engaging and innovative programming to accompany the exhibition. We extend our deep appreciation to our Audio-Visual and Graphics team, led by Wade Thomas and Susan Perrigo, whose extraordinary commitment, critical eye and enviable problem solving skills are evident in every dimension of this project. We are also indebted to our Registrars, Jenny Wilson, Amber McBride and Susan Sirovyak, who assisted with shipping arrangements and coordinated the immense number of objects in the exhibition with aplomb; and to our Preparation department, Glen Flanderka, Jim Stamper, Ken Labun and their team, who approached the numerous installation challenges that the exhibition presented with enthusiasm and flair.

This publication is the result of a collaboration between the Vancouver Art Gallery and Information Office; we are grateful to Derek Barnett and Jonathan Middleton for their thoughtful approach to the content and inspiring mandate to reconceive publishing in the twenty-first century. It was a pleasure to work with Derek Barnett again and we thank him for his prescient ability to capture the essence of the project in his publication and exhibition design, providing continuity between the book and the presentation in the Gallery. Trevor Mills, Rachel Topham and Maegan Hill-Carroll of our Photo Imaging department, as always, did a wonderful job preparing the images for this publication. Rachel in particular worked tirelessly to ensure that each image looked its best; her unerring eye and aesthetic decisions are apparent throughout. Danielle Currie, Amy Luo and Zoë Chan worked diligently to secure reproduction rights for the many images in the book and exhibition. Our copyeditors, Meaghan McAneeley and Emma Conner, refined the publication through their edits and feedback.

Throughout the development of this exhibition and publication we received advice and assistance from curators, writers, archivists, artists and colleagues whom we would like to thank: James Benning, Gene Bernofsky, Jonathan Braun, James Connell, Upe Flueckiger, Becky Fullerton, Rick Gardiner, Jocelyn Gibbs, Gillian Harris, Richard Kallweit, Elizabeth Kundert-Cameron, Hana Lani, Michael Lis, Chip Lord, Waverly Lowell, Dylan Lustrin at neugerriemschneider, Berlin, Chris Marino, Michael McNamara, Tim Neuger, Gerry Parker, Linda C. Parker, the Seth Peterson Cottage Conservancy, Jean-Luc Pilon, Anna Reynolds, Clark Richert, Diana Saverin, Curtis Schreier and Lindsay A. Stokalko. We would like to thank the Design History Society for the Research Exhibition Grant which enabled Jennifer M. Volland to travel to Norway to conduct research that informed the scope and curatorial conception of the project. We also extend our gratitude to the lenders of the exhibition: Art, Design & Architecture Museum, UC Santa Barbara; Morris and Helen Belkin Art Gallery; Canadian Centre for Architecture; Environmental Design Archives, University of California, Berkeley; Filson; Richard Johnson Gallery; neugerriemschneider; Partisans; Patkau Architects; Pendleton; Roots Canada; Scott & Scott Architects; and UUfie. Their willingness to lend drawings and objects from their collections enriched the exhibition tremendously.

Cabin Fever would not have been possible without the financial contribution of Naudia and Mark Maché and we are grateful for their support.

Finally, we would like to thank the artists, architects and writers whose work is represented on these pages – this project has benefited immensely from your creativity and enduring engagement with the multifaceted and omnipresent cabin.

Jennifer M. Volland, Bruce Grenville and Stephanie Rebick

Cover images (from left to right, top to bottom): Refugee Cottages, Camp 9, Lobos Square, San Francisco, CA, 1906, Courtesy of the California History Room, California State Library, Sacramento, California; Britton & Rey, *Sunday Morning: Log Cabin* (detail), c. 1908, Library of Congress, Prints and Photographs Division; Ant Farm, *Inflatocookbook* (detail), 1973, Courtesy Chip Lord and Curtis Schreier, Photo Courtesy of the Environmental Design Library, University of California, Berkeley; Lower Swedish Cabin, Darby, PA (measured drawings), 1937, Historic American Buildings Survey, Library of Congress, Prints and Photographs Division; Richard Johnson, *Ice Hut #180, Beaverton, Lake Simcoe, Ontario, Canada*, 2008, Courtesy of the Artist; A.O. Wheeler Hut, Glacier National Park, BC, c. 1950, Photo: Hans Gmoser, Whyte Museum of the Canadian Rockies, Hans Gmoser Fonds (V68/pa-707); Map of the North American Subarctic, Adapted from Harold E. Driver and William C. Massey, *Comparative Studies of North American Indians*, 1957, p. 170, Courtesy of Jean-Luc Pilon; Elizabeth Parker Hut, Yoho National Park, BC, 1956, Whyte Museum of the Canadian Rockies, Bob Hind Fonds (V46/28/1); Steve Baer, *Dome Cookbook* (detail), 1969, pff NA2790.B3 1969. Courtesy of The Bancroft Library, University of California, Berkeley; 1840 Presidential campaign handkerchief, 1840, Rare Books and Special Collections Division, Library of Congress, Prints and Photographs Division; FBI Unabomber sketch, 1995; Andrew Geller, Reese House (elevations), Bridgehampton, NY, 1956, Andrew Geller Architectural Archive, Collection of Jake and Tracey Gorst; Millions of Acres: Iowa and Nebraska, 1872, Library of Congress, Rare Book and Special Collections Division, Printed Ephemera Collection; *Lincoln Logs Design Book* (detail of cover), c. 1923, brochure, Photo: Maegan Hill-Carroll, Vancouver Art Gallery; Clard Svenson inside Theater Dome, Drop City, Trinidad, CO, 1967, Denver Public Library, Western History Collection, X-7739; Ken Isaacs, *How to Build Your Own Living Structures* (detail), 1974, Photo: Trevor Mills, Vancouver Art Gallery; Ken Isaacs, *Culture Breakers, Alternatives & Other Numbers* (detail), 1969, Photo: Trevor Mills, Vancouver Art Gallery; "Mrs. Oleo Margarine" with daughter "Melissa," Drop City, Trinidad, CO, 1965, Denver Public Library, Western History Collection, X-7737; Henry David Thoreau, *Walden; Or, Life in the Woods* (title page), 1854, Library of Congress, Prints and Photographs Division; **Back Cover Images (from left to right, top to bottom):** Steve Baer, *Dome Cookbook* (detail), 1969, pff NA2790.B3 1969. Courtesy of The Bancroft Library, University of California, Berkeley; Olson Kundig, Delta Shelter, Mazama, WA, 2005, Photo: Benjamin Benschneider, Courtesy of Olson Kundig; John Campbell, John Campbell's Leisure House (rendering), Published in *Interiors*, January 1951, Photo: Trevor Mills, Vancouver Art Gallery; Olson Kundig, Delta Shelter, Mazama, WA (sketch), 2005, Courtesy of Olson Kundig; Patkau Architects, La Petite Maison du Weekend, Wexner Center for the Arts, Columbus, OH (elevations), 1998, Courtesy of Patkau Architects; Conrad E. Meinecke, *Your Cabin in the Woods* (detail), 1943 [reprint edition], Published by Black Dog & Leventhal, 2016; Bo Helliwell, Illustrations of Leaf House published in *Architectural Design*, 1978, Courtesy of Michael McNamara; Conrad E. Meinecke, *Your Cabin in the Woods* (detail of cover), 2016 [reprint edition], Published by Black Dog & Leventhal; John Campbell, John Campbell's Leisure House, San Francisco Arts Festival, 1951, Photo: Ernest Braun; Desolation Peak Lookout, North Cascades National Park, WA, 2009, Photo: Pete Hoffman; Conrad E. Meinecke, *Your Cabin in the Woods* (detail), 2016 [reprint edition], Published by Black Dog & Leventhal; Walden Pond (manuscript survey), 1846, Courtesy of Concord Free Public Library; Harrison & Tyler Campaign Emblem, 1840, American Cartoon Print Filing Series, Library of Congress, Prints and Photographs Division; Britton & Rey, *Sunday Morning: Log Cabin* (detail), c. 1908, Library of Congress, Prints and Photographs Division; Rudolph Schindler, Bennati Cabin, Lake Arrowhead, CA (detail of floorplan), 1934–37, R.M.

Schindler Papers, Architecture and Design Collection, Art, Design & Architecture Museum, UC Santa Barbara, CA; Ant Farm, *Inflatocookbook* (detail), 1973, Courtesy Chip Lord, Curtis Schreier, Photo Courtesy of the Environmental Design Library, University of California, Berkeley; Caroline M. Kirkland, *A New Home, Who'll Follow? Or, Glimpses of Western Life* (title page), Courtesy University of California Libraries; Mark Twain, *Roughing It* (illustrations), 1872; Ken Isaacs, *How to Build Your Own Living Structures* (detail), 1974, Photo: Trevor Mills, Vancouver Art Gallery; MacKay-Lyons Sweetapple Architects Limited, Cliff House, Tomlee Head, NS, 2010, Photo: Greg Richardson, Courtesy of MacKay-Lyons Sweetapple Architects Limited; "Coupoles Géodésiques pour L'Habitat Hippie" (detail of illustration), *l'architecture d'aujourd'hui*, December 1968–January 1969, Photo: Trevor Mills, Vancouver Art Gallery; University of Colorado, College of Architecture and Planning, Colorado Building Workshop, Outward Bound Micro Cabins, Leadville, CO (plan), 2015; Lincoln Logs (Advertisement), c. 1950s, Photo: Maegan Hill-Carroll, Vancouver Art Gallery; **1, 43 (bottom):** Helen Dowe at Devil's Head Fire Lookout, Pike National Forest, CO, 1919, Forest History Society, Durham, NC; **2–3:** 50'× 50' pillow during production of *Whole Earth Catalog* supplement, Saline Valley, CA, 1970, temporary installation, Photo: Curtis Schreier, Courtesy of University of California, Berkeley Art Museum and Pacific Film Archive; **4–5:** MacKay-Lyons Sweetapple Architects Limited, Cliff House, Tomlee Head, NS, 2010, Photo: Greg Richardson, Courtesy of MacKay-Lyons Sweetapple Architects Limited; **6–7:** Elizabeth Parker Hut, Yoho National Park, BC, 1956, Whyte Museum of the Canadian Rockies, Bob Hind Fonds (V46/28/1); **10–11, 123 (top), 185, 186 (left):** Marcel Breuer Papers, Special Collections Research Center, Syracuse University Libraries; **11 (top), 218 (bottom):** Courtesy of Scott & Scott Architects; **11 (middle), 143–149:** Photo: Julius Shulman © J. Paul Getty Trust. Getty Research Institute, Los Angeles (2004.R.10); **12:** Image (G-00754) Courtesy of the Royal BC Museum and Archives; **13 (top):** Image (C-09277) Courtesy of the Royal BC Museum and Archives; **13 (bottom), 33–35, 56 (bottom), 116–17, 130–31, 133:** Historic American Buildings Survey, Library of Congress, Prints and Photographs Division; **14:** © Dennis Stock/Magnum Photos; **15, 237 (top left and middle):** Urs Peter Flueckiger; **16:** © Varley Art Gallery, Town of Markham, Photo: Rachel Topham, Vancouver Art Gallery; **17, 122 (bottom), 151, 156 (bottom), 186 (left), 188 (top left), 189 (bottom right), 195 (middle), 282–84:** Trevor Mills, Vancouver Art Gallery; **18, 19, 20 (bottom), 42, 52 (bottom), 55 (right), 62, 67, 74–75, 124:** Library of Congress, Prints and Photographs Division; **20 (top):** blickwinkel/Alamy Stock Photo; **21:** Jennifer M. Volland; **22–23:** Photo: C.C. Curtis, Kaweah Cooperative Colony Papers, Beinecke Rare Book & Manuscript Library, Yale University; **23:** Dennis Frates/Alamy Stock Photo; **24, 28 (bottom), 29, 30–31:** Zach Moser; **25 (top):** Chris Felver/Getty Images; **25 (bottom):** Photo: Lyle Sowls, Courtesy of the Aldo Leopold Foundation, www.aldoleopold.org; **28 (top), 152:** © Sunset; **36 (top):** Gary Corbett/Alamy Stock Photo; **36 (bottom left):** Randy Duchaine/Alamy Stock Photo; **36 (bottom right):** Nova Scotia Archives (1987-453); **37:** Published in Frederic Irland, "Sport in an Untouched American Wilderness," *Scribner's* 20 (1896); **38:** City of Vancouver Archives, CVA 783-169; **38–39:** Image (I-298903) Courtesy of the Royal BC Museum and Archives; **39 (top):** City of Vancouver Archives, CVA 783-176; **39 (bottom):** City of Vancouver Archives, CVA 783-168; **40:** City of Vancouver Archives, CVA 783-172; **43 (top left):** Glenbow Archives NA-4868-184; **43 (top right):** Glenbow Archives NA-3961-4; **43 (middle):** Library and Archives Canada/1971-271 NPC/K-5735; **44:** Art & Architecture Collection, Miriam and Ira D. Wallach Division of Art, Prints and Photographs, The New York Public Library, Astor, Lenox and Tilden Foundations; **46:** Performance Image/Alamy Stock Photo; **47:** © Parks Canada; **48:** Adapted from Harold E. Driver and William C. Massey, *Comparative Studies of North American Indians*, 1957, p. 170, Courtesy of Jean-Luc Pilon; **50:** Originally published in *Quinze ans sous le Cercle Polaire : Mackenzie, Anderson, Youkon*, 1889, p. 216; **52 (top):** Canadian National Exhibition (Toronto, Ont.)/Library and Archives Canada/PA-045081; **53:** Image (C-09506) Courtesy of the Royal BC Museum and Archives; **54:** Courtesy Special Collections, UC Davis Library [Eastman's Originals Collection - Group 7]; **55 (left):** Courtesy Special

Collections, UC Davis Library [Eastman's Originals Collection - Group 94]; **56 (top)**: Photo: Frank Palmer, Library of Congress, Prints and Photographs Division; **57**: Image (D-01764) Courtesy of the Royal BC Museum and Archives; **58, 60**: © CORBIS/Corbis via Getty Images; **59**: Printed Ephemera Collection, Library of Congress, Special Collections Division; **61 (top)**: Library and Archives Canada/C-052819; **61 (bottom)**: Canada. Dept. of Interior/Library and Archives Canada/PA-034285; **63, 65**: Courtesy University of California Libraries; **67**: Vintage Images/Alamy Stock Photo; **66–67**: New York State Archives. Education Dept. Division of Visual Instruction. Instructional lantern slides, 1911-1925, A3045-78, Lantern slide DnAE9; **72**: Photography Collection, Miriam and Ira D. Wallach Division of Art, Prints and Photographs, The New York Public Library; **73, 261–275**: Farm Security Administration - Office of War Information Photograph Collection, Library of Congress, Prints and Photographs Division; **76**: Jean Blackwell Hutson Research and Reference Division, Schomburg Center for Research in Black Culture, The New York Public Library, Astor, Lenox and Tilden Foundations; **78 (top)**: Image (NA-03870) Courtesy of the Royal BC Museum and Archives; **78 (bottom)**: Glenbow Archives NA-2222-1; **79 (top)**: Glenbow Archives NA-944-6; **79 (middle)**: Glenbow Archives NA-4428-6; **79 (bottom)**: Jack R. Wrathall/Library and Archives Canada/PA-096144; **81**: Photo: Major James Skitt Matthews, City of Vancouver Archives, M-3-36.1; **82**: Image (F-06161) Courtesy of the Royal BC Museum and Archives; **82–83**: Image (A-08199) Courtesy of the Royal BC Museum and Archives; **84–85, 108–109, 109 (middle)**: Courtesy of the California History Room, California State Library, Sacramento, California; **87**: Pete Hoffman; **88**: © Estate of Harold Vail; **91–92**: Buddy Mays/Alamy Stock Photo; **94**: Glenbow Archives S-20-147; **96**: Photo: Hans Gmoser, Whyte Museum of the Canadian Rockies, Hans Gmoser Fonds (V68/pa-707); **98–104**: Courtesy of Richard Johnson; **105**: Photo: Jessie B. Cook, San Francisco Subjects Photography Collection, PC-SF, California Historical Society; **106 (top)**: Keith Beaty/Toronto Star via Getty Images; **106 (middle)**: Library and Archives Canada/1971-271 NPC/79255; **106 (bottom)**: Colin McConnell/Toronto Star via Getty Images; **107 (top)**: Photo: Walter Curtin, Library and Archives Canada/1981-262 NPC; **107 (middle left)**: © Library and Archives Canada. Reproduced with the permission of Library and Archives Canada. Source: Library and Archives Canada/Walter Curtin Fonds; **107 (middle right)**: Hemis/Alamy Stock Photo; **107 (bottom), 114 (bottom right)**: Copyright ©1993 by Lester Walker. Reprinted by arrangement with The Overlook Press, Peter Mayer Publishers, Inc. www.overlookpress.com. All rights reserved.; **108, 109 (top)**: San Francisco History Center, San Francisco Public Library; **110–111**: California State Library; **112 (top)**: Whyte Museum of the Canadian Rockies, Mary Schäffer Fonds (V527/ps-269); **112 (bottom)**: Glenbow Archives S-20-24; **112–113**: Joanne Chui; **113 (top left)**: The Alpine Club of Canada Archives; **113 (top right)**: Image (I-66786) Courtesy of the Royal BC Museum and Archives; **114 (top)**: Culture Club/Getty Images; **114 (middle), 115 (bottom right)**: Reproduced with permission of the author; **114 (bottom left), 115 (top), 125**: Courtesy of Concord Free Public Library; **115 (bottom left)**: Chronicle/Alamy Stock Photo; **118–119**: R.M. Schindler Papers, Architecture and Design Collection, Art, Design & Architecture Museum, UC Santa Barbara; **120, 220 (left and middle), 221 (bottom left and right), 222**: Maegan Hill-Carroll, Vancouver Art Gallery; **122 (top)**: Department of Mines and Technical Surveys/Library and Archives Canada/PA-023175; **123 (bottom left)**: Anshen & Allen Collection, University of California, Berkeley, Environmental Design Archives; **123 (bottom right)**: Gottscho-Schleisner Collection, Library of Congress, Prints and Photographs Division; **132**: Carol M. Highsmith's America, Library of Congress, Prints and Photographs Division; **134–35**: Published by Black Dog & Leventhal; **136–39**: Courtesy Schoeler & Heaton Architects Inc.; **140 (left)**: CBC Still Photo Collection/John de Visser; **140 (right)**: CBC Still Photo Collection/Harold Whyte; **153 (top)**: Henrik Bull Collection, Environmental Design Archives, University of California, Berkeley; **153 (middle), 154**: Photo: Ernest Braun, George T. Rockrise Collection, Environmental Design Archives, University of California, Berkeley; **153 (bottom)**: The Denver Post via Getty Images; **155**: © Eve Arnold/Magnum Photos; **156 (top), 159 (top right), 159 (bottom)**: © Dennis Stock/Magnum Photos; **157 (top)**:

Denver Public Library, Western History Collection, X-7737; **157 (bottom left), 241**: Denver Public Library, Western History Collection, X-7739; **157 (bottom right)**: Photo: Gene Bernofsky, University Archives, Kenneth Spencer Research Library, University of Kansas Libraries; **158**: Courtesy of Environmental Communications; **160 (top)**: Photo: Myron Wood, © Pikes Peak Library District, 002-5768; **160 (bottom)**: Denver Public Library, Western History Collection, X-7740; **162–163**: Photo: Trevor Mills, Vancouver Art Gallery, Courtesy of the Vancouver Art Gallery Library; **164**: Courtesy Chip Lord, Curtis Schreier, Photo Courtesy of the Environmental Design Library, University of California, Berkeley; **165, 242 (top)**: pff NA2790.B3 1969. Courtesy of The Bancroft Library, University of California, Berkeley; **166–67**: Photo: Trevor Mills, Vancouver Art Gallery, Courtesy of Sara Isaacs; **168–69**: Dan Scott/Vancouver Sun; **170 (top left), 225**: Richard Howard; **170 (top right)**: © Allen Ginsberg/CORBIS/Corbis via Getty Images; **170 (bottom left)**: Ron Bull/Toronto Star via Getty Images; **176–78**: Diana Saverin; **179**: AP Photo/Elaine Thompson, File; **180**: © Alec Soth/Magnum Photos; **181**: Rick Wilking/Reuters Pictures; **187**: © Ezra Stoller/Esto; **188 (bottom left), 189 (top and bottom left), 192**: Ernest Braun; **188 (right)**: Look Magazine Photo Collection, Library of Congress, Prints and Photographs Division; **190–91**: Courtesy of the Seth Peterson Cottage Conservancy; **194, 298, 299 (top and middle)**: Photo: Benjamin Benschneider, Courtesy of Olson Kundig; **195 (top)**: Jason Koxvold; **195 (bottom)**: Ford Yates; **197**: Alain Rumpf; **202–03**: American Cartoon Print Filing Series, Library of Congress, Prints and Photographs Division; **204**: Ed Clark/The LIFE Picture Collection/Getty Images; **208 (left)**: Library and Archives Canada/1971-271 NPC/ K-5568; **208 (right)**: City of Toronto Archives, Fonds 217, Series 249, File 137; **208–09**: City of Toronto Archives, Fonds 124, File 11, Item 9; **209**: Ron Bull/Toronto Star via Getty Images; **210–13**: Noah Kalina for Cabin Porn; **216–17**: © MIR, Courtesy of Snøhetta; **218 (top), 219 (bottom)**: Photo: Andrew Pogue, Courtesy of mwlworks architecture+design; **219 (top)**: Frank Oudeman/OTTO; **220 (top), 221 (top)**: Copyright Gestalten 2013; **220 (bottom)**: Copyright Gestalten 2014; **224**: The National Trust Photolibrary/Alamy Stock Photo; **226 (left), 228 (middle), 228–29**: Courtesy of Roots Canada; **226 (right), 228 (bottom), 229 (top left and right)**: Photo: Mike Seehagel, Courtesy of Camp Brand Goods; **227, 228 (top)**: Photo: Stephen Wilde, Courtesy of Herschel Supply Co.; **230 (left)**: Photo: Pop Jenks, Park City Museum, Pop Jenks Collection.1987-2-9; **230 (right), 231**: Courtesy of Bjarke Ingels Group; **232**: Chad Ziemendorf; **233**: Jasper Sanidad; **234–35**: Photo: Jonathan Friedman, Courtesy of Partisans; **236**: Photo: Denny Mingus, Courtesy of Urs Peter Flueckiger; **237 (top right and bottom)**: © ITAC, Photo: Nicholas Steffens; **238 (top and middle)**: Courtesy of Michael Fox and Juintow Lin; **238 (bottom), 239, 297, 302–03**: Jesse Kuroiwa; **242 (left), 242–43**: Clark Richert; **243 (top)**: Drop City Photo Archives: Richard Kallweit; **244, 245 (bottom left and right), 248**: Michael McNamara; **245 (top)**: Anne Louise Bonner; **246–47**: Courtesy of Patkau Architects; **251**: © Varley Art Gallery, Town of Markham, Photo: Trevor Mills, Vancouver Art Gallery; **252**: Vancouver Public Library, Accession Number 2222; **253**: Vancouver Public Library, Accession Number 16720; **255**: Vancouver Public Library, Accession Number 2258; **256–57**: Vancouver Public Library, Accession Number 16763; **258–59**: Vancouver Public Library, Accession Number 2271; **277–79**: James Welling; **280–81**: Courtesy of Vikky Alexander; **288–89**: Rachel Topham, Vancouver Art Gallery; **290–91**: James Benning; **292–95**: UMJ, Nicolas Lackner; **298–99**: Photo: Tim Bies, Courtesy of Olson Kundig; **299 (bottom right)**: Courtesy of Olson Kundig; **300–01, 304**: Photo: Greg Richardson, Courtesy of MacKay-Lyons Sweetapple Architects Limited; **310–11**: Grading and Timber Gang, Crowsnest Pass, BC, 1898, Glenbow Archives NA-919-34; **312–13**: UUfie, Lake Cottage, Kawartha Lakes, ON, 2013, Photo: © Naho Kubota; **314**: First Memorial Hut, Jasper National Park, AB, 1929, Whyte Museum of the Canadian Rockies, Alpine Club of Canada Fonds (AC1P/2-7); **315**: Anshen & Allen, Diamond Mountain Cabin, Squaw Valley, CA, 1967–60, Anshen & Allen Collection, University of California, Berkeley, Environmental Design Archives, Photo: Ernest Braun; **316–17**: Olson Kundig, Delta Shelter, Mazama, WA, 2005, Photo: Tim Bies; **318–19**: Abbot Pass Hut, Rocky Mountains, AB, 2017, Photo: Jason Pineau.

Published in conjunction with *Cabin Fever*, an exhibition organized by the Vancouver Art Gallery, curated by Jennifer M. Volland, Bruce Grenville and Stephanie Rebick, and presented from June 9 to September 30, 2018.

Editors: Jennifer M. Volland, Bruce Grenville and Stephanie Rebick
Curatorial Assistant: Amy Luo
Editing: Emma Conner and Meaghan McAneeley
Design: Derek Barnett, Information Office
Publication coordination: Stephanie Rebick
Digital image preparation: Rachel Topham, Vancouver Art Gallery
Rights and reproductions: Zoë Chan, Danielle Currie, Amy Luo
    and Stephanie Rebick
Printed in Belgium

© 2018 Vancouver Art Gallery

ISBN 978-1-927656-39-6 (Vancouver Art Gallery)
ISBN 978-1-988860-00-8 (Information Office)

Visionary Partner for Scholarship and Publications:
The Richardson Family

Major exhibition support generously provided by:
Naudia and Mark Maché

Vancouver Art Gallery
750 Hornby Street, Vancouver, BC V6Z 2H7
www.vanartgallery.bc.ca

Vancouver
Artgallery

The Vancouver Art Gallery is a not-for-profit organization supported by its members, individual donors, corporate funders, foundations, the City of Vancouver, the Province of British Columbia through the British Columbia Arts Council, and the Canada Council for the Arts.

Information Office
202–4580 Main Street, Vancouver, BC V5V 3R5
www.informationoffice.ca
www.distributionoffice.ca

**Information
Office**

Library and Archives Canada Cataloguing in Publication

Cabin fever (Vancouver, B.C.)
    Cabin fever.

Published in conjunction with an exhibition held at the Vancouver Art Gallery from
    June 9 to September 30, 2018.
Curated by Jennifer M. Volland, Bruce Grenville, and Stephanie Rebick.
Co-published by Vancouver Art Gallery.
ISBN 978-1-927656-39-6 (hardcover : Vancouver Art Gallery).—
ISBN 978-1-988860-00-8 (hardcover : Information Office)

    1. Dwellings—Canada—History—Exhibitions. 2. Dwellings—United States—
History—Exhibitions. 3. Dwellings—Social aspects—Canada—History—Exhibitions.
4. Dwellings—Social aspects—United States—History—Exhibitions. 5. Dwellings—
Canada—History—Pictorial works—Exhibitions. 6. Dwellings—United States—
History—Pictorial works—Exhibitions. 7. Exhibition catalogs. I. Volland, Jennifer
M., 1970–, organizer, editor II. Grenville, Bruce, organizer III. Rebick, Stephanie,
organizer IV. Vancouver Art Gallery, issuing body, host institution V. Title.

NA8470.C35 2018   728.7'30971   C2018-901846-1